D0444389

"The great challenge of this era is to l   ꓳ   ꓶnto alignment with the rest of the natural world. Business, with its resources and capacity for innovation, has both the opportunity and the responsibility to facilitate the transformation of industrial society. The Natural Step provides an elegant framework, a compass, to guide us on the road ahead. *The Natural Step for Business* is a powerful tool for all seeking a new mental model, documented with the actual experience of successful corporations, to move their business into a sustainable future." — Maurice F. Strong, Secretary-General, United Nations Conference on Environment and Development; Chair, The Earth Council; former Chairman and CEO, Ontario Hydro

"The question confronting leaders in all sectors is how to build enterprises that can prosper by operating in greater harmony with the natural environment. *The Natural Step for Business* illuminates principles to guide this quest. Even more important in these times of momentous transition, it examines four successful corporations quietly leading by example. I believe this book will eventually stand out as a watershed of sorts, not only as a provocative glimpse of what is being accomplished by a few, but as a spark to the imaginations of a great many more." — Peter M. Senge, Senior Lecturer, MIT; Chairperson, Society for Organizational Learning; Author, *The Fifth Discipline: The Art and Practice of the Learning Organization*

"The Natural Step is a lucid, science-based way to marry sustainability with value. Now we have practical examples of how leading businesses are using its principles to create exceptional competitive advantage." — Amory B. Lovins, Director of Research, Rocky Mountain Institute

"At Mitsubishi Electric, we have pursued sustainable development by utilizing The Natural Step as the compass to guide our way together with the implementation of an environmental management system. This book provides easy-to-understand concepts of lasting value because it helps people see the relationship between their daily activities and larger environmental issues." — Tachi Kiuchi, Managing Director, Mitsubishi Electric Corporation; Chair, Future 500

THE NATURAL STEP
FOR BUSINESS

WEALTH, ECOLOGY, AND
THE EVOLUTIONARY
CORPORATION

Brian Nattrass and Mary Altomare

Foreword by Karl-Henrik Robèrt
Afterword by Paul Hawken

NEW SOCIETY PUBLISHERS

To further the dialogue about business and sustainability, you can contact Brian Nattrass and Mary Altomare via e-mail at: innostrat@aol.com

Cataloguing in Publication Data:
A catalog record for this publication is available from the National Library of Canada and the Library of Congress.

Cover design by Miriam MacPhail.

Printed in Canada on acid-free, partially recycled (20 percent post-consumer) paper using soy-based inks by Best Book Manufacturers.

New Society Publishers acknowledges the support of the Canadian government's Book Publishing Industry Development Program and the British Columbia Arts Council in the publication of this book.

Inquiries regarding requests to reprint all or part of *The Natural Step for Business: Wealth, Ecology, and the Evolutionary Corporation* should be addressed to New Society Publishers at the address below.

Paperback ISBN: 0-86571-384-7

To order directly from the publishers, please add $4.00 to the price of the first copy, and $1.00 for each additional copy (plus GST in Canada). Send check or money order to:

New Society Publishers,
P.O. Box 189, Gabriola Island, BC V0R 1X0, Canada.

New Society Publishers aims to publish books for fundamental social change through nonviolent action. We focus especially on sustainable living, progressive leadership, and educational and parenting resources. Our full list of books can be browsed on the world wide web at: http://www.newsociety.com

The Natural Step for Business is part of NSP's Conscientious Commerce series.

NEW SOCIETY PUBLISHERS
Gabriola Island, British Columbia, Canada

*As a guiding star, a compass, for our environmental work,
we have adopted the [Natural Step] four System Conditions for a
sustainable society. Everyone who has attended IKEA's environmental
training has learned of the importance of these conditions. Each of us
in our various roles must now seek to put these into practice,
within the framework of IKEA's business idea.*
Anders Moberg — *President, IKEA*

*What it's all about, really, is to utilize the resources that we have on this
planet in the best way. That is part of our vision. We say that we are
turning from a resource over-consuming society to a resource-saving
society and that the environment discussion is really about taking care of
resources in a better way. Everybody still acts as if these resources were
unlimited, and as if we will always find other sources. But they will hit the
funnel as described by The Natural Step. By focusing on these items —
energy, water and waste — we are creating competitive advantages.
We are also saving the environment.*
Roland Nilsson — *CEO, Scandic Hotels*

*Interface is committed to shifting from linear industrial processes to
cyclical ones. To do this, we use a compass to guide us, and a
set of tools to help us. They are both the result of The Natural Step.
Interface will use four fundamental principles of science described
by The Natural Step as a guide to reduce its impact and footprint
upon the planet. We believe that institutions that continuously
violate these principles will suffer economically.*
Ray Anderson — *CEO, Interface*

*The Natural Step is one of the easier things to get people to
buy into even though they may not be able to remember what the
four System Conditions are. Once they've been exposed to them,
they have an instinctive understanding of what is being talked about.
It's easier to get people to equate to this as opposed to other
management concepts that are designed to motivate people.
This is one that you can internalize quickly.*
Jim Quinn — *CEO, Collins Pine Company*

DEDICATION

To my daughter Sarah,
whose life, and those of the children of tomorrow,
is my inspiration for engaging in this work;
and to my father and mother with gratitude for
providing me with the many opportunities and insights
that helped make this path possible.
BN

To those I hold most precious, Staci, Kristen, and Mingo,
and especially Kylee and Sydney, tomorrow's children,
who will inherit the world we are creating;
and to my parents, brother, and sisters
for teaching me to love, question, and dream.
MA

Finally, to each other
for the deepening courage, commitment,
and love that is emerging
through our shared lives and work.
BN & MA

TABLE OF CONTENTS

PART ONE: DESIGNING THE FUTURE

PART TWO: THE BUSINESS OF SUSTAINABLE DEVELOPMENT

PART THREE: THE EVOLUTIONARY JOURNEY

LIST OF FIGURES

ACKNOWLEDGEMENTS

A
LTHOUGH WE ARE THE STORYTELLERS, the real credit for the content of
this book is the deeply inspiring work of others. The Natural Step orig-
inated with its pioneering founder, cancer researcher and physician Dr.
Karl-Henrik Robèrt and his principal collaborator, physicist Dr. John
Holmberg. Visionary businessman/author Paul Hawken has been chiefly
responsible for bringing The Natural Step to North America and is a source of
continual inspiration to us. It is, of course, the innovative work of the business
people described in this book, especially the men and women of IKEA, Scandic
Hotels, Interface, and Collins Pine, that provides its real content. They very gen-
erously opened their doors to us and granted us the time and the opportunity
to pursue the research which is the foundation of this book. Corporate sustainability consultant Susan Burns shared her knowledge with us and contributed
Chapter 9 on environmental management systems. To all of these people we are
deeply grateful.

The first company to adopt The Natural Step, to experiment with it and to
discover its utility in business, and the first of our case studies, is IKEA. We are
very grateful to the co-workers of IKEA who shared their time and expertise. We
especially thank Russ Johnson and Kalle Nilsson who made our work with
IKEA as fruitful as it was. In addition, we thank Carina Andersson, Glenn
Berndtsson, Magnus Bjork, Chriztel Carleson, Mats Flygare, Bjorn Frithiof,
Magnus Guselin, Ingemar Hallberg, Anders Lennartsson, Erik Linander, Didi
Malabuyo, Marty Marsten, Dan McCulloch, Peter Olofsson, Cecilia Svensson,
Sven Olof Trulsson, Marianne Wir, and John Zurcher who shared their time and
stories with us.

We particularly thank Roland Nilsson and Ola Ivarsson at Scandic Hotels
for sharing Scandic's environmental vision, achievements, aspirations, and challenges; and Mia Olden for her kind assistance in coordinating our many meetings. We extend special thanks to Jan Peter Bergkvist and the entire staff at the
Scandic Hotel Bromma for their warm hospitality. In addition, we thank Unni
Astrom, Gunnar Brandberg, Ethel Capelle, Steve Davidson, Charlie Eldh, Emil

Gammeltoft, Kerstin Goransson, Marie Hallander, Tommy Hansson, Kristina Helin, Ken Hopper, Helene Jendelin, Pia Lonnroth, Monia Orstal, and Katri Savolaninen. We also thank Peter Havéus and Staffan Persson of Sophus Berendson, an important supplier to Scandic Hotels.

We express our heartfelt gratitude to Ray Anderson of Interface, Inc. for sharing his vision with us, and special thanks go to Charlie Eitel, Michael Bertolucci, and Jim Hartzfeld. We also thank Nicole Armstrong, Jo Ann Bachman, Tim Barnes, David Black, Chris Carson, Cheryl Eaton, Kay Gordy, David Gustashaw, Buddy Hay, Dan Hendrix, Michael Hutton, David Hobbs, Joyce LaValle, Mac McGowan, David Oakey, Mindy O'Gara, Daniel Price, Bill Reynolds, Jim Rowe, and Linda Timms.

We are particularly grateful to Jim Quinn of Collins Pine for being so generous with his time, and to Connie Grenz for keeping us informed about the fast pace of developments in 1998. In addition, our special thanks to Nancy L. Helseth, R. Wade Mosby, Larry Potts, Dale Slate, Cami Waner, and W. Travis Wilson.

We extend our special gratitude to Mats Fack and Jimmy Sjoblom of Sånga-Säby for sharing with us their trail-blazing work in utilizing The Natural Step four System Conditions as the basis for a useful and innovative system of environmental metrics.

In addition, we extend heartfelt thanks to Nick Sonntag, Executive Director of the Stockholm Environment Institute, and his gracious wife, Linda, for their enduring friendship and warm hospitality; to Dr. Rigmor Robèrt for sharing so much with us during our months in Sweden; and to all of the staff at The Natural Step in Sweden, particularly Kerstin Abrahamsson and Magnus Huss, for their very helpful advice, co-operation, and interest in this project. We also thank Leif Johansson, CEO of Volvo, Mats Lederhausen, CEO of McDonald's of Sweden, Bertil Rosquist, Environment Director of McDonalds of Sweden, and Göran Carstedt, Managing Director of the Society for Organizational Learning for sharing with us their insights and experience regarding The Natural Step.

The genesis of this book is Brian's doctoral research in Learning and Change in Human Systems at the School for Transformative Learning, California Institute of Integral Studies in San Francisco. Brian is deeply grateful to the head of his dissertation committee, Dr. Ralph Metzner, for his guidance and inspiration; to Dr. Alexander Laszlo for his introduction to the field of evolutionary systems design; and to Dr. Lynn Tanner for his example of bringing academic discipline into the results-oriented world of business.

There are countless others to whom we owe gratitude for their constant support and interest in this project. We thank you all, particularly Tony Barrett, Kelly Hawke Baxter, Beth Beloff, Catherine Gray, John Hagen, Jill Rosenblum, and Dr. Bryan Smith for taking the time to read parts of the manuscript and to provide insightful suggestions on ways to improve it. Thanks to Bob Willard for allowing us to read and quote from his unpublished paper on sustainability and business. Finally, we extend special gratitude to Christopher and Judith Plant of New Society Publishers for their faith in us and for their enduring patience and good nature.

FOREWORD

Karl-Henrik Robèrt
Founder of The Natural Step

MY EARLIEST IDEAS ABOUT THE NATURAL STEP began in the late 1980s when I was working as a medical doctor and cancer-treatment researcher. During those years, I saw many things that confused me about how we as human beings take care of our habitat. On the one hand, messages from the mass media and the general public made it sound as if people were more interested in getting richer and driving their cars faster than in preserving our environment for the sake of their children's future. On the other hand, I saw an endless stream of concerned parents come into the hospital with their cancer-diseased children. And these parents were prepared to do anything for their children. So, something was wrong here: how could both of these descriptions of human nature be true? Despite this deep concern for our children's well-being and futures, we seemed to handle the problem of maintaining our environment by fighting instead of cooperating. Was there some way, I asked myself, that we could learn to reach some consensus on how to change?

I was not only passionate in the beginning — I was obsessed. When I first started out, I felt a very clear sorrow in my heart and fear about the destruction of the environment. I am a cell scientist, and I see the cell as a metaphor for the whole Earth, as there must be a balance of all flows in both the cell and the Earth for each to survive. What I see is that humankind is running into a funnel of declining life-sustaining resources and increasing demands. The converging walls of the funnel represent the globally declining productivity of renewable resources per capita. More and more resource input is required for each unit of production from forests, agricultural land, and fishing waters. At the same time, the declining vital life-sustaining resource base of nature is exposed to climate change and increased concentrations of pollutants. Finally, the population of the world is increasing, projected to reach 10 billion people in the next generation, while the traditions that keep our cultures together are getting weaker and weaker.

Many people are blaming business. It is easy to understand why. A large part of the destruction we see is either directly attributable to business activities, or indirectly to the consumption of the products and services that business provides. On the other hand, even for a restorative society it is not difficult to see the potential that exists in business to slow the convergence of the walls of the funnel and to accelerate the opening of the funnel. Business is the economic engine of our Western culture, and if it could be transformed to truly serve nature as well as ourselves, it could become essential to our rescue. Perhaps there are even quite simple solutions just waiting to be discovered. Perhaps the strategies and traditions of our firms — developed in another and relatively simpler time — are simply not relevant anymore. If so, could they be exchanged for new traditions and strategies, which would combine protection of the common good with a clear self-interest to do so? How much legislation would be required? To what extent can we expect a profound and desirable transformation of our business corporations to occur of their own free will?

There are many driving forces other than legislation. Many big transnational companies have already suffered economically from public stigmatization due to unethical ecological and/or social behavior. There are also many examples of big transnational companies that have benefitted from taking a clear social and ecological stand and from the international dissemination of such standards, thus leveraging the companies' impact for the public good. In addition, there are many examples of business corporations that have suffered economically from increased resource costs, increased costs for waste management, new rules from international business agreements, etc. Part of the economic pressure that many firms are beginning to encounter is due to increased competition from proactive business corporations that are learning how to anticipate and avoid problems far in advance of their competition.

Will businesses expand their focus beyond short-term profits to long-term goals for our common good? Will the driving forces be strong enough? Or will we need tougher legislation? Most likely, a successful transition will require a combination of these factors. It is even reasonable to expect that proactive and successful strategies implemented by some corporate actors will support the development of constructive and proactive legislation to accelerate change in other companies. In any event, it seems desirable to develop effective strategic and tactical tools to ensure that business for the common good will pay off in the short term as well as in the long term.

Whether we expect to see tougher legislation or tougher and tougher competition from proactive companies, the question of whether the resource funnel may in any way influence tomorrow's markets is, of course, rhetorical. And it is likely that intelligent strategies to avoid problems — whether induced by legislation or tough competition from proactive firms — will be virtually the same. So, the interesting question is: *how* will the market change? It seems obvious that good business in times of expected, profound change should avoid hasty or precipitous solutions in the long run, and avoid investment strategies that will lead to dead ends. Each step in the right direction should provide return on investment quickly enough and sufficient enough to fuel the transition further ahead. In short, when tackling the problems at hand, how can a company align short-term with long-term objectives in a step-by-step manner allowing each step to pay off? And how can companies avoid the creation of new problems when they solve the old ones?

It is obvious that sustainable development requires a sufficiently broad perspective. From an overall point of view, the ultimate starting point would be a framework given by first-order principles for ecological, economic, and social sustainability for the whole ecosphere. Thereafter, the consequences of this framework can be drawn for the individual business corporation. Finally, programs for transition should be launched in which the following two aspects are combined:

1. Each investment provides as flexible a platform as possible for subsequent investments in the direction given by the framework; and

2. Highest priority is given to "low hanging fruits," i.e. investments that are believed to give rapid returns on investment; this finances and empowers the steps that follow which, in turn, become the next flexible platform from which additional low hanging fruits are chosen in an iterative process.

The Natural Step is an environmental not-for-profit organization I started in Sweden in 1989. The objective of The Natural Step was to address these problems by seeking the advice and expertise of a growing circle of scientists, economists, business leaders, and other stakeholders in society. I wondered if it would be possible, if the participants in this dialogue represented the community well enough, to develop relevant and solid, shared mental models for the definition of sustainability based on first-order principles of sustainability. Could such models then be used for problem-solving and investment strategies? If so, would it be possible to demonstrate a competitive advantage from using such models?

To that end, a number of scientific reports and dissertations, as well as teaching tools and good examples of the application of these tools, have been published. The dialogue has spread internationally and Natural Step organizations have been launched in the United States, Canada, the United Kingdom, Australia, New Zealand, and the Netherlands. Japan and South Africa are now in the process of establishing Natural Step organizations. In parallel with these developments, a growing number of business corporations around the world have started to gain experience from allowing global sustainability in the future to be a guiding force of business today. Up to this point, the implementation of The Natural Step principles in business has been anecdotal or described in annual reports or the statements of individual business leaders. Until now there has been no systematic study of the implementation procedures of The Natural Step concepts, and consequently, there have been no answers to the following questions:

1. What has motivated specific companies to integrate ecological sustainability into their business strategies and operations?

2. Why have they chosen The Natural Step framework as the most effective means to accomplish this?

3. How exactly have specific companies used The Natural Step framework? How does it relate to corporate change, visioning, strategic planning, day-to-day operations, etc.?

4. How has The Natural Step framework been implemented?

5. What factors contribute to the successful integration of The Natural Step framework into business operations?

6. What measures or indicators of success exist with respect to the implementation of The Natural Step framework?

7. What lessons and tools can be derived from the experience of the companies using The Natural Step framework, and how can these be made available to other companies?

Brian Nattrass set out to answer these questions, and many others, in his dissertation research. He and Mary Altomare have translated the insights gained through that research into this book. They have done this in a comprehensive and elegant study of four innovative and successful business corporations that have adopted The Natural Step framework. It is my belief that this study is the first in a long series of similar studies to come. In my mind there are few more challenging and demanding scientific tasks than to study systematically the driving forces behind sustainable development along with strategies, tools, stumbling blocks, common denominators for success, and other important aspects of sustainable development in every-day business. And it is yet another challenging task to make these findings easy to understand and relevant to a wide audience. I am deeply grateful to Brian Nattrass and Mary Altomare for giving themselves the demanding task of producing the first implementation study of The Natural Step framework in business. They have answered many questions that we have had, and posed new and important questions for future studies.

PART ONE

DESIGNING THE FUTURE

In an age when the speed, intensity, and complexity of change increase constantly and exponentially, the ability to shape change — rather than being its victims or spectators — depends on our competence and willingness to guide the purposeful evolution of our systems, our communities, and our society.
Bela H. Banathy
*Designing Social Systems
in a Changing World*

CHAPTER 1

The Challenge of Design:
An Introduction

The journey to a different future must begin by defining the problem differently than we have done until now....The task is not to find substitutes for chemicals that disrupt hormones, attack the ozone layer, or cause still undiscovered problems, though it may be necessary to use replacements as a temporary measure. The task that confronts us over the next half century is one of redesign.
Theo Colborn, Dianne Dumanoski, John Peterson Myers
Our Stolen Future

N 1628, ONE OF THE GREATEST WARSHIPS ever designed, the powerful man-of-war Vasa, pride of the King of Sweden, abruptly sank at the beginning of its maiden voyage with a full crew and many noble and illustrious guests on board. It had suddenly reached the limits of its woefully inadequate design when hit by a squall while still in its home port of Stockholm. Despite the frantic efforts of its increasingly desperate crew, once the limits of the ship's design had been exceeded and overwhelmed, nothing that they could do in their frenzy would be sufficient to stop a disaster that could have been avoided.

Today, more and more people throughout the world are becoming concerned that the basic design of our entire industrial society is both faulty and inadequate for the long-term voyage that is the dream of humanity. The precious cargo of our family and friends, the multitude of other life forms, and all that we hold dear is in danger while we maintain our present course. From eminent scientists in leading research institutes with the most sophisticated global climate computer models to Earth-wise shamans embodying the collective wisdom of some of the planet's oldest surviving indigenous peoples, urgent warnings are signalling the approaching, yet still avoidable, collision with the limits imposed by the natural world.

Our industrial economy, indeed any human economy, is contained within and dependent upon the natural world. The natural world is not separate from the human economy. All of our basic life needs — breathing, drinking, and eating — are entirely dependent on the continuing capacity of the natural world to provide us with pure, uncontaminated air, water, and food. We are totally dependent upon what visionary businessman and author Paul Hawken and others call "ecosystem services." These are the services valued at trillions of dollars annually, provided at no cost by nature, such as global oxygen production, regulation of climate, detoxification and recycling of human wastes, regulation of the chemical composition of the oceans, maintenance of soil fertility, protection against cosmic and ultraviolet radiation, and countless other services – none of which have adequate technological substitutes.

Unfortunately, the natural world is becoming more and more impaired everywhere on the planet in its capacity to continue to provide us with the vital services we need to exist and to thrive with dignity and pleasure. The reality is that in many parts of the world, and for vast and growing numbers of people, life no longer provides much dignity or pleasure. Evidence is mounting that living systems throughout the world are in increasing jeopardy. For example, Lester Brown and others report that "unless humanity stabilizes the global atmosphere that we have been steadily altering for more than a century, virtually every ecosystem on Earth will be at risk."[1]

Yet there is another way, a better way. The emerging conflict of humanity with the rest of the natural world need not be inevitable if we use our insight, muster forces globally, and act now. A small yet growing number of leading business people from around the globe have heard and understood the warnings of our cultural look-outs, those scientists, shamans, and other people of wisdom, whose vision can pierce the mists of the future more clearly than most of us. It is these perceptive business people who have made a remarkable discovery: if we align the business economy with the economy of nature, there are still great profits to be made — profits made in ways that enhance rather than endanger the future of life on Earth.

There need be no conflict or compromise between commercial profits and the environmental health and well-being of humanity and other life forms if the design of commerce is aligned with the inherent design of the natural world. Prominent architect and designer William McDonough and his colleague, industrial chemist Dr. Michael Braungart, express it this way: "If people are to prosper within the natural world, all the products and materials manufactured by industry must after each useful life provide nourishment for something new.... Products composed of materials that do not biodegrade should be designed as technical nutrients that continually circulate within closed-loop industrial cycles — the technical metabolism."[2] Humanity must rediscover its ancient ability to recognize and live within the cycles of the natural world. We have done this since the birth of our species, and it is only comparatively recently that we have veered off course.

The focus of this book is the insights of a passionate and dedicated cancer physician, Dr. Karl-Henrik Robèrt of Stockholm, and the application of his insights by leading–edge business people who have understood the urgent need to change the design parameters of our global industrial system. The Natural Step, founded by Dr. Robèrt and subsequently endorsed by some of the world's leading scientists, provides a comprehensive definition of an environmentally sustainable society that is easily understood and grounded in natural science. — Implementing it on a corporate level, practitioners of The Natural Step employ methods similar to those of the quality movement and concepts from learning organization theory, both of which are respected by many business people.

This book does not have the space to adequately explore the topics of organizational learning and change, particularly the five learning disciplines as described by Peter Senge in his best-selling book *The Fifth Discipline* and further elaborated by Dr. Senge and his colleagues in the *Fifth Discipline Fieldbook* series. However, our research has shown us that for those business corporations that make the commitment to sustainable development, the understanding and practice of the organizational learning disciplines will be the indispensable prerequisite of a successful transformation to sustainability. We touch briefly upon the learning organization as a metaphor in Chapter 2; — for more in-depth reading, refer to the Resources in the back of the book.

This book does not describe at length the ecological drama that is now being played out in virtually every region of this planet. We assume the reader has some familiarity with the issues or can quickly gain it. There are many quality books and reports, far too numerous to list here, that describe and document the environmental, societal, and economic trends that are shaping the markets of the future. For example, refer to *The Ecology of Commerce* by Paul Hawken, *The Choice: Evolution or Extinction?* by Ervin Laszlo, *Our Stolen Future* by Colburn et al, the annual *State of the World* and *Vital Signs* series by the Worldwatch Institute, and to the books and websites listed in Resources.

What this book does deal with is the business journey to sustainability. The very concepts of "sustainability" and "sustainable development" are relatively new, and there is debate about their precise definitions. A consensus definition does not exist. A commonly cited definition came out of *Our Common Future*, the 1987 report of the World Commission on Environment and Development (the Brundtland Commission). According to the commission, development is sustainable "if it meets the needs of the present without compromising the ability of future generations to meet their own needs."[3] The vagueness of this definition raises several questions: How are needs (present and future) defined? How are those needs prioritized? What about equity (now and in the future) and the just distribution of resources? Carl Frankel, in his insightful book *In Earth's Company*, explores the evolution of the concept, and finds that once we get beyond the Brundtland Commission's definition, sustainability is characterized in terms of harmonizing three elements: economics, environment, and social equity. As Frankel observes, "Growth is to be pursued in a manner consistent with long-term environmental protection and social fairness."[4]

John Elkington, in his recent work *Cannibals with Forks*, cites Herman Daly's definition that to be sustainable, a society needs to meet three conditions: "its rates of use of renewable resources should not exceed their rates of regeneration; its rates of use of non-renewable resources should not exceed the rate at which sustainable renewable substitutes are developed; and its rates of pollution emissions should not exceed the assimilative capacity of the environment."[5] As is pointed out in the next chapter, the very concept of sustainability arose because of our growing awareness that human activities appear to be reaching thresholds that are unsustainable with respect to the natural environment that supports those activities. We are beginning to understand that crossing some of these thresholds may be irreversible.

The need to develop a more precise definition of sustainability and related concepts such as sustainable development and sustainable growth has been a driving force behind the work of Dr. Karl-Henrik Robèrt, his colleague, physicist Dr. John Holmberg, and other scientists and researchers affiliated with The Natural Step. As Dr. Robèrt has commented, "Everyone talks about sustainability, but no one knows what it is." It is precisely this dilemma that he sought to clarify, a search which resulted in the identification of four "System Conditions" that define societal sustainability. The very issue of how we can clearly conceptualize a sustainable society is at the heart of The Natural Step framework described in Chapters 2 and 3.

Carl Frankel speaks of "the great divide"[6] that exists between two categories of corporations in their attitudes toward "the environment." On one side of the great divide are those companies and individuals who have come to understand that their relationship to the natural world affords a true business opportunity for the corporation, that properly approached, it can represent a source of new profits and creativity. On the other side of the divide are those companies and individuals who still regard the environment as merely a cost to the corporation, something to be dealt with through regulatory compliance and risk management surely, but rarely an opportunity for innovation and new revenues, with a kind of second-class status amongst the corporate echelons.

The central thrust of this book is to describe how four successful and dynamic companies, two of them global in nature, one principally European and one principally American — IKEA, Scandic Hotels, Interface, and Collins Pine — are learning to integrate sustainable development at both the strategic and operational levels for improved performance and profitability. These companies, described in Chapters 4–7, have shown marked improvement in each aspect of their relationship to sustainability's triple bottom line: profits, people, and planet. For these corporations, the environment has attained first-class status within their organizations. These companies have crossed the great divide to the positive side, where sustainable development takes its place in the executive suite with the other core competencies of the corporations.

As we will examine in the chapters to follow, benefits to the companies that have integrated The Natural Step framework into the heart of their corporate strategy and operations include improved competitiveness, lowered costs, enhanced profits, greater resource productivity, enhanced new product innovation, improved staff morale, reduced staff turnover, lower environmental impact, and greater market share.

In the last section of the book, Chapters 8–10, we summarize the major lessons and tools that emerged from our research on these four companies. These chapters detail what we've learned, along with a vision of what corporations can become — and need to become — in order to contribute to the healthy continuation of the communities of which they are a vital part. We include here a very useful chapter written by corporate sustainability consultant Susan Burns that describes the relationship between The Natural Step framework and environmental management systems; this concept is gaining popularity worldwide as an effective resource for management in the movement toward corporate sustainability. In the final chapter, we explore what we mean by an evolutionary corporation.

A Synopsis of Our Argument

1. The whole structure of industrial society is based on a faulty design. Ours is a take-make-waste society that violates the conditions for sustainable human life on Earth. To understand the problem, we need to take a natural systems view of our society and its relationship to the environment.

2. Although the elements of the problem are complex in their many dimensions, the core issues are easy to understand through the intellectual framework developed by The Natural Step.

3. It is likely not too late for industrial society to take action, if we act now. There is no more time for business as usual. It is not necessary or

important to assign blame. It is necessary to take action, to change our present unsustainable course.

4. Humanity is now able to take its evolution into its own hands by conscious choice and design. This is a basis for hope. Some innovative people and companies are already taking conscious evolutionary action, and some of those are using The Natural Step in that process.

5. We can learn from these innovative people and companies to discern glimpses of the evolutionary path forward. The Natural Step can act as a kind of corporate compass to assist organizations in their voyages of discovery, the corporate odyssey which both Collins Pine and Interface describe as their "journey to sustainability."

6. Companies that take on a higher purpose to their business mission create an empowered workforce of energized and motivated people, which makes the company stronger and more profitable. Those conscious, innovative companies that are redesigning the way they do business to include caring for the Earth are what we call "evolutionary corporations."

The creative leading-edge businesses described in the following pages are creating the basis of real long-term wealth for tomorrow. IKEA, Scandic Hotels, Interface, and Collins Pine share their driving motivations and initial steps to a new form of business — "natural capitalism", as Paul Hawken calls it. This book is also about leading thinking in the natural sciences and its integration into the practice of business by some of the world's most progressive corporations. This is also about our culture, our evolution, and the very crucial juncture we have reached. Finally, this is a book about the power of the individual, the power of commitment, and the power of taking a stand for what you passionately believe.

CHAPTER 2

A New Framework
for Management

*The world we have created today as a result of our thinking
thus far has problems that cannot be solved by thinking
the way we thought when we created them.*
Albert Einstein

*Metaphor encourages us to think and act in new ways.
It extends horizons of insight and creates new possibilities.*
Gareth Morgan — *Images of Organization*

ALL THEORIES OF ORGANIZATION and management are based on implicit images or metaphors, according to Gareth Morgan in his seminal work *Images of Organization.*[1] These metaphors inform our understanding of reality by highlighting certain aspects of that reality while ignoring others. We use metaphors to understand reality much as we use a picture frame. The frame calls our attention to what is inside its border, while we tend to ignore everything that is outside of it.

In *Vital Lies, Simple Truths,* an analysis of the psychology of self-deception at the individual, organizational, and societal levels, Daniel Goleman points out that our metaphor-frames provide us with a context to interpret reality.[2] They tell us how to understand and react to what is going on around us. Anything outside the frame, by definition, does not deserve attention. These "out-of-the-frame" aspects of reality become individual, organizational, and social blind spots.

The dominant framework that has guided most organizational and management thinking in the 20th century has been based on the "organization-as-machine" metaphor. According to this metaphor, an organization is a rational, technical entity. Like a machine, an organization is designed to operate as a network of parts, which are further specified as networks of precisely defined jobs. Jobs are linked together in a chain of command, and the organization operates in a "command and control" fashion. This framework for thinking, this mental model, has been both useful and successful for organizing human activity. Otherwise it would not have survived and thrived as long as it has. Nonetheless, it has important limitations that are becoming increasingly significant in a rapidly changing business environment. For example, very little attention is given to the human aspects of an organization. People are treated as replaceable parts. Knowledge and decision-making power reside with those in authority, who sit at the top and operate through a chain of command to ensure that the "parts" operate efficiently and mechanistically to achieve the organizational goals they set. As a result, according to Morgan, "mechanistically structured organizations have great difficulty adapting to changing circumstances because they are designed to achieve predetermined goals; they are not designed for innovation."[3] In an age characterized by accelerating and dramatic change, corporations organized around a mechanistic metaphor are at a distinct disadvantage.

Because this well-worn metaphor no longer fits the reality being experienced by many businesses, new metaphors are capturing considerable attention. Prominent among these is the learning organization or "organization-as-brain" metaphor. This metaphor sees organizations as complex systems that are capable of learning. Not only do organizations process information about current circumstances, a function vital to every aspect of the organization, they are also able to imagine different possibilities that go beyond the present state. The ability to learn and innovate is spread throughout the organization. Knowledge and decision-making power resides in individuals and teams constituted to learn. Morgan comments: "Intelligent learning systems use information about the present to ground their activities in a business reality. But they are also skilled in spotting the 'fracture lines,' signals, and trends that point to future possibilities. They are skilled at imagining and anticipating possible futures and acting in the present in ways that help make those futures realities."[4] Learning is a continuous process that takes place at the individual, team, and organizational level. We do not intend that our reference to "the learning organization" be interpreted as refering to an objective reality, to a thing, but rather as refering to a constant process of developing toward an ideal.

Learning organizations are able to respond to a rapidly changing environment because they embrace change as the norm. In contrast to the skills required in a context of the rigid mechanistic certainty implied in the organization-as-machine metaphor, the learning organization must develop competencies in

- Creating compelling aspirations and a shared vision that energizes and inspires organizational stakeholders;
- Scanning and anticipating changes in the wider environment;

- Questioning, challenging, and changing operating norms and assumptions; and

- creating new strategic directions and patterns of organization.[5]

How does this contribute to competitive advantage? According to Stuart Hart from the University of North Carolina, "Researchers in the field of strategic management have long understood that competitive advantage depends upon the match between distinctive internal (organizational) capabilities and changing external (environmental) circumstances."[6] To realize and maintain competitive advantage when these external circumstances are changing rapidly, an organization must develop internal capabilities to quickly and constantly scan its environment, anticipate change, develop the appropriate strategies and skills, and put them into action. Rather than rely on directives that come through the chain of command, the learning organization develops corporate values and aspirations that are aligned with the personal values and aspirations of the members of the organization. These provide a compelling force that guides diverse activities toward a common vision no matter how rapidly the external environment is changing. Many more minds contribute knowledge, creativity, and innovation to the process.

Learning to be a learning organization is no easy task because conventional management thinking and management structures are still strongly influenced by the organization-as-machine image. Becoming a learning organization often requires a fundamental shift in corporate culture, in the way people interact and collaborate, in the way they think and view their internal systems and interrelationships, and in the way they organize work. The real power of the learning organization is the ability to create vision, purpose, and direction as the motivating force for action. For many companies, this is not only very new and exciting, but also frightening territory.

The growing popularity of the learning organization as an organizational metaphor indicates that it is meeting some important perceived needs in today's business environment. As learning organizations, corporations are able to envision different futures and to act more quickly and flexibly in the face of change than their machine-model compatriots. They operate in greater dynamic relationship with their business environments. Is this enough to ensure that a corporation can act intelligently, create the most viable vision, effectively read the correct signals from the environment, and act with appropriate speed in the most effective direction?

Much depends upon what is included in the frame of the business environment and what is ignored. As Hart points out, there is a serious omission in management theory. It "systematically ignores the constraints imposed by the biophysical (natural) environment. Historically, management theory has used a narrow and parochial concept of environment that emphasizes political, economic, social, and technological aspects to the virtual exclusion of the natural environment. Given the growing magnitude of ecological problems, however, this omission has rendered existing theory inadequate as a basis for identifying important emerging sources of competitive advantage."[7]

In other words, we still have a perceptual blind spot. Although industry takes place within, and depends upon, natural systems and cycles, these factors have, since the beginning of the industrial revolution, been outside the frame of business reality. As long as nature was so big and human activities proportionally so small, it was possible for societies to work quite well despite this perceptual omission. We could depend upon the Earth's abundance to provide all of our raw material needs; to meet our requirements for clean water, healthy air, and fertile soil; and to recycle, process, or simply store our wastes. Because we did not really understand how the Earth's systems work, it was hard to imagine how human society could affect the Earth to the point of altering the very systems upon which our continued health and survival depend. This was simply outside the frame of reality for us as individuals and organizations. We have acted blindly, and despite advances in environmental knowledge, we continue to act as though the Earth's capacity to absorb our garbage, wastes, effluents, pollutants, and toxins is infinite.

Goleman suggests that the future prospects of the planet are intimately linked to the human capacity for self-deception. He reminds us that even the most ecologically concerned among us do not really know the net effect on the planet of how we live and carry out our many enterprises. And, for most of us, being oblivious to the relationship between our daily decisions and the effect of those decisions on the natural environment "allows us to slip into the grand self-deception, that the small and large decisions in our material lives are of no great consequence."[8]

However, today we continue to remain oblivious only if we choose to do so. Scientific evidence documenting the effects of human activities on natural systems is compounding. We have moved from being products of evolution to being drivers of evolution. Our frame needs to change to incorporate a larger view. Once proportionally insignificant to the health of the planet, or even merely to whole ecosystems, human systems are now unexpectedly contributing to Earth and climate changes on a scale of geologic proportions. This means that we are having an impact on the planet at a scale akin to the forces of the Earth itself.

Human society, with its exponentially increasing population and its far-reaching technology, has become an evolutionary force on a planetary scale. The compelling evidence of this is not restricted to obscure scientific journals — it is publicly and widely available. The environmental effects of human activities are consistently featured on radio and television, from daily news reports to special editions and programs. They are featured prominently and regularly in articles in newspapers and magazines. Our purpose here is not to detail the evidence of human impacts on the natural environment, but to acknowledge that these effects are increasing dramatically and cumulatively. Several factors contribute to this, such as increases in global population, the spread of industrialization, increased affluence that produces even greater demands for resources, and the belief that we are separate from nature, exempt from natural constraints, or too small relative to natural systems to make a difference. As it becomes ever more evident that the effects of human activities on nature are beginning to harm the health and well-being of human communities all over our planet, we can no longer deceive ourselves into thinking this isn't the case. Very soon, it will become mandatory to include these factors in the frame of day-to-day business because the distress of the natural world is already thrusting itself ever more forcefully into the frame of our personal and social realities.

The question then is: how do companies build the knowledge base and the competencies necessary to fully integrate the natural environment into their business framework? It seems clear that they should use the tools and the disciplines being developed to help organizations become learning organizations, for it will certainly take such organizations to change the operating norms and assumptions that have guided business in the 20th century. Yet something more is required. We need to integrate the natural environment into the frame of our business reality in a realistic and operational way. It is no longer sufficient to be a smart organization, one that can scan the commercial environment, detect variations, and react accordingly. If we restrict ourselves to reacting to signals when it comes to human impact on the natural environment, we may well end up focusing our organizational resources just on minimizing the pain of irreversible damage. Our business organizations need to become conscious of the evolutionary role business plays in the future of the planet and to take responsibility for that role. What we need now is a new metaphor. We call that metaphor the *evolutionary corporation.*

The new management framework of the evolutionary corporation applies the competencies developed through organizational learning to a wider view of business reality: ecological factors are integral to the business frame of the 21st century. The evolutionary corporation understands that competitive advantage in tomorrow's markets will require building strong core competencies in the development of environmentally benign, even restorative, products, processes, and systems. The evolutionary corporation is conscious of, and accepts responsibility for, the ecological effects of its business decisions at every level of corporate activity. These will range from what kind of paper to use to how products are designed, used, and disposed of, to where and how to build facilities, among countless other common operational decisions. This corporation is also intent not only on financially surviving but on thriving, because it is only by being successful that it can influence our current evolutionary trajectory.

The companies that have embraced this path are pioneering a task that is at once both profoundly simple and profoundly complicated: the integration of natural systems and natural laws into the frame of their business reality. It is, on the one hand, a simple task because the natural laws that constitute the larger frame of reality are already known. There is general scientific consensus about these laws. Although we may ignore them, we cannot change them or make them go away. We briefly describe these scientific principles in Chapter 3.

On the other hand, their corporate task is profoundly complex because it requires re-thinking many of the fundamental assumptions, and in many cases re-designing products, processes, and systems that form the core of their business world. They are unleashing creativity and innovation to design a new future, one based on a new premise: in the 21st century, companies that learn from and imitate nature in order to operate in harmony with natural laws will be more successful and profitable than those that don't. The evolutionary corporation operates with a wider vision of its purpose, an expanded definition of its business environment, and a sense of evolutionary responsibility. This task is both daunting and enormously exciting. It engages the very best in human ingenuity while it invites us to be humble in view of the immensity of what we still do not know.

When it comes to the environment, leading edge companies are on a steep learning curve. Environmental awareness seemed to first dawn in the 1970s with the advent of Earth Day, burgeoning environmental legislation in many countries, the first U.N. Environmental Conference in Stockholm, and Love Canal, among many other infamous contamination events. According to Carl Frankel in his book *In Earth's Company*, this was the "era of compliance:" "During this period, good corporate citizenship consisted of simply obeying the law. Corporations routinely proclaimed that it was company policy to meet all regulatory requirements."[9]

In the 1980s, particularly in 1984, a new type of environmental awareness and call for responsibility was ushered in with the accidental release of 15,000 gallons of deadly methyl isocyanate from a Union Carbide plant in Bhopal, India. Frankel notes: "Earlier eco-catastrophes like Love Canal and Times Beach paled before Bhopal. Literally overnight, it became clear to business executives and the general public that corporate environmental practices had to change."[10] This marked the dawn of the "beyond compliance era," one of public accountability, pollution prevention, and fast, and often expensive, learning. As Bruce Piasecki comments in *Corporate Environmental Strategy*, "Since the tragic release at Bhopal, India, corporations worldwide have experienced an avalanche of change. Some of this change is reliable; some of it is questionable; all of it is costly and consequential."[11]

The third era of environmental awareness began in the 1990s and is characterized by terms such as "eco-efficiency" and "dematerialization." Companies are moving beyond pollution prevention that focuses on reducing environmentally harmful outputs, to eco-efficiency which looks at "industrial metabolism." Frankel notes: "Eco-efficiency strategies run the gamut from energy-efficiency retrofits to the use of recovered and recoverable materials, to what has become known as 'dematerialization' (e.g., reducing the amount of materials used, for instance by making packaging thinner and lighter.)"[12]

The fourth era, which is dawning now at the turn of the millennium, must extend even beyond eco-efficiency and continuous improvements in environmental performance to a new guiding vision, one that we believe requires a new framework for business reality. Frankel suggests four keystones of this new era:

• Progress toward zero waste: rather than seeking to reduce waste, companies will come as close as possible to eliminating it altogether.

• Whole systems thinking: addressing problems at the level of the entire system, rather than the parts, using a design approach that allows strategists to conceive something completely new rather than simply to extrapolate the future from the present.

• Looking beyond internal operational sustainability and making the world's problems the company's problems.

• Moving beyond the focus on environmental issues to a focus on sustainable development.[13]

Although these corporate developmental phases are set within the context of a particular historical period, not all companies are entering, or have entered, each phase, or era, at the same time. Far from it! In the era of eco-efficiency, for example, there are countless organizations that are just beginning to consider what it means to move beyond compliance, and countless others for whom environmental management still means mere compliance with the law. On the other side, there are already early adopters of a sustainable development (fourth era) approach to business. These companies are far advanced on the learning curve and are developing the core competencies of the future that will set the standards for those who follow.

Figure 2.1 summarizes some of the stages, management innovations, attitudes toward change, and other elements that contribute to industry's learning curve as it moves toward greater integration and explicit mainstreaming of the environmental aspects of business. Set in the context of Frankel's four phases, the figure highlights some of the ways industry has responded to the transformation of what is relevant to the business framework.

Figure 2.1 — Industry's Sustainability Learning Curve

	Before 1970s	1st Era COMPLIANCE	2nd Era BEYOND COMPLIANCE	3rd Era ECO-EFFICIENCY	4th Era SUSTAINABLE DEVELOPMENT
		1970s	1980s	1990s	2000s
		Pollution Control/Compliance			
		Pollution Prevention/Waste Minimization			
			Stakeholder Participation		
			TQEM*/Environmental Management Systems		
				Product Stewardship/DFE/LCA*	
				Environmental Cost Accounting	
					Integrated Management Systems
					Design for Sustainability
CORPORATE RESPONSE	Unprepared	Reactive	Anticipatory	Proactive	High Integration
INDUSTRY GOALS	None	Regulatory Standards	Cost Avoidance • Impact Reduction • Pre-emption of Regulation • Leadership • Legitimacy Protection • Partnerships • Competitive Edge	Profit Centre Approach • Eco-efficiency • Dematerialization • Strategic Environmental Management	Explicit Mainstreaming of Environmental Goals • DFE/LCA* Systems • Environmental Cost Management • Resource Productivity • Products of Service • Culture change

Source: Adapted from Beloff, 1998; Frankel, 1998; and Richards and Frosch, 1997

*for explanations of abbreviations see text.

During the first era, which focused on compliance, industry went from being basically unprepared, with no strategic goals regarding environmental issues, to an attitude of complying with legal requirements. The movement was essentially from an inactive attitude to a reactive one. As environmental legislation increased, companies reacted by setting their environmental goals according to regulatory standards.

With the advent of the second era, marked by the Bhopal incident, companies became more anticipatory in their environmental strategy. Their strategic focus and environmental frame was geared to avoiding costs, reducing potential impacts of environmental factors through pollution prevention, and preempting legislation.

The third era marks a period of emerging integration where environmental management is reframed again, and begins to be viewed not just as a "cost center" but as a "profit center." It is becoming accepted as a legitimate business factor, one that leads to competitive advantage and positive bottom-line impacts. As such, the focus is cutting current costs through reducing inputs and waste, while also creating opportunities through innovation.

In the fourth era, industry moves into a process of deeper integration where products and processes are designed on environmental criteria ("design for environment" or DfE, and "design for disassembly" or DfD); the full lifecycle of products is taken into account and is described as "cradle-to-cradle" rather than "cradle-to-grave" because the product never becomes waste — instead, it is reused or recycled in some way. Outputs are reframed. Companies sell the service or quality of their products rather than the actual material from which their products are constructed.

Closed loop processes become the norm. Companies proactively take on the challenge of designing a sustainable future. Environmental goals become as normal and essential to business as accurate financial accounting or quality control. The culture of the corporation changes to accommodate and create a new ecologically sustainable way of doing business.

In the first, second, and third eras, the natural environment is perceived as something outside the company. The relationship between the enterprise and the natural environment corresponds to this outlook: "ignore it" (first era – inactive); "react to it" (second era – reactive); or "predict changes arising from it" (third era – anticipatory). In the evolutionary perceptual reframing of the fourth era, an enterprise recognizes that it is a part of nature and consciously integrates its vision and operations with natural cycles and processes.

The Natural Step Framework

How *does* the proactive company design the future? The Natural Step provides a simple yet elegant framework to integrate environmental issues into the frame of business reality and to move the company toward sustainable development. The framework's purpose is to explain systems in the simplest way so an organization can deal with complexity without either getting lost in it or denying that it exists. It includes four core processes:

- Perceiving the nature of the unsustainable direction of business and society and the self-interest implicit in shifting to a sustainable direction;
- Understanding the first-order principles for sustainability, i.e., the four System Conditions;
- Strategic visioning through "back-casting" from a desired sustainable future; and
- Identifying strategic steps to move the company from its current reality toward its desired vision.

The Natural Step framework is used to develop a new shared mental model of business reality, one that integrates environmental considerations into strategic business decisions and day-to-day operations. It provides a common language to talk about sustainability and facilitates the creation of shared goals that move the company in a sustainable direction. These attributes allow scientists, strategists, experts and non-experts, technicians, production line personnel, marketing and sales people, and accountants at all levels within an organization to learn together effectively and to implement actions that lead to a robust and sustainable future.

Despite the complex nature of today's environmental realities, the primary components of the global situation that we confront concerning the natural environment can be visualized simply. Imagine the walls of a giant funnel. The upper wall is resource availability and the ability of the ecosystem to continue to provide services. The lower wall is societal demand for resources that are converted into goods and services such as clothes, shelter, food, transportation, etc., and ecosystem services such as clean water, clean air, and healthy soil. As aggregate societal demand increases and the capacity to meet those demands decreases, society as a whole moves into a narrower portion of the funnel.

As the funnel narrows, there is less room to maneuver and there are fewer options available. The inactive company that remains oblivious to the changing environmental realities is likely to hit the wall and go out of business. The reactive company waits until it gets clear signals from the environment, often by running into the wall, and then it must react quickly or fail. Often, options for action that would have been possible earlier, and usually at much less expense, are no longer available. There is little time for experimentation or strategic corrections.

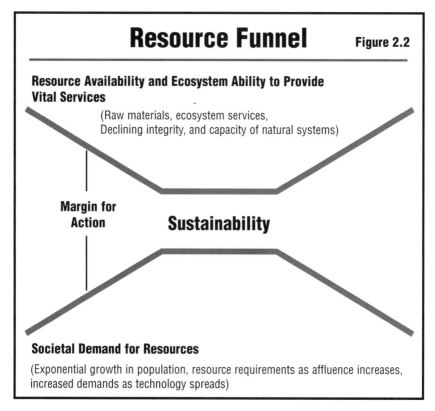

Resource Funnel
Figure 2.2

Resource Availability and Ecosystem Ability to Provide Vital Services

(Raw materials, ecosystem services, Declining integrity, and capacity of natural systems)

Margin for Action

Sustainability

Societal Demand for Resources

(Exponential growth in population, resource requirements as affluence increases, increased demands as technology spreads)

The viability of solutions is often only tested by running into dead-ends or other environmental or social constraints. Changes may be dramatic and costly.

The anticipatory company forecasts the future based on past trends. It has no clear vision of sustainability because it is extrapolating its future from the conditions of the present, which are not ecologically sustainable. Thus, it is vulnerable to sudden and unanticipated changes in the external market as the walls of the funnel close. While it may adjust slowly as it reads new signals from the environment, it is still in danger of hitting the wall if its corporate vision does not become aligned quickly enough. Like the reactive company, it may find itself suddenly faced with dramatic and costly changes with little or no time to set a corrective course.

The goal of a sustainable organization or a sustainable society is to direct its activities and investments to the center of the funnel rather than towards the wall. The strategic, proactive company seeks first to understand the larger environmental and social realities that are creating the funnel effect and, based on this understanding, assesses its current reality with respect to this broader systemic perspective. This means that the company must understand what is required for society in general and its operations in particular to be sustainable.

With this perspective firmly in mind, the company can project itself into the future with investments strategically targeted toward the opening in the funnel and create an ideal vision of itself as a truly sustainable company. Once this desired condition is envisioned, the company can back-cast to determine the steps required to reach the desired state. Each step is planned to become a platform for future steps. In contrast to forecasting, by which present methods are extrapolated into the future, back-casting allows for a departure from present, unsustainable extrapolations in order to attain new goals and define truly new conditions. Back-casting is particularly useful when

- the problem to be studied is complex;
- there is a need for major change;
- dominant trends are part of the problem;
- the problem to a great extent is a matter of externalities; and
- the scope is wide enough and the time-horizon long enough to leave considerable room for deliberate choice.[14]

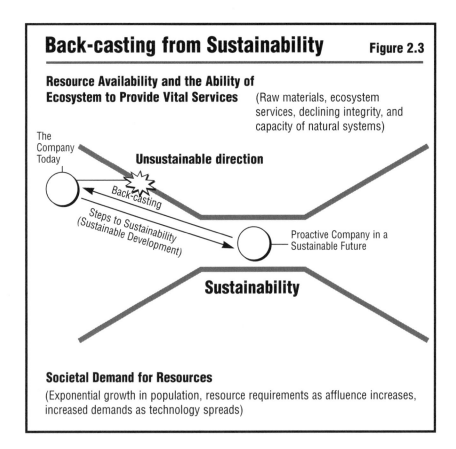

Back-casting from Sustainability — Figure 2.3

Resource Availability and the Ability of Ecosystem to Provide Vital Services (Raw materials, ecosystem services, declining integrity, and capacity of natural systems)

The Company Today

Unsustainable direction

Back-casting

Steps to Sustainability (Sustainable Development)

Proactive Company in a Sustainable Future

Sustainability

Societal Demand for Resources
(Exponential growth in population, resource requirements as affluence increases, increased demands as technology spreads)

To design for sustainability, the company needs to understand what is required for society to be sustainable and what constitutes an ecologically sustainable and integrated human/nature system. Any system is defined by its fundamental principles. With this in mind, Robèrt sought to articulate the first-order principles for sustainability.

Robèrt understood that one of the first challenges we face is learning how to think in systems, that is, to think in wholes. He developed the following metaphor to help clarify both the concept of thinking in wholes and the problem of identifying first-order principles. He likens the way that we think about environmental issues to a tree. Currently we are focused on the many leaves of the tree while ignoring the trunk and the branches, which are the first-order principles of the system. He develops the metaphor this way:

> We are confronted with a series of seemingly unrelated questions: Is the greenhouse effect really a threat, or will it actually prevent another ice age? Is economic growth harmful, or does it provide resources for healing the environment? Will the costs of phasing out non-renewable energy sources outweigh the benefits? Can communities, regions, or countries accomplish anything useful on their own, or must they wait for international agreements?
>
> In the midst of all this chatter about the "leaves," very few of us have been paying attention to the environment's trunk and branches. They are deteriorating as a result of processes about which there is little or no controversy; and the thousands of individual problems that are the subject of so much debate are, in fact, manifestations of systemic errors that are undermining the foundations of human society.[15]

The trunk is a stable entity that provides the framework for the system. The overall principles, found in the trunk and the branches, are immutable and non-negotiable. They must hold if the tree is to continue to thrive, just as first-order principles must hold if the system is to continue to operate effectively. The leaves are all the consequences and activities of the system. They are the variety of designs, ideas, and strategies that arise from the first-order principles. These are negotiable.

Robèrt explains further:

> By "first-order principles" of an object or a system, we mean the "core" principles that define the object or the system. All other principles or details of the system can be described, or ordered, in line with those principles. Soccer or chess, for instance, are defined by the first-order principles of these game systems — the objectives and the rules of the games — not by various exercises, strategies, and skills to become a good player. But in order to become a good player, the starting point is

to learn about the objectives and rules. This is the easy part. After that, the more advanced and demanding training to become a good player begins. All the strategies and skills are then elaborated as consequences of the first-order principles. This means, that by "first-order" we do not mean "more important" than anything else. It is just the logical starting point in making more sense of, and coordinating in a strategic way, the other important parts of the system.

Planning toward sustainability by back-casting from first-order principles for sustainability and distinguishing such principles from the various means or measures to meet them (like "renewable energy", or ISO 14001) promotes:

- Simplicity without reduction: it makes it simpler to deal with complexity, yet doesn't simplify in the sense of disregarding any of the complexity.
- Validity at any scale and activity: it is simpler to coordinate various parts and details into a comprehensive whole.
- The creation of a shared mental framework: it is generally easier for teams or groups of people to share the first-order principles of a vision than it is for them to share detailed pictures of the vision.
- Non-prescriptive problem solving: creativity is supported if experts in various fields share the framework for planning, but are allowed to be free within that framework.
- Thinking upstream in cause-effect chains: upstream causes of any problem can more easily be properly understood and addressed. Analyses of detailed "downstream problems" then flow more logically. This supports problem-solving without creating new problems for the future.
- Measurability: it is easier to elaborate non-overlapping indicators that are based on critical flows in a wide enough perspective.

Using the metaphor of the tree, we could say that a company needs to learn to identify when it is in the leaves and how to constantly refer back to the trunk and branches, the first-order principles, when designing its sustainable future. But we could also use another metaphor: if a company plans to create a vision of itself as a sustainable enterprise, it needs to move its investments and development toward the opening of the funnel. How can a company know what boundaries define that opening? By focusing on essential, non-negotiable principles about which scientists can agree. This systems perspective makes it possible to build a framework of four fundamental conditions a society must meet to be ecologically sustainable.

The Four System Conditions for Sustainability

The primary purpose behind the development and articulation of the four System Conditions was to find a framework for discussing sustainable human activities through a set of non-overlapping first-order principles. Ironically, the very concept of sustainability did not become meaningful until we began to imagine that human activities could create a condition of ecological unsustainability. For that reason, to derive the first-order principles, we ask in what ways human activities can possibly deteriorate or destroy the complex ecological system on which we all depend. We then determine that these activities would not occur in a sustainable society. Although we can imagine what an unsustainable society looks like, we cannot define in detail how the sustainable society looks because there are infinite ways in which such a society could evolve. However, we can describe the framework within which that evolution must take place.

The mechanisms through which human activities can deteriorate, or otherwise negatively affect, nature are then translated into statements concerning the minimum environmental criteria a society must meet to be sustainable:[16]

Figure 2.4

The Four System Conditions

In order for a society to be sustainable, nature's functions and diversity are not systematically:

1 *...subject to increasing concentrations of substances extracted from the Earth's crust;*

2 *...subject to increasing concentrations of substances produced by society; or*

3 *...impoverished by overharvesting or other forms of ecosystem manipulation.*

And,

4 *resources are used fairly and efficiently in order to meet basic human needs worldwide.*

In a sustainable system, society does not systematically draw upon renewable resources faster than they can be regenerated. A sustainable society does not systematically reduce the productive capacity of nature by overharvesting, eroding the soil, or otherwise detrimentally manipulating green surfaces. It does not leak compounds in such amounts, and of such quality, that their concentration systematically increases in nature. In a sustainable society, population is stabilized and resources are used efficiently and fairly to meet basic human needs. In a sustainable society, the driving forces of social and economic development are organized around, and operate in ways that conform with, the rules of the system.

How does a company know if it is moving in the direction of sustainability unless it has an idea of what will keep the funnel open? This is where first-order principles — the four System Conditions — are essential. From these principles we can describe the operating principles of a sustainable society. The System Conditions and some of the scientific principles underlying them are described further in Chapter 3.

Applying The Natural Step Framework

The four companies profiled in Part Two have integrated the environment into their business reality using The Natural Step framework. The companies recognize that the economy and the environment are integrally linked and that nature's limits have both significant economic consequences and opportunities for their businesses. They use this knowledge to guide their company's planning and investment strategies and to increase their long-term viability and competitive advantage. They understand that important economic benefits can be gained by learning to operate in harmony with nature and by guarding against a collision with the limits imposed by natural laws or by society's reactions to negative environmental effects, i.e., the walls of the funnel.

Using the concept of the funnel again, we can see how everyday business realities create pressures that are closing the walls. They are

- Competition, costs, shortages of raw materials, expenses, natural disasters, and environmental clean-up, etc.;
- Customer pressure from more environmentally concerned citizens, boycotts, and bad publicity;
- Regulations (environmental, health and safety, and community right to know), standards (ISO and others)[17], fees (for pollution, disposal of waste, and violations);
- Increased competition for the best employees, employee loyalty, health, and need for meaningful work.

Changes from these pressures are likely to appear suddenly as threshold effects in a non-linear fashion. This means that the slower the market reacts the larger (not smaller) the difference in future stakes between proactive and reactive companies will probably be. Proactive companies can prepare themselves and avoid sudden and perhaps overwhelming demands for solutions. With this understanding, a company invests toward the future market, that is, toward the opening of the funnel. The strategic organization makes itself less economically dependent on practices, products, and processes that reinforce or perpetuate the mechanisms that disrupt or destroy natural systems. The company that ignores the walls of the funnel, that does not include the realities of the natural world into its business frame, is likely to be blindsided by these realities, often at a high cost.

The Natural Step framework can be applied at any scale from board-level strategic decision-making to day-to-day operations on the shop floor. We have identified three basic interrelated applications for the framework: strategic visioning, building a learning platform, and integrating sustainable practices through employee involvement, action, innovation, and continuous learning.

Strategic Visioning

If a company accepts the definition of reality contained in the four System Conditions, then the purpose and operations of the specific business enterprise may need to be re-evaluated, and re-envisioned, and possibly redesigned to be more compatible with that framework. This level of application generally occurs first at the upper executive levels of the business, and is eventually communicated to all shareholders, employees, suppliers, and customers. The process is similar to that used to create shared vision and compelling aspirations described in the growing literature about learning in organizations.[18] The distinction is that the company's vision is set within the framework of a sustainable society. Back-casting combined with the System Conditions provides a valuable tool for incorporating sustainability into strategic visioning.

Building a Learning Platform

The learning process provides the platform upon which all other applications are built. Through education and training, employees develop the conceptual framework, the shared mental model, that makes it possible to explore what is sustainable and unsustainable behavior. Learning is also an integral part of the strategic visioning process. It is necessary to learn what is required for sustainability before a sustainable future can be realistically envisioned. Once the strategic visioning process is done, The Natural Step framework is developed into an educational program tailored to the specific business enterprise. All employees participate in this program. For some specialized areas, additional, more advanced training is often developed where the System Conditions are examined in greater detail.

Integrating Sustainability into All Business Functions

All companies have two categories of flows: matter and energy. In realistic terms, over time these are comprised of hundreds of thousands of flow components moving through a business. During a typical day, each employee will make dozens, often hundreds, of decisions involving flows into or out of the corporation. This may range from the mundane, such as the use of electricity, water, paper, coffee, and so on, to larger transportation, manufacturing, and inventory purchasing decisions. Thus, every employee is a resource gatekeeper. For real change to take place, every employee needs a common language and a shared mental model to contribute effectively to the company's sustainability vision. In addition, they need to be involved in translating that mental model of sustainability into daily work practices.

The Natural Step framework can be used to assess the environmental impact of every element of a company's operations. Employees are empowered to make changes, to experiment, and even to make mistakes in the course of learning how to operate more resource effectively and efficiently. Processes are established to reinforce learning until operating within the conditions of sustainability becomes second nature.

At this level of application, the goal is to move from awareness generated through education to practice, and then to integrate what is learned through practice into a continuous learning process that constantly feeds back into practical applications. Environmental impacts are no longer treated as special considerations that must be given to decisions and activities but are taken for granted as the way business is conducted. In other words, the full integration of The Natural Step framework into the operation of business means that working within the framework of these first-order principles is inherent at all levels of business operations from the executive office to the reception desk, warehouse, and shop floor. This integration shows up in product and process design, measurement systems, and bottom-line impacts.

The Link Between Business Conduct and Ecological Sustainability

Why would business perceive its interests to be linked to ecological sustainability? Interface, Inc., a Fortune 1000 company with annual revenues in excess of US$1 billion, answers this question:

> We need to understand the basic laws of nature and how they will affect the future of this and all companies. Just as we watch for long-term trends that could adversely impact our employees and shareholders, we

have studied the consequences of our continued assault on nature and have determined that unless we change, we may be responsible for catastrophic losses to ourselves and others. Our concern for the environment is not a short-term attempt to improve our image, but a strategic change necessary to guide our corporation into and through the 21st century.[19]

The strategic self-interest of corporations involves being astute about the current reality in which their operations take place and being aware of the trends, opportunities, and risks that will affect their operations and profits in the future. Every successful business enterprise must take these factors into account. A company that ignores the realities of its total business environment is unlikely to stay in business. What does The Natural Step offer business with regard to understanding current reality?

Fundamental scientific laws, such as the laws of thermodynamics and other physical and natural laws, impose certain non-negotiable limits upon human activities. The logical process, based upon scientific rationality, through which The Natural Step derived the first-order principles of sustainability, is transparent and continues to be subject to scientific peer review. In Sweden, the development of the four System Conditions occurred with extensive input from the scientific community, was debated publicly, and has been presented in respected scientific journals. Formal meetings of professional scientists and engineers to review the science behind The Natural Step have taken place in North America, the United Kingdom, and Australia.

Such a meeting of 21 prominent scientists and engineers from the United States and Canada, which included members of the U.S. National Academy of Sciences and one Nobel Prize winner, took place in the United States in 1997 and resulted in the following statement, to which all of the scientists and engineers present added their signatures:

> We believe that without solutions to the problems addressed by The Natural Step, both human civilization and biological diversity are seriously threatened. The development of appropriate solutions to these problems requires the support and contributions of the global community of scientists and engineers.
>
> We further believe that the application of The Natural Step's Four System Conditions is a valid approach for addressing these problems, and is especially useful for organizing information regarding sustainability. To be effective, the Conditions must also be augmented by the evaluation of the environmental impacts of specific substances and practices.

We urge The Natural Step to continue to engage scientists and engineers fully in the application, testing, and improvement of the System Conditions and all other aspects of its programs.[20]

Why should business care that its operations continue to violate the principles of a sustainable society? Why should it care that waste is accumulating in all living systems in the world? Why should it care that resources are being used up at a rate greater than that at which they can be replenished? Interface answers these questions in its *1997 Sustainability Report:*

> We believe that institutions that continuously violate these principles will suffer economically. The walls of the funnel will continue to impose themselves in the form of environmentally concerned customers, stricter legislation, higher costs and fees for resources and waste, and tougher competition from companies who anticipate the narrowing limits and adjust accordingly. The failure of institutions and businesses to begin to address sustainability not only leads to hitting the funnel wall — wasted effort, energy, money, and resources — but further constricts the funnel itself in the long run."[21]

The more fully a business enterprise accepts The Natural Step framework as a valid description of the reality within which it operates — and upon which its present and future prospects depend — the more likely it links its self-interest to sustainability. The educational program of The Natural Step presents the framework in a simple and logical form. Because the approach is so basic, the validity of this mental model is difficult to discredit, albeit still possible to ignore. Ignoring this reality, however, does not make it any less true. As society continues to ignore it, the walls of the funnel are necessarily narrowing and the margin for action is decreasing accordingly.

As the cases presented in this book show, business enterprises that have adopted The Natural Step framework believe they gain considerable competitive advantage. By adapting their products and processes within the System Conditions framework now, they avoid having to adapt later at greater cost, in less time, as the walls of the funnel close in on business and society.

Journey to Sustainability

Even if a business enterprise accepts the need to move toward sustainability, it must still operate within the other realities of its business milieu in order to remain profitable. How does a business move toward ecological sustainability and simultaneously retain or improve its profitability, and what does The Natural Step offer to assist in this process?

The Natural Step framework acts as a compass with which to navigate the journey to sustainability. It enables a corporation to steer toward a richer and deeper understanding of its business, one where cyclical industrial processes mimic and integrate with natural cycles. The way ahead suggested by The Natural Step is illustrated by a statement from Anders Moberg, President of IKEA, that appears on all of the company's environmental reports and action plans: "It may not be possible to do everything you would like to do right away, but at least make a start and do what you can do — now!" The essence of this message is that while the path to becoming a sustainable company — an evolutionary corporation — is a long journey consisting of countless small steps, the most important step is to start.

The Natural Step framework facilitates the journey to sustainability, first, by describing the features by which we can recognize our destination, second, by pointing out the direction to travel, and third, by providing a compass to keep us on track. Although several important steps can be taken within current competencies, processes, and technology, many steps require the development of new ones. Rather than leading to changes overnight that ignore other current realities, the process encouraged by The Natural Step is to first make the evolutionary decision to become a sustainable corporation, then to move forward steadily, step by step, in the direction of sustainability, maintaining and enhancing profitability and shareholder value in the process.

CHAPTER 3

Scientific Background to The Natural Step

*Each industrial process and each economic activity involves the
transformation of materials and energy from one form to another.
Thermodynamics provides very specific rules and limits
which govern these transformations.*
Tim Jackson
Material Concerns

THE PURPOSE OF THIS CHAPTER is to briefly summarize the basic scientific principles, evolutionary context, and cyclical metabolic principles that form the scientific underpinnings of The Natural Step. This is followed by a description of the four System Conditions, also referred to as the first-order principles of sustainability. The interested reader is encouraged to pursue further study into the research papers of Professors Robèrt and Holmberg and their colleagues which are referred to in the Resources section at the end of this book.

The Natural Step begins with two fundamental assumptions. The first is an ethical assumption that destroying the future capacity of the Earth to support life is fundamentally wrong. The second is a biophysical and societal assumption that humanity cannot tolerate continual degradation of the environment. Robèrt notes: "We may and do argue about what levels we can survive within, but no one argues that we can survive with continuous loss or degradation in living systems."[1] The rules of the biophysical world cannot be amended, changed, or negotiated; the laws of nature ultimately supersede human-made laws.

A fundamental purpose of The Natural Step as an organization has been to extend knowledge to all levels of society about the basic science that describes the boundaries of the system that sustains all life on our planet now. This approach is based on the assumption that a new shared mental model of how the world works is necessary for society to make intelligent decisions about sustainability. Robèrt and others note:

> The scientific background to our principles is not new — indeed they derive their force from the most basic laws of science. All physicists know and accept them (first and second laws of thermodynamics and the principle of matter conservation). But the voting public does not understand them, and often the scientists themselves fail to see how these laws set the context for sustainable development.[2]

Robèrt approached the description of this shared mental model from the perspective of cellular biology, the area of his expertise, training, and daily work as a cancer researcher. Plants and animals, including humans, share a common evolution. Not only are all humans and other animal life forms made of cells, but plant cells and animal cells share common characteristics. He points out:

> Other than plants' ability to photosynthesize, plant cells and animal cells are strikingly similar. In the simplest terms, they both consume resources and create waste, and they both have depended on each other for their biological evolution. As we descend the ladder of complexity in plant and animal life, going from the level of cell structure at the molecular level, the differences between plants and animals become less and less detectable, and we begin to see all living things as equally part of nature; they are nature. Even in DNA, the genetic blueprint that determines the identity of all life forms, animals and plants are alike. Both life forms are constructed using the same set of genetic building blocks; it is only the combination of these building blocks that determines the particular life form.[3]

For people to understand what is required to create a sustainable society, it is fundamental to understand the physical laws that make possible and constrain life; the evolutionary context of biological life on this planet; and the cyclical principle that governs the metabolism of cells, organisms, and societies. This basic scientific background is well known to scientists. However, the relevance of this background to sustainability and to the day-to-day life decisions of individuals and the investment, production, distribution, process, and other daily business decisions of companies and other organizations is not as commonly understood. We continue to ignore this basic understanding at our peril.

Basic Scientific Principles Underlying The Natural Step

The following basic scientific principles serve as the foundation for The Natural Step framework:

1. Matter and energy cannot be created or destroyed (according to the first law of thermodynamics and the principle of matter conservation).

2. Matter and energy tend to disperse (according to the second law of thermodynamics). This means that sooner or later matter that is introduced into society will be released into natural systems.

3. Material quality can be characterized by the concentration and structure of matter. What we consume are the qualities of matter and energy — the concentration, purity, and structure of matter, and the ability of energy to perform work. We never consume energy or matter because it is neither created nor destroyed.

4. The net increase in material *quality* on earth is produced by sun-driven processes. Photosynthesis is the only large-scale producer of material quality.

1. Matter and Energy Cannot Be Created or Destroyed

Among the most important of the laws that govern energy and material transformations in all physical systems are two important conservation laws upon which physicists agree. The first law deals with energy. Energy exists in a number of different forms including gravitational energy, chemical energy, electrical energy, heat, light, and motion, all can be measured in the same energy units called joules. These different forms of energy are constantly being transformed from one type into another. According to the law of conservation of energy, also known as the first law of thermodynamics, energy is neither destroyed nor created during these transformations. The total energy input always matches the total energy output.

The principle of matter conservation deals with matter: the conservation of atoms during material transformations. According to this principle, the atoms of the material inputs to a transformation process are conserved so that they are exactly the same in the material outputs. The only exceptions to this rule are nuclear reactions. This means that all material resources we exploit and transform through human activities must end up somewhere — if not in products, then in the environment.

In summary, the Earth is a closed system with respect to matter. This means that the overall mass of the Earth remains constant: we have the same volume of matter now as we did 4.5 billion years ago. In other words, nothing disappears — it just takes a different form. For example, as gasoline is used in a car, it doesn't disappear, it simply changes to a different form — much of it as molecular garbage, that although invisible, exists nonetheless.

2. Matter and Energy Tend to Disperse

The first law of thermodynamics explored above refers to the quantity of energy during transformation. It indicates that the total quantity of energy remains the same before and after transformation. The second law refers to the availability of energy to perform useful work. It indicates that the quantity of energy becomes less and less available to perform useful work as it passes through successive transformations. Energy becomes more dissipated and less useful. This is referred to as the entropy of a system. States with greater entropy are those where less energy is available to perform useful work. States with low entropy have more available energy. The second law of thermodynamics is the underlying mechanism behind our experience that energy and material transformations operate to reduce the available energy in the system and increase the dissipation of matter throughout the system.

3. Material Quality Can Be Characterized by The Concentration, Purity, and Structure of Matter

The laws that state that nothing is created or disappears apply to everything: to matter and energy. The only thing that can disappear is the quality or value of matter. The spontaneous tendency of energy and matter to dissipate as described in the second law of thermodynamics is what changes or diminishes material quality. Because nothing disappears and everything tends to disperse, a carpet turns to dust and a car turns to rust, and not the reverse. Dust does not reassemble into a carpet or rust into a car. As matter disperses, it loses its concentration, purity and structure — its order. Biological and economic value come from concentration and structure. A bottle of pure ink has economic and functional value as does a bathtub filled with pure water. As the ink is dripped into the water, it disperses and both lose their economic and functional value. The contaminated water in fact develops a negative economic and functional value as it becomes a disposal problem, while the quantity of water and ink remain the same before and after they are mixed together.

4. The Net Increase in Material Quality on Earth Is Produced by Sun-driven Processes

The very existence of continued life on Earth seems to contradict the second law of thermodynamics. Instead of declining into a greater entropic state, the Earth abounds with more and more complex biological organization. This is possible because of the continuous flow of available energy from the sun. The increase in entropy resulting from energy and material transformations is exported from the system in the form of low-grade heat energy. Input energy is needed to counteract the tendency of materials to dissipate. Through the slow process of evolution, the global ecosystem has developed a complex interactive network of material cycles to accomplish this: for example, the carbon cycle through which dissipated carbon is transformed into fixed carbon through photosynthesis, the process by which green cells transform solar energy into chemical energy. Solar input provides the supply of high-quality energy that maintains the ecological balance. The global material cycles provide the process through which degraded materials are returned naturally to available states using this solar input.

To summarize, while the Earth is a closed system with regard to matter, it is an open system with respect to energy. This is the reason why the system hasn't already run down with all of its resources being converted to waste. The Earth receives light from the sun and emits heat into space. The difference between these two forms of energy creates the physical conditions for order in the biosphere — the thin surface layer in the path of the sun's energy flow, in which all of the necessary ingredients for life as we know it are mingled.

Green plant cells are the primary producers of this order through photosynthesis. They capture solar radiation to concentrate and structure dispersed matter. Green cells are the only ones that produce more order than they consume. Humans and other animals always consume more order than they create.

The Evolutionary Context

Life as we know it evolved on this planet within the possibilities and constraints of the physical laws described in the preceding section. Life continues as an evolving system of increasing complexity and organization. According to our current understanding of the birth and evolution of the universe, the abundance and variety of life and life forms on Earth arose from an evolutionary story dating back billions of years.

If we look back only 4.5 billion years, ignoring for now the billions of years it took for cosmic and stellar evolution, the Earth consisted primarily of a swirling stew of compounds: cyanides, carbon dioxide, methane, ammonia, and so on — an atmosphere certainly hostile to life as it exists now. Approximately 3.5 billion years ago, the first plant cell appeared, most likely in the Earth's earliest oceans. The first cells were prokaryotic, which means they had no nucleus. Yet through their life processes, these primitive cells very slowly and over a very long time contributed to the process of detoxifying the biosphere of compounds such as hydrogen sulfide, carbon monoxide, and hydrogen cyanide. This alteration in the biosphere was critical to the evolution of life as we know it. According to Eriksson and Robèrt,

> Detoxification of the biosphere has not occurred entirely by converting "disorganized material" into building blocks for the creation of natural resources. Cells have also contributed to detoxification, using other,

much slower processes. Heavy metals such as lead, mercury, and cadmium were removed from the biomass by the comparatively slow process of biomineralization and through passive accumulation in cells. Subsequently, the metals were trapped in sediments and fossil deposits.[4]

The detoxification of the atmosphere[5] was accompanied by a gradual enrichment of the atmosphere with oxygen, a by-product of the production of organic molecules from the evolution of blue-green algae, prokaryotic cells that employ a photosynthetic mechanism.

> Additional quantities of oxygen [were] also released through the deposit of carbon, originating from CO_2 into sediments. This oxygen was first tied up in new chemical bonds, such as the oxidation of iron and other materials. Only after these "oxygen sites" had been saturated could the concentration of oxygen in the atmosphere increase. As the amount of oxygen increased, the ozone layer in the stratosphere was established. It protected the Earth's surface from ultraviolet radiation, and made it possible for eukaryotic life forms to survive, and eventually to emerge from the seas and colonize land.[6]

Eukaryotic cells are more complex than prokaryotic cells. They have nuclei and respiration systems. These early plant cells evolved so slowly that even after two or three billion years they were still primitive. The first green plants appeared about 1.5 billion years ago. Photosynthesis that was initiated by blue-green algae was further developed by green plants. This ability to capture energy from the sun and to convert it into chemical energy by plants is the foundation on which all life is built.

Between 0.7–1 billion years ago, the first animal cells appeared. Some of the energy captured by green plants began to be consumed by animal cells in increasingly complex food chains and webs. The evolutionary process continued to be fueled by a constant supply of ordered energy from the sun. Both plant and animal life forms grew increasingly complex and diverse and the giant cycles of which they are a part, and which they helped create, expanded. Ericksson and Robèrt observe:

> During the past 500 million years, the two main families of eukaryotic organisms, plants and animals, have exchanged matter in growing biochemical cycles, giving rise to the enormous diversity and complexity of the biosphere. The green plants capture solar [energy] in the process of photosynthesis and make it available to all forms of life. The plants, themselves, do not take up more matter from their environment than they need for their work of construction. . . During the past 500 million years, the interchange of matter between plants and ani-

mals has formed the basis of an accelerating evolution that has led to the rich natural diversity of which humans are a part.[7]

In evolutionary terms, the arrival of our human-like ancestors is relatively recent, occurring only an estimated two million years ago. To put this timeline into perspective, David Brower created an analogy that places evolutionary time in a form that we can more easily conceive, the time span of one week:

> Sunday at midnight, the Earth is created. There is no life until Tuesday noon. Millions upon millions of species come during the week, and millions of species go. By Saturday morning at seven, there's been enough chlorophyll manufactured for the fossil fuels to begin to form. Around four in the afternoon, the great reptiles come on stage. They hang around for a long time, as species go, until nine-thirty, a five-hour run. The Grand Canyon begins taking shape eighteen minutes before midnight. Nothing like us shows up for another fifteen minutes. No Homo Sapiens until thirty seconds ago. Let the party begin! A second and a half back, we throw the habits of hunting and gathering to the winds, and learn to change the environment to suit our appetites. We get rid of everything we can't eat as fast as we possibly can, and that's the beginning of agriculture.

> A third of a second before midnight, Buddha; a quarter of a second, Jesus Christ; a fortieth of a second, the Industrial Revolution; an eightieth of a second, we discover oil; a two-hundredth of a second, how to split atoms.[8]

In the short time span since humans discovered how to use concentrated energy resources such as fossil fuels and nuclear power, rapid changes have occurred. Humans now have access to tremendous flows of matter primarily (80 percent) driven by fossil fuels that are the result of billions of years of evolution. We are flooding the biosphere with waste, a by-product of our activities, which puts us at risk of changing the precious oxygen-rich atmosphere that makes life as we know it possible.

The scope of human impact on the environment has become an evolutionary force on a planetary scale. However, unlike the evolution of the complex systems that make up the biosphere, the changes being created by our complex and growing human societies are taking place not over the course of billions or even millions of years, but over the course of decades. Natural resources are shrinking and plant and animal species are being made extinct at a rate faster than any time in human history. Meanwhile, carbon dioxide and other pollutants in the atmosphere and oceans are reaching alarming levels. As a rapidly increasing human population strives to duplicate the consumption patterns of the industrialized nations, the scope of this impact is likely to increase while the time for life to adapt to these changes decreases. Robèrt comments:

> After 3.5 billion years of evolutionary growth, during which we aligned ourselves with the balanced, cyclical patterns of nature, we have begun to reverse direction. Now instead of turning resources into waste and then reconverting waste back into resources, we turn matter into junk in a linear dead-end process. If we continue in this way, we can expect to see our habitat blighted more and more by a deadly combination of both visible and molecular garbage: rusting car wrecks, mercury fumes, sulphurous acid rain, greenhouse gases, freons and so on. Although the visible garbage is certainly an eyesore, it is the molecular refuse that poses the most danger to all life on Earth for it acts as an irritating, abrasive gravel in the sensitive machinery of the ecosystem.[9]

In essence, we are in danger of running in reverse the very process of evolution that created the possibility for present life forms.

The Cyclic Principle

Billions of years of evolution have resulted in highly complex systems and cycles that maintain biological life on Earth. Eriksson and Robèrt remind us:

> Plant cells are unique in their ability to synthesize more structure than is broken down elsewhere in the biosphere. The perpetuation of this process requires the recycling of wastes. However, modern industrial societies are obsessed with the supply side, ignoring the principle of matter's conservation and neglecting to plan for the entire material flow. As a result there has been an accumulation of both visible and invisible garbage (pollution), which disturbs the biosphere and reduces stocks of natural resources. Furthermore, due to complexity and delay mechanisms, we usually cannot predict time parameters for the resulting socio-economic consequences or the development of disease. To continue along this path of folly is not compatible with the maintenance of wealth, nor with the health of humans or the biosphere. Rather than address the millions of environmental problems one at time, we need to approach them at the systemic level. It is essential to convert to human life-styles and forms of societal organization that are based on cyclic processes compatible with the Earth's natural cycles.[10]

Human societies are spreading over the entire planet at a rapid rate and at the expense of other species. Currently close to six billion people, the human population is expected to increase to at least 10 billion in the next generation. Eriksson and Robèrt observe:

> Society can be viewed as having a metabolism of its own based not only on solar energy flows and cyclic material flows but also on one-way flows of energy and materials from the Earth's interior to its surface. The industrialization that has made it possible to support a large human population has, to date, been characterized by this linear processing of energy and materials. That process has become a geophysical force, causing profound changes in the biosphere, some of them irreversible.[11]

Building on the foundation of basic scientific laws and the assumption that humans cannot tolerate the continual degradation of our life support systems, the cyclic principle arises. It can be summarized simply:

1. Waste must not systematically accumulate in nature; and

2. The reconstitution of material quality must be at least as large as its dissipation.

The cyclic principle holds that matter must be processed in cycles. Consequently, the societal metabolism — the process of transforming energy and matter due to human activities — must also be integrated into the sun-driven cycles of nature for society to be sustainable in ecological terms. To avoid the systematic accumulation of waste in nature, we must know the mechanisms through which waste can accumulate. Robèrt and others point out that if waste is systematically accumulating in the biosphere at the expense of resources, it can only be due to three overall mechanisms, which don't overlap functionally:

1. Waste is increasing because matter is systematically introduced to the biosphere from the Earth's crust at a higher rate than it is redeposited back.

2. Waste is increasing because it is produced by society at a higher rate than that by which it can be deposited in the Earth's crust or be used as building blocks in nature.

3. Waste is increasing because nature itself is turned into waste (such as greenhouse gases) while, at the same time, its sun-driven capacity to process waste into resources is diminished.[12]

A fourth mechanism is social, and acts as an accelerator on all these mechanisms: a wasteful and unfair handling of resources with respect to human needs.

Rationale Behind the System Conditions

Society can be seen to have a metabolism that is embedded in, and dependent upon, the larger cyclic metabolism of nature. The model for sustainability developed by The Natural Step begins with the cyclic character of the natural system and asks in what ways human activities can deteriorate or destroy that system. The mechanisms through which human activities can deteriorate or otherwise negatively influence nature are then translated into statements concerning the minimum requirements a society must meet to be sustainable, exist in a balanced relationship with the greater flows of nature.

In nature's cycle, green plants are the primary producers of ordered matter. Unlike animal cells, they contain chloroplasts that enable them to use solar energy directly. Green plants concentrate and structure decay products. All other production, including the production of human cells, is secondary, not directly sun-driven and therefore dependent on photosynthesis in green plants for the restoration of order. Order is consumed by animal cells and the output of this process is recycled into ordered matter by plant cells. There is no waste in the sense that garbage is accumulating in the system. There is also a flow of matter between the biosphere and the Earth's crust. Matter from the crust is introduced into the biosphere through volcanic eruptions and weathering, and returned to the crust through sedimentation; however, these flows are small and slow in contrast with the large and fast sun-driven living cycles.

In a sustainable society the flows are in balance and nature can reconstitute order at the same rate it is consumed. Society does not allow concentrations of matter from the Earth's crust to increase. Society does not allow concentrations of human-made compounds to build up in nature. Society draws on renewable resources no faster than they can be regenerated, and does not reduce the productive capacity of nature by detrimental manipulation of green surfaces. Human society is efficient, population is stabilized, and basic human needs are met.

Robèrt and Holmberg further clarify the System Conditions as follows:

1. The societal influence on the ecosphere due to accumulation of material from the Earth's crust is covered by the first principle. It implies that the flows of substances from the Earth's crust to the ecosphere must not systematically be larger than the flows back into the Earth's crust. The balance of flows must be such that concentration[13] of substances from the Earth's crust do not systematically increase in the whole ecosphere or in part of it, such as the atmosphere or ecosystems, etc. Besides the upstream influence on this balance through the amounts of mining and choices of mined mineral, the balance can be influenced by the quality of final deposits and the societal competence to technically safeguard the flows through recycling.

2. The societal influence on the ecosphere due to accumulation of substances produced in society (such as synthetic organic compounds not found in nature) is covered by the second principle. It implies that the flows of societally produced molecules and nuclides to the ecosphere must

not systematically be so large that they cannot either be integrated into the natural cycles within the ecosphere or be deposited into the Earth's crust. The balance of flows must be such that concentrations of substances produced in society do not systematically increase in the whole ecosphere or in parts of it, such as the atmosphere or ecosystems, etc. Besides the upstream influence on this balance through production volumes and characteristics of what is produced, such as degradability of the produced substances, the balance can be influenced by the quality of the final deposits and the societal competence to technically safeguard the flows through reuse, recycling, etc.

3. The societal influence on the ecosphere due to manipulation and harvesting of funds and flows of natural resources within the ecosphere is covered by the third principle. It implies that the resource basis for (i) productivity in the ecosphere such as fertile areas, thickness and quality of soils, availability of fresh water, and (ii) biodiversity is not systematically deteriorated by overharvesting, mismanagement, or displacement.

4. The internal societal metabolism and the production of services to the human sphere is covered by the fourth principle. It implies that if the societal ambition is to meet basic human needs everywhere, today and in the future, while conforming to the restrictions with regard to available resources given by the first three System Conditions, then the use of resources must be efficient. If we are more efficient, technically, organizationally, and socially, more services with the possibility of meeting more human needs can be provided for a given level of influence on nature.[14]

The System Conditions provide a model for sustainability that creates a framework for society's activities and makes societal metabolism compatible with the overall conditions of its underlying natural resource base. Any sustainable society would meet these principles as a minimum requirement. Figure 3.1 provides a summary of the System Conditions, showing some of their implications and the way they are linked to some of the basic scientific assumptions in this chapter.

The first three System Conditions describe the mechanisms through which human activities can deteriorate, disrupt, or destroy the natural cycles on which life on Earth depends. The fourth System Condition is a conclusion about human society drawn from the other three Conditions. It is relative to System Conditions one to three and cannot be described in absolute terms. With respect to System Condition four, Robèrt suggests that there is probably no limit to resource efficiency for the satisfaction of human needs. But if System Condition four is not met sufficiently, global society will not be able to meet the other three System Conditions either.

Figure 3.1

Summary of the Rationale Behind the TNS System Conditions

	System Condition	Meaning	Rationale
1. STORED DEPOSITS	Substances from the Earth's crust must not systematically increase in the ecosphere.	Fossil fuels, metals, and other minerals must not be extracted at a faster pace than their slow re-deposit and reintegration into the Earth's crust.	If this condition is not met, the concentrations of substances in the ecosphere will increase and eventually reach limits - often unknown - beyond which irreversible changes occur. *Nothing disappears and everything disperses.*
2. SYNTHETIC COMPOUNDS AND OTHER SOCIETALLY-PRODUCED MATERIAL	Substances produced by society must not system-atically increase in the ecosphere.	Substances must not be produced at a faster rate than that at which they can be broken down and integrated into cycles of nature or redeposited into the Earth's crust.	If this condition is not met, the concentration of substances in the ecos-phere will increase and eventually reach limits - often unknown - beyond which irreversible changes occur. *Nothing disappears and everything disperses.*
3. ECOSYSTEM MANIPULATION	The physical basis for productivity and diversity of nature must not be systematically diminished.	We cannot harvest or manipulate ecosystems in such a way that productive capacity, ecosystem services, and diversity systematically diminish.	Our health and prosperity depend on the capacity of nature to reconcentrate and restructure wastes into new resources. *Human activities need to work in harmony with the cyclic principle of nature.*
4. SOCIO-ECONOMICS	There must be fair and efficient use of resources with respect to meeting human needs.	Basic human needs must be met with the most resource-efficient methods possible.	Unless basic human needs are met worldwide through fair and efficient use of resources, it will difficult to meet conditions 1-3 on a global scale.

Corporations are important contributors to, and drivers of, the societal metab-olism. They are also clearly dependent upon ecosystem resources in terms of material and vital ecosystem services. The cases in Part Two illustrate how four companies are beginning to integrate this understanding into how they conduct their business.

PART TWO

THE BUSINESS OF SUSTAINABLE DEVELOPMENT

We have the capacity and ability to create a remarkably different economy, one that can restore ecosystems and protect the environment while bringing forth innovation, prosperity, meaningful work, and true security. The restorative economy unites ecology and commerce into one sustainable act of production and distribution that mimics and enhances natural processes.
Paul Hawken — *The Ecology of Commerce*

INTRODUCTION TO THE CASE STUDIES

PART TWO TELLS THE STORIES of why four companies became motivated to embed ecological sustainability into their business, why they chose The Natural Step framework to help them do so, and how they use that framework in their operations. There are numerous companies incorporating sustainability into their operations without using The Natural Step, and there are many companies using The Natural Step that are not included in this volume. Constraints on time and space dictated our choices.

We conducted a handful of in-depth case studies rather than take a cursory look at many companies to understand the motivations, timing, process, challenges, and results for each company. We wanted to hear from a cross-section of employees — from the production line to the CEO — and not just from the environment or public relations departments. Our choice of companies to study was based on the following factors:

Diverse Industry Groups and Sectors. The chosen companies represent diverse industry groups from primary, secondary, and tertiary sectors: IKEA (retail/distribution, secondary sector); Scandic Hotels (service/hospitality, tertiary sector); Interface (manufacturing, secondary sector); and Collins Pine (natural resource extraction, primary sector). These distinctions are not always clear. For example, IKEA and Collins Pine are also involved in some manufacturing and Interface is increasingly involved in distribution. Nonetheless, their primary categories represent the main identities of each company.

A Range of Experience with Implementing The Natural Step Framework. We wanted to view the process at different stages. IKEA was one of the very first corporations to introduce the framework in 1990; Scandic Hotels adopted it in 1993; Interface in 1996, and Collins Pine in 1996. The cases are presented in chronological order.

Diverse Sizes. In the most recent year for which figures are reported, IKEA had revenues in excess of US $7 billion and employed more than 40,000 people worldwide; Interface had revenues of approximately US $1.1 billion and employed more than 7,400 people worldwide; Scandic had consolidated revenues of roughly US $700 million and employed nearly 7,500 people; and Collins Pine had revenues of around US $230 million and employed about 1000 people.

Publicly Traded and Privately Held Companies. Scandic Hotels and Interface are publicly traded, Scandic Hotels on the Stockholm Stock Exchange and Interface on the NASDAQ exchange in the United States. IKEA and Collins Pine are privately held.

Operations in Diverse Market and Cultural Contexts. Collins Pine operates primarily in the U.S.; Scandic Hotels in northern Europe; and IKEA and Interface operate globally. IKEA and Scandic are both Swedish-based organizations, although IKEA has executive offices in Denmark. Interface and Collins Pine are both U.S.-based organizations. Interface has its headquarters on the East Coast in Atlanta and Collins Pine has its headquarters on the West Coast in Portland.

The personal and corporate stories of these companies are "works in progress." All four companies have independently characterized their process as journeys of many steps. They are each aware that they are just at the beginning of this journey and that they, along with almost all other organizations in our society, have a long way to go. They know from experience that they will make mistakes along the way. They share an urgency and seriousness about what they are doing, and a willingness, even eagerness, to share what they are learning. Each company is determined that it will grow robustly and will lead, not follow, its competition. They all believe this can be done without sacrificing the Earth's capacity to continue to provide the vital materials and services on which our well-being and that of future generations depend.

Wherever possible, we used the words of the people interviewed to recount the substance of the story and to illustrate key points. In conducting our research, we organized information around seven points:

1. The background and history of the company.

2. The company profile today.

3. Motivations for integrating environmental issues into business thinking.

4. Motivations for adopting The Natural Step framework.

5. Ways in which The Natural Step framework was introduced and is being used.

6. Ways in which environmental aspects in general and The Natural Step framework in particular are being embedded in both strategy and day-to-day operations.

7. The benefits, lessons, and effects of adopting The Natural Step framework.

We approached our research with as few preconceived ideas about the outcome as possible. Admittedly, our bias was that The Natural Step framework was an innovative organizational technology. Our approach was inductive: to observe and record the stories and perceptions of the people most directly involved in changing the way their companies do business, and to see what patterns emerged and what lessons might be applicable to other companies. Although we preferred to encounter positive and inspiring stories, we were prepared for disappointment and committed to report whatever we found. We felt that whatever the result, the potential learning would make the effort worthwhile.

CHAPTER 4

IKEA:
"Nothing is Impossible"

Sustainability is the key word for the future. Our ambition is to work step by carefully thought-out step, and with great respect, towards a business based on sound ecological principles. It is not enough to be friendly toward the environment — we must adapt to it.
Anders Moberg — President, IKEA

RIDING THE INTERCITY EXPRESS into the beautiful lake and forest country of southern Sweden, we found it difficult to imagine that we were approaching the center of operations for the world's largest retailer of home furnishings. As the pine and birch trees, lakes, and farm lands sped by the rushing train, we could imagine ourselves in the countryside of Wisconsin, Minnesota, or Ontario, where, indeed, tens of thousands of Swedes had settled in the great out-migrations of the 19th century. Today, the outflow is millions of Scandinavian-designed household products destined for the global marketplace. Founded in 1943 by then 18-year old Ingvar Kamprad as a simple mail order business operated from a farm in this same Swedish countryside, by 1997 IKEA had achieved annual worldwide sales in excess of US $7 billion. One could not help wondering by what intriguing interplay of personality, market and historical forces this home furnishings colossus had arisen from the unlikely and aptly named area of Småland ("Small Land") in this land of forests and farms in the south of Sweden.

IKEA's Swedish founder, Chairman, and still dominant presence, Ingvar Kamprad has stated many times over the more than half-century life of his creation that the soul of his company is to be found in the traditional and enduring handmade stone fences characteristic of rural Småland. Each of these solid fences is built from thousands of individual rocks, each lifted one by one from the rocky soil of the Swedish countryside. Rooted in the soil, built one stone at a time, made with intention and much effort over the years, these solid stone walls serve as a continual symbol of IKEA's spirit.

The very name, IKEA, helps co-workers remember their roots as the four letters of the name are derived from the first letters of four words: Ingvar Kamprad Elmtaryd Agunnaryd. Elmtaryd is the name of the farm on which Ingvar Kamprad was raised and Agunnaryd is the name of the village in which the farm was located. IKEA's driving purpose is "to provide a better everyday life for the majority of people." As the company's farflung operations extend in product lines, complexity, and geography far beyond its humble beginnings in Småland, its mission statement and the vision of its founder are familiar landmarks by which to navigate through new opportunities, challenges, and markets.

The founding values of the IKEA culture are outlined in a booklet written by Kamprad called *Testament of a Furniture Dealer* given to every IKEA employee. These values include simplicity, humility, and honesty in internal relations among co-workers and in external relations with suppliers and customers; risk-taking, daring to be different, always questioning assumptions and asking "why"; and daring to take responsibility. For IKEA, grown in the soil of frugal Småland, doing more with less and providing value for money are key foundation stones. Today this is called "resource efficiency," obtaining good results with minumum inputs. Waste of resources is considered a "mortal sin" at IKEA. In the IKEA family, the core values are to support one another and to exercise freedom of action and the responsibility that goes with it.

Kamprad believes that the fear of making mistakes is the "enemy of evolution." The challenges of a rapidly changing world and expanding markets are viewed as opportunities; the word "impossible" is absent from IKEA's dictionary. "Strategic mistakes", i.e., unsuccessful initiatives in pursuit of the company's goals, are regarded as "learnings." There is a realization and an acceptance that mistakes not only happen, but are necessary in an entrepreneurial company such as IKEA.

IKEA Today

In the lifetime of its founder, IKEA has successfully grown into a profitable and complex global system of more than 40,000 co-workers with 150 stores in 28 countries, 14 major distribution centers, and approximately 2,300 suppliers in more than 64 countries. Worldwide, more than 168 million people visited IKEA stores in 1998. Clearly a robust company, IKEA has seen its revenues grow steadily (Figure 4.1).

The IKEA group is owned by a Dutch foundation, Stichting Ingka, of which Ingvar Kamprad is Chairman. The management services to the IKEA Group are provided by IKEA International A/S located in Humlebaek, Denmark, the international headquarters for IKEA, which is managed by the President of the IKEA Group, Anders Moberg. The operations of the IKEA Group are based on

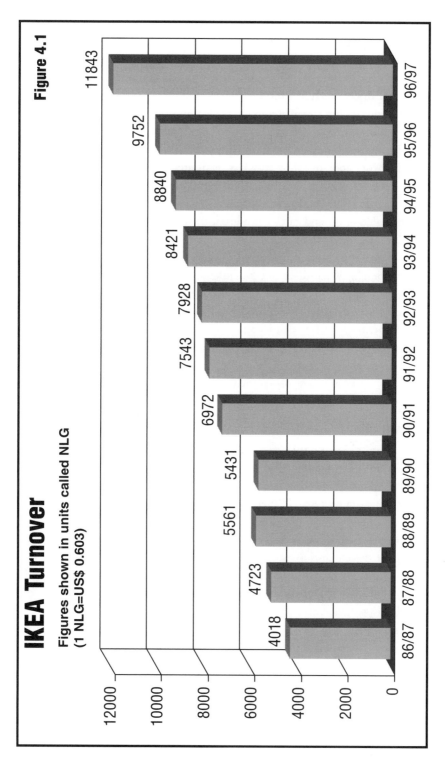

Figure 4.1

IKEA Turnover

Figures shown in units called NLG
(1 NLG=US$ 0.603)

four basic functions: the product range (design and development), trading (purchasing), wholesale (distribution), and retail (sales).

The product-range company, IKEA of Sweden, often referred to as the "heart of IKEA," has overall responsibility for the competitiveness and effectiveness of the entire IKEA product range in all IKEA markets. It also has the overall responsibility to ensure goods availability in the stores and warehouses. Trading has the overall responsibility for purchasing activities including relationships with suppliers, product quality, service levels, and delivery information. The functions of wholesale and retail are organized into three regions: North America, Europe, and Asia Pacific. Wholesale with its commercial and supply-support function has the overall responsibility for all warehousing activities, the phasing in and out of products, delivery information, and the transportation of goods within IKEA. Retail companies are responsible for marketing and sales in each local market.

In general, IKEA does not manufacture its own products, but works through a complex network of suppliers around the world. However, in the past few years, IKEA has acquired a number of its own factories, some of which function as training units and set standards for other suppliers for production economy, quality, and environmental awareness. To secure supplies and help suppliers develop, IKEA is also partnering as joint owners or financiers in a number of countries including Poland, Slovakia, Russia, Romania, and Bulgaria.

Crisis in the Market

Signals from the marketplace initially raised IKEA's environmental awareness. In the mid-80s, customers, especially in Germany, IKEA's largest market, began to ask new questions, such as: "Are IKEA's bookshelves made from wood from tropical rainforests? Is there anything toxic in the lacquers IKEA used? Do IKEA's halogen lamps cause cancer?" According to Karl-Olof Nilsson, Group Staff Environmetal Affairs, IKEA's product and material experts initially thought these questions were "sometimes strange." In fact, what IKEA personnel ultimately discovered was that questions such as these signalled that the "majority of people" were starting to worry. They were becoming more concerned about the environmental and health effects of products.

IKEA hit its first environmental wall in the mid-80s. In 1981, Denmark established a new law regulating the maximum emissions allowed from formaldehyde off-gassing in particleboard, which is a core component of many IKEA products. According to Nilsson, although the law seemed very strange to IKEA at that time, they simply requested that their suppliers follow it. The Danish authorities decided to test compliance with the new law and found that furniture companies were paying very little attention to it. Being one of the largest companies operating in Denmark, and with headquarters located there, IKEA became the focus of a new and aggressive public campaign. The government tested products from IKEA and found that some products had formaldehyde emissions above the legislated limit. A television program drew dramatic attention to the issue. IKEA was sued for violating Danish laws and assessed a fine. The fine, however, was minimal compared to the damage done to IKEA's image and sales, which temporarily dropped by about 20 percent in the Danish market.

The formaldehyde issue was quickly referred to IKEA's quality department. Russel Johnson, then head of quality, moved into action. IKEA immediately set up a large testing laboratory for its products, that today is one of the most sophisticated of such facilities in Scandinavia. They began testing samples from their suppliers and introduced stringent new requirements for suppliers to meet. For suppliers to meet those standards, the investigation had to go deeper. IKEA's suppliers, scattered throughout the world, use particleboard and plywood from numerous manufacturers. IKEA went to these manufacturers and was advised that they could not solve the problem alone because they, in turn, used numerous manufacturers of the glue, which turned out to be the source of the formaldehyde. IKEA took the investigation to the glue manufacturers and still could not find a satisfactory solution. Eventually they ended up going directly to chemical giants such as ICI and BASF in Germany to find a way to reduce the level of formaldehyde off-gassing in IKEA products. In the course of this investigation, Johnson believes that IKEA actively contributed to finding solutions for the entire European furniture and particleboard industry.

In addition to the formaldehyde crisis, IKEA became aware in the late 1980s that it was being criticized more often for more environmentally-related issues. For example, IKEA began to receive criticism for its packaging waste and for the use of PVC plastic which had become a big issue in Germany. PVC, once considered to be an excellent material, had come under environmental scrutiny particularly after a large fire in the plastic industry traced dioxins to the combustion of PVC. Unexpected criticism was also launched against IKEA's famous catalog, then the biggest circulation color catalog in the world. Criticisms were voiced about the number of trees felled each year for pulp to make the catalog's paper, and for the use of chlorine in bleaching that pulp because the chlorine residues released into rivers and seas endangered marine life, particularly in the Baltic Sea. The company was also criticized for the amount of waste produced in the making of the catalogs and from discarded catalogs. These environmental issues were new and confusing for the company. IKEA began to recognize that environmental concern was a new market reality.

Then in 1992, IKEA faced yet another and totally unexpected formaldehyde crisis. This time it was in IKEA's largest market, Germany, and with one of its biggest sellers, the globally popular Billy bookshelf, which represented many millions of dollars per year in revenue to IKEA. Tests conducted by an investigative team from a large German newspaper and television station found formaldehyde emissions for the Billy bookshelf to be just slightly higher than the legislated requirement. This time the culprit was not the particleboard itself — which was the part of the bookshelf that was actually regulated by law — it was the lacquer on the bookshelves. The regulatory details did not matter to the press. The impact of the coverage mattered a great deal to IKEA. Glenn Berndtsson, current head of IKEA's quality division, recalls: "It was in all the newspapers and all the television stations throughout the world: 'the deadly poisoned bookshelves.' From Hong Kong to Australia. We had to put a stop on all sales of Billy bookcases. We stopped production worldwide."

Berndtsson estimates that the direct cost just to track the bookshelves and correct the situation was between US $6 million and US $7 million at that time, not counting the cost for diverted manpower, lost sales, lost production by suppliers, or the costs and time it took to persuade customers to return to IKEA to buy the bookshelves. Altogether, this one incident cost IKEA and its suppliers tens of millions of dollars to correct. IKEA was learning an important and costly lesson. As Erik Linander, former Environmental Coordinator for IKEA of Sweden, reflects:

> IKEA was top of the line in Europe, and I think one of the best companies in the world, with regard to formaldehyde problems. But from that day on, we realized that the environment is not only a technical and a legal affair but an emotional media affair. We were prepared for the technical. But when the media put in the headline 'the deadly poisoned bookshelves,' I think that day we woke up.

Johnson explains that early on, Kamprad defined the mission of the company: to create a better everyday life for the majority of people. If environmental problems such as pollution and health effects are becoming more of a worry for everyday people, they must also be a concern for IKEA. "If people see IKEA as a company that is polluting the environment, creating wastes or emissions, or wasting resources, then we are not living up to our mission as it is understood by people now in the late 1980s and 1990s. That's a very strong matter. We are meeting customers face-to-face every day. As a company built on the mission to create a better everyday life for the majority of the people, of course we must take environmental issues seriously."

IKEA and The Natural Step

Prior to the 1992 German formaldehyde incident, IKEA had already begun to examine its stand on environmental issues. In 1989, Anders Moberg, President of the IKEA Group, asked Russel Johnson, head of quality for the IKEA Group, to take on the task of mapping out which environmental questions were relevant to IKEA, which might affect their operations, and conversely, what impact IKEA might have on the environment. Moberg told Johnson: "Environment is not just a new fashion, it will not just fade away, it is the new reality and we have to adapt to it." He asked Johnson to draft an environmental policy as a basis for discussion for the IKEA Group management.

Johnson had no knowledge in the environmental area nor did the members of the environmental task force that he pulled together to work on the environmental policy. Nilsson, a member of that pioneering group, recalls that when the task force was formed, they realized that they had to go outside the company to learn more about environmental issues. They went to authorities in several countries where IKEA does business, particularly Germany and Sweden, to learn about anticipated regulation. They conferred with environmental organizations, universities, and scientists that were involved in research relevant to IKEA's business. Finally, they learned from other companies that had already started to work with environmental issues in a structured way. Altogether it took more than a year for the task force to complete the analysis.

In January 1990, Johnson presented his first report to the group management. The report detailed a number of environmental issues relevant to IKEA and presented a first draft of the environmental policy. Johnson told the group management that he realized that neither he nor IKEA had the competence to address these environmental issues. IKEA could not sort these issues out alone. He proposed that the environmental task force would organize an environmental day for the IKEA group management and group staff with someone who could help them make sense out of these issues. Johnson decided that Dr. Karl-Henrik Robèrt, then working as a medical doctor and director of cancer research at a major hospital in the Stockholm area, was the appropriate person for this task. At that time, although still practising medicine, Robèrt had a growing reputation for balanced environmental thinking after the well-publicized launch of his Natural Step organization in 1989 under the patronage of the King of Sweden.

IKEA's first environmental day was held at the beginning of June, 1990. Johnson recalls that a number of the corporate executives present at the meeting were quite suspicious. They were accustomed to environmental activists talking only about problems and blaming industry. Robèrt, however, was different. Johnson explains: "He presented a quick story of how the Earth looked three billion years ago, how it has evolved, and how we are now running the evolutionary picture in reverse. He showed us that the situation is really serious, but that it's not too late, and that we can change it. It is companies, enterprises, that can make the difference."

The group management agreed that environmental issues were becoming more important to IKEA's business. They adopted the first environmental policy for a one-year trial period in 1990. In 1991, IKEA's Board approved the current IKEA environmental policy.

The challenge remained to make the environmental policy an operational reality. The next assignment of the task force was to develop an environmental action plan. By early 1992, it was ready. In April 1992, Moberg hosted a two-day environmental seminar for IKEA's top management to increase their environmental awareness and to get their acceptance of the proposed environmental action plan. At this seminar, IKEA's environmental task force presented its analysis of IKEA's relationship with the natural environment. Nilsson recalls: "We stated that we had discovered that we at IKEA were environmental gangsters, that we were a threat to the environment. We were violating the possibilities of having a sustainable society." The task force used only three overheads to present the results of their analysis. One slide contained IKEA's success figures such as increased sales and new stores opened the previous year. The second slide pointed out that IKEA had distributed some three million cubic metres of future waste in the previous year. The third slide was a hand-drawn illustration of IKEA's relationship with the environment. Nilsson describes it as follows:

It showed how IKEA takes natural resources such as fossil fuels, minerals, metals, etc. and transports these resources, often in many stages and often in many directions, to a facility where they are transformed into products. The transport process uses fossil fuels, produces emissions, and requires roads that take up green spaces. The production process also produces other effects such as emissions into water, air, and soil; the use of energy; and the production of other wastes. Then again, the products are transported, in many cases to a central warehouse and in some cases to a store. The IKEA store, where the product goes, uses energy, takes up land, and produces wastes. In that store, IKEA markets its products and the customer brings him or herself to the store, hopefully buys IKEA products, and transports him or herself and the product back home. Again polluting transport is used. The first thing the customer must do is get rid of the packaging material, so that becomes waste rather quickly. And, at some stage, hopefully later rather than sooner, the product itself becomes waste.

The environmental task force summarized their findings by telling IKEA's top management that when they analyzed how IKEA works, how other companies work, and how society works, they realized that "what we are doing is actually transforming resources into waste. The process is measured at the cash register where we measure turnover. What we are actually measuring there is the rate at which we are transforming resources into waste." After the task force analysis was presented, Robèrt introduced The Natural Step framework as a way to begin reconceptualizing and redesigning the relationship between IKEA and the natural environment.

IKEA's environmental task force had conducted significant research on environmental issues with numerous organizations covering a range of approaches and knowledge. The reason they chose The Natural Step approach is summarized by Johnson: First, Robèrt delivered a positive message, that IKEA could make a difference because it influences people in countless ways. It is an important value in the IKEA culture to make a difference in the world. The second factor is structure. Johnson remarks, "The Natural Step provided a compass, a means to orient us to move ahead. We can use these System Conditions to test the changes we want to make, to see how the proposed change relates to these System Conditions."

After the seminar, the group management approved IKEA's first environmental action plan beginning with education and training.

Education and Training

As part of its new environmental action plan, IKEA's senior management elected to use The Natural Step as the foundation for developing an environmental training program to be given to all employees. In consultation with The Natural Step, the environmental task force developed training material geared specifically to IKEA's business and culture. A video was created to deliver a message from Anders Moberg about the importance of incorporating environmental matters into IKEA's business strategy and operations. This message reinforced that environmental issues were important to IKEA and that this was consistent with IKEA's culture. The training was designed as either a 10-hour or a 16-hour program over two days. The 10 hour program was designed for co-workers working in the sales organization, and the 16-hour program was for co-workers working with product development and purchasing. Specialized training was designed to meet the demands of specific work areas.

IKEA decided on a "train-the-trainers" approach to disseminating the environmental education. Trainers were chosen from each IKEA department. They attended an intensive week-long trainers' seminar and received a trainers' kit consisting of a manual and overhead slides. The seminar curriculum included the principles of The Natural Step and descriptions of IKEA's environmental policy and action plan together with information about how different aspects of IKEA's operations were affecting the environment.

Although the training design team made every effort to simplify the language in the materials so that it was applicable at all levels of the organization as well as at all educational levels, the first trainers' seminar revealed the need to simplify even further. At the end of the seminar, each trainer had to present a component of the training for a practice session. Some of the trainers were assigned the task of giving The Natural Step portion of the training. Nilsson reports that they came back with swollen eyes after a sleepless night and said "No, we'll skip that part, it's much too complicated." He comments: "I started to think about this and very spontaneously came up with a description that has helped us very, very much."

A three-part approach was developed to learning the fundamentals of The Natural Step. First, a summary of the scientific principles behind The Natural Step in four short statements; second, the four System Conditions expressed in action language;[1] and third, an outline of eight key concepts that are related to the four System Conditions and that can be used to guide day-to-day decisions. He summarized these three components as follows:

Four fundamental scientific principles underlying the four System Conditions

1. Everything spreads.
2. Nothing disappears.
3. Concentration and structure give value.
4. Green cells concentrate and give structure.

Four System Conditions

1. Cease using resources from the Earth's crust.
2. Stop using unnatural, persistent substances.
3. Allow space for nature and the natural cycle.
4. Harmonize use of resources with natural regeneration.

Eight key concepts to translate the System Conditions into possible actions or bases for decisions

1. *Renewable:* Change over to renewable raw materials and energy sources (System Condition one).
2. *Degradable:* Use substances and materials that are easily broken down in nature and converted into new resources (System Condition two).
3. *Sortable:* Construct products so that the constituent materials can be easily separated for recycling (System Condition four).
4. *Nature:* Refrain from all unnecessary intrusions into nature and the eco-cycle (System Condition three).
5. *Save:* Always ask yourself whether you can avoid or cut back on your use of resources (System Condition four).
6. *Quality:* Choose products with a long useful life, which can be repaired if they break (System Condition four).
7. *Efficiency:* Plan use of materials, energy, technology, and transport to achieve maximum benefit for minimum expenditure of resources (System Condition four).

8. *Reuse:* The greatest savings in our use of resources can be achieved by reusing them (System Condition four):

a. Reusing products (i.e., using the same product several times).

b. Recycling materials (i.e., using used material as raw material for a new product).

c. Incinerating materials to release the energy content, such as using for heating purposes. This is only acceptable if the gases emitted are such that nature can deal with them. Dumping waste on garbage tips or pumping it into rivers, lakes, and seas is not an alternative in a sustainable society.

According to Nilsson, "the four fundamental principles provide the scientific background. They address why we have the situation we have today. The four System Conditions describe what we have to do about it. The eight key terms provide guidance on how to do it." Once these distinctions were made and discussed, Nilsson recalls, "all of a sudden everything, to everybody's big surprise, was quite clear!" Participants could see the functional use of the information and the way it related to IKEA. For the training to become effective, it was essential, first, to connect the various components of the training material, and second, to link that material to IKEA's daily business decisions and activities.

IKEA's initial company-wide environmental training strategy in the early 1990s was three-fold:

1. The training would proceed in the company's four functional areas, starting with product development, then purchasing, and finally wholesale and retail.

2. It would be a "top–down" training strategy where management would receive training first. For example, Anders Moberg ensured that his management team was trained. Each member of the management team was to ensure that his or her management team was trained. Then each member of those management teams was responsible for seeing that his or her area of responsibility received training.

3. The training applied what IKEA calls the "grandfather principle." This meant that when IKEA of Sweden (product development and product range company) had their training session for their management team, it was convened by the managing director of that company, and Anders Moberg, as president of the company and each managing director's boss, provided the introduction to the training. This process, showing the support at the highest executive levels of the company, was duplicated at all levels to communicate that this training and these issues were highly important to IKEA and to be taken seriously by each worker.

IKEA's goal was to provide full training to all co-workers directly invloved in product development or in direct contact with suppliers or customers — about 90 percent of IKEA's 20,000 employees at that time. All other co-workers were offered the opportunity of attending a shorter version of the training. They started with their major environmental training in 1993, and, including the retail side, the majority of the training was done by 1995. However, by the end of 1997, the coverage of the training program in IKEA stores around the world was uneven. In general, where there was higher demand and higher interest about environmental issues in the market, such as in Germany, the training rate was as high as 90 percent of the co-workers in a store. In other cases, it was closer to 50 percent.

In the process of launching a worldwide education campaign in this area of new learning, IKEA has learned some valuable lessons. In the beginning, the education team was so involved in providing the training to all co-workers that little emphasis was placed on what steps should occur after the training. Nilsson reflects that they counted on the training to be the stimulus for action, but it was not that easy. Training had to be reinforced through practice and action. That is, workers needed opportunities to experiment with different ways to do their jobs and management needed to support suggestions and ideas generated after the training about how IKEA could conduct business with more environmental responsibility. Another lesson they learned was to make sure concrete results can be shown very quickly to co-workers to keep the fire of their enthusiasm burning. It is important to take advantage of "low hanging fruits" to demonstrate that something is being done, that progress is taking place.

After five years of experience, IKEA is developing its Natural Step-influenced environmental education in three general categories:

1. Basic training for all co-workers to create awareness, understanding and know-how, and refresher training for co-workers who took part in the extended training in 1993-95 that will include information on what has occurred in IKEA since that time and what is being planned for the future.

2. Professional training for (a) specialists to increase knowledge about the environmental aspects in IKEA's functional areas. (For example, IKEA has developed a program for transport buyers and transport planners who need to know more about the environmental aspects of the transport sector.); (b) environmental coordinators and environmental trainers. It develops more extensive environmental knowledge, and greater capacity to help co-workers see the connections between their day-to-day work and the natural world; and (c) for suppliers.

3. Master training, which is more advanced training for co-workers that support the professionals, to develop either a very deep knowledge in one or a few areas, or a very broad general knowledge.

Initial Steps

For most companies, working with the concept of sustainability and the fostering of an environmental consciousness is a new area requiring the development of new knowledge and new competencies. IKEA is no exception. In the course of IKEA's journey, the company has made mistakes as well as built upon its many successes. IKEA's environmental concerns are clearly connected to signals received from a changing marketplace, but they go beyond that. IKEA's vision involves a better everyday life for the majority of people. Originally that vision meant that the majority of people should be able to afford attractive and durable home furnishings. Today the vision embraces choosing a path that will help achieve a sustainable society in ecological balance.

It was easy to recognize the need for integrating environmental concerns into business thinking. It was more difficult to imagine how the changes would actually happen. As early as the April 1992 presentation of the environmental task force to the top management at IKEA, the challenge was obvious. When Robèrt presented The Natural Step framework at that meeting, one of IKEA's top managers responded: "Thank you very much, you have just ruined our business idea." The discussion that followed acknowledged that IKEA would clearly have to start changing direction, but environmentally friendly products were known to cost more money and thus were out of the question for IKEA. Then one manager suggested that IKEA start by producing an "eco-range" that might be more expensive than other parts of the range, but that would still be less expensive than what anyone else could produce. People began to come to agreement around this idea.

IKEA set out to create a line of products under the new name of "Eco-Plus", consisting of products that had one or more environmental advantages. Erik Linander, at that time Environmental Coordinator for IKEA of Sweden, was deeply involved in this effort. He went out to all of IKEA's business areas to initiate the program. He quickly learned that it was an extremely difficult task. Immediately questions arose about how to compare different products such as a sofa and a glass, and what criteria should be used. Linander started building up criteria, looking for something that went beyond ISO 14000 "because ISO 14000 doesn't explain how you find the product criteria that have environmental value." The more Linander searched, the more questions arose.

Despite the many problems, the project team identified several possibilities to be included in the Eco-Plus line working with The Natural Step System Conditions as the core criteria. After they selected the product line, questions arose as to how they were going to market the product, how long the products were likely to remain environmentally adapted, what would happen in one or two years when technology or knowledge changed? In addition, by creating a more expensive eco-line, IKEA was in danger of inadvertently drawing negative attention to the rest of its product range. Linander recalls that internally, people remarked: "That's good, you're talking about a hundred products, that's good. How about the other 7,000? Aren't they good?" Without intending to, the more expensive Eco-Plus line had, in a sense, created an elite line of furniture that was contrary to IKEA's guiding vision to provide a better everyday life for the majority of the people. Despite its merits and IKEA's best intentions, the Eco-Plus line was not the way to proceed. IKEA was not being forced to produce the collection. They had time to experiment, time to learn.

An Evolutionary Moment

Part way into the development of the new Eco-Plus line, IKEA decided to reassess and change its strategy. Putting marketing aside for a moment, they asked how IKEA could make the best contribution to a better environment. They concluded that a few products of a very high environmental standard would not make much of a contribution. The best thing to do was to focus on the products already in the range or being designed for the range that had potential to be the best sellers. They reasoned that everything that IKEA could do to reduce their environmental impact in those products would make a greater contribution than if they sold 10,000 eco-sofas. According to the new strategy, it is not a matter of taking five or 15 percent of the product range and making it environmentally the best, *it is taking the whole range and improving it step-by-step.*

In retrospect, we can see that this fundamental insight marked IKEA's evolutionary shift toward true ecological sustainability. *This change in strategy meant that environmental thinking would be integrally connected with the IKEA business vision and operations.* It needed to be connected with daily work, with product design and specification, with analysis of the environmental effects of a product through its whole life-cycle, with choice of suppliers and supplier relations, and with the hundreds of thousands of daily decisions made by tens of thousands of IKEA co-workers around the world. According to Linander, this meant that environmental improvements would occur in a much less dramatic way, but would take place in many, many small steps integrated into daily planning and operations. Everyone needed to be involved because these "small green steps" needed to occur at all levels of the organization. In this way, environmental thinking would be interwoven into how IKEA co-workers conducted the company's business.

Stairway to Sustainability

One of the most practical sustainability initiatives arose from co-workers in IKEA of Sweden where the product range is designed, specified, and developed.

As a result of the mandate to integrate environmental thinking into operations, Björn Frithiof, head of law and standards at IKEA of Sweden, helped innovate an approach that has since been adopted by all business areas as a basic IKEA operational model. Originating in the textile division, the model presents a way of operationalizing the idea of "small green steps."

Textiles represent between 15 and 20 percent of IKEA's entire product range. In a US$7 billion dollar company, this represents a significant business item with potentially important environmental impacts all the way down the supply chain. As Figure 4.2 illustrates, the step model developed by textiles is a system that classifies the entire textile range into four groups based on the environmental standard that each product or supplier has attained.

The first step, or level, ensures that all of IKEA's textile products are tested in internationally recognized textile laboratories to verify compliance with IKEA's basic requirements. This assures that there are no harmful substances in the products and that the customer can feel safe using them. This is the minimum requirement that all IKEA textile products must meet. All IKEA suppliers of textiles must comply with this requirement. The standards of the first green step mean that all textiles produced for IKEA must meet the following minimum criteria: lead free, cadmium free, no PCPs, no AZO-dyestuffs, strict limitations on formaldehyde, no PVC, and no moth-proofing except per International Wool Society recommendations.

The second step calls for tougher production standards. This step begins to incorporate a lifecycle view of the product. The first step specifies that there is nothing toxic or harmful in the product that will affect the customer. The second step applies criteria concerning the way the product is produced to reduce any negative affects on the environment at the production stage. At this level, IKEA requires that no chlorine bleach and no organic solvents are used in the production process, that heavy metal residue is kept to a minumum, and that the pH stays within a range of 4.5–7.5.

The third step demands minimal environmental impact throughout the product's entire lifecycle. It takes into consideration factors such as waste-water treatment at the manufacturing site, the use of PCBs, and the reduction or elimination of other harmful emissions. It also takes into account what happens when the product has served its lifetime, ensuring that it can be recycled and that it won't be harmful if it is deposited or incinerated.

The fourth step goes back even further in the chain to the source of raw materials. At this step, IKEA seeks sources of organically grown material such as cotton and flax. This is an ideal toward which IKEA is aspiring.

IKEA Textiles: Four Green Steps towards Greater Environmental Responsibility

The entire range is classified into four groups based on environmental status.
Once this is completed, goals are established (FY98). The aim is to continually take "small green steps" to improve each product's environmental status.
Moving up a step involves fulfilling additional or tougher requirements.

IKEA basic requirements
- Lead free
- Cadmium not allowed
- PCPs not allowed
- AZO - dyestuffs not allowed
- Formaldehyde
  - Children's articles: 30ppm
  - Skin contact: 100ppm
  - Other: 300ppm
- No PVC
- Moth-proofing not allowed or per IWS recommendations

Cultivation
Production
Customer

- Non-chlorine bleached
- No organic solvents
- Minimum heavy metal residue
- pH within range of 4.5 - 7.5
- Tougher FA requirements:
  - Children's articles: 30ppm
  - Skin contact: 30ppm
  - Other: 100ppm

Cultivation
Production
Customer

- Water treatment system
- AZO - dyestuffs not allowed
- No PCBs used
- Minimum pesticide residue

(This level corresponds to Natural Cotton/Linen)

Cultivation
Production
Customer

Certified organically grown
Entire chain from cultivation to finished product is carried out under controlled conditions and with minimum impact on the environment

Cultivation
Production
Customer

Figure 4.2

Originally, the four-step process developed by textiles was configured in three steps: the first step safeguarding the customer; the second step ensuring environmental and human safety during production; and the third step going back to how the fibers are originally grown. Textiles extended it to four steps because suppliers complained that it wasn't possible to make the kind of leaps IKEA required. So IKEA made two steps out of the second step. By working with all suppliers to move them progressively up these steps, textiles is working with its entire product range rather than singling out just a few articles to be environmentally friendly.

The stair model is now being adapted to, and adopted by, other functional areas within IKEA and is being applied to IKEA's relationship with suppliers outside the textile area. It is an example of how education led to involvement, innovation, and operational integration.

Employee Participation

Because IKEA's culture provides so much room for autonomous action, no single model of involving employees was applied after the initial company-wide environmental education process. The level of engagement of co-workers turned out to be quite variable and depended upon the initiative of the workers in any particular operating unit. Through experience, IKEA has learned that for them to build a shared mental model and language, education is a necessary but not a sufficient condition to stimulate involvement. In addition, a company operating in many countries must take different societal and cultural contexts into account.

In 1993-94, for example, IKEA North America developed a strategy to make the core IKEA values relevant to the North American setting. IKEA's environmental values were not presented as a separate program, but as fundamental to IKEA's core values. According to Göran Carstedt, then President of IKEA North America and member of the IKEA Group executive committee, The Natural Step-influenced environmental education provided for all co-workers in the United States and Canada was a powerful vehicle for blending these cultural values. As a result of the largest training program IKEA North America has ever implemented, co-workers became energized, environmental ambassadors were designated in every store, and numerous activities were initiated. Co-workers developed a sense of pride and convergent values with their company. However, despite the success of the initial launch, interest and energy waned over time. As a result, IKEA North America learned that to keep co-workers energized, it is necessary to constantly relaunch and renew initiatives, and to view change as a step-by-step process, each development acting as a step to the next level.

In 1998, IKEA North America relaunched its environmental education initiative. The general philosophy behind the new initiative is, first, to make IKEA's environmental action plan and policy credible internally to its own employees.

Second, it is not part of IKEA North America's plan to advertise itself as environmentally friendly. According to their business plan, their overall goal is to be perceived as an environmentally responsible company without necessarily advertising themselves as such. According to Didi Malabuyo, Assistant to the Sales and Marketing Manager for North America, who has been centrally involved in the relaunch activities, it is essential that IKEA employees believe in the company's efforts and that this must be demonstrated not just in words, but also in actions. Once employees are convinced of IKEA's intentions and actions, it will become natural to convey this information to the customer.

As part of the environmental relaunch, every IKEA facility, store, and warehouse in North America designated an environmental coordinator who participated in an intensive training course. The intensive training was done in June 1998 in three locations: Philadelphia, Toronto, and Los Angeles. The local environmental coordinator was then responsible for training his or her co-workers. To facilitate this process, IKEA North America staff in Philadelphia developed a simple training tool, including a set of PowerPoint™ slides, that covers IKEA's approach to the environment, The Natural Step framework, and examples that make the information relevant to everyday life.

These training activities are also based on a staircase model: at the first step, as part of their orientation, all new employees learn that IKEA has an environmental policy, what that policy is, and what it means. They receive an introduction to the environmental action plan. They learn who the environmental coordinator is and where they can go for information. The second step, which takes place within the first month of employment, is the basic environmental training. At the third level, if additional environmental training is desired, people can attend the intensive training provided to environmental coordinators.

In addition to the training, environmental coordinators form a North American network and meet monthly by teleconference. The purpose behind the network is to provide the support that was lacking in the first launch of the education program, to link the coordinator in the store to the Environmental Coordinator for North America and through that linkage to connect them with the overall IKEA Environmental Network coordinated through IKEA's international headquarters in Humlabaek, Denmark.

Another important difference in this relaunch is that IKEA North America has made the environmental coordinator a full-time position, whereas previously it was only part of the position handled by the customer service manager. Besides monthly teleconferencing, John Zurcher, the Environmental Coordinator for North America, is working with the local environmental coordinator in each store to set up a working committee in the store to create an environmental action plan and to provide support, generate ideas, and encourage on-going action.

Integration: Actions and Results

The key to operationalizing sustainability is to integrate it into daily decisions and practices, to make environmental aspects a normal part of working methods. Education is the necessary foundation for the effective integration of environmental considerations into the frame of business reality. However, without actual involvement of the workers, education remains in the realm of theory. These two ingredients, education and involvement, are essential for success. Building on these, IKEA has identified five key areas to focus the task of integrating environmental criteria and awareness into its business operations.

1. The Environmental Adaptation of the Product Range

IKEA has become increasingly aware of how much there is to learn about how the materials and substances in their products can affect health and the environment. Currently, IKEA is working with Chalmers University in Göteborg, Sweden, to produce a material inventory of all their products using the four System Conditions and lifecycle analysis as their framework. The goal is, first, to identify what material is being used today and, second, which materials they will need to eliminate over both the short and long term. The knowledge gained through this initiative will be used to improve the environmental performance of existing products as well as to inform the design of new products. Because the IKEA product range is so extensive, with more than 10,000 product lines currently, the project is expected to take between one and two years. IKEA is also working with Kingston University in the U.K. to look at designing furniture from an environmental perspective, including the concepts of dematerialization and design for disassembly.

The stair model for the adaptation of the product range can be summarized as follows:

First, inventory the materials in the product. Second, analyze the material and determine what needs to be, or can be, eliminated and by when. Third, increase the percentage of products that use fewer materials and materials that are not harmful to the environment. Fourth, ensure that the materials used are 100 percent recyclable or are third-party certified, and that the product can be easily disassembled for future recycling.

Producer responsibility legislation — regulation that makes producers liable for taking back products at the end of their lifecycle — is of particular concern to IKEA, particularly with respect to furniture. IKEA believes that eventually the majority of countries will introduce some form of voluntary or legislated producer responsibility for furniture. In Sweden, discussions about the parameters for producer responsibility for furniture have been taking place since May of 1995, and some form of producer responsibility legislation is expected. In Germany it is no longer legal to dispose of old furniture at dumpsites. IKEA is working on the product development side to design and construct furniture for future disassembly and recycling. In Switzerland, IKEA's store in Spreitenbach has been offering customers the service of recycling their old sofas and armchairs since 1994. This service is offered at a charge that is less than customers would have to pay for disposing of the furniture at a dumpsite. In 1996, this service was expanded to allow customers purchasing home furnishing articles at IKEA to return all types of furniture including kitchen units, white goods, and flooring. In both Sweden and Switzerland, IKEA is working with local recycling companies to explore the feasibility and logistics of recycling materials from discarded furniture. The discarded furniture will be recycled for use as raw material for new products. What cannot be recycled will be used for energy recovery.

2. Sustainable Forestry

Approximately 75 percent of the raw material for IKEA's products, packaging, and catalogs comes from forests. This makes sustainable forestry a very important issue to IKEA. IKEA has become actively involved with various organizations in establishing principles for sustainable forestry. It is a founding member of the Forest Stewardship Council and was a member of the working group for the Swedish Forest Stewardship Council in developing their criteria for sustainability. IKEA has dedicated one full-time position to making an inventory of IKEA's current use of wood, including how much wood IKEA uses and from what sources. IKEA's ultimate goal is to use wood products sourced only from sustainably managed forests.

3. Environmental Work with Suppliers

The manufacturing of products creates some of the greatest environmental impacts. IKEA directly manufactures less than 10 percent of the products it sells. The balance is produced by some 2,300 suppliers in more than 60 countries. IKEA is initially focusing its environmental lens on its largest suppliers as it estimates that approximately 20 percent of IKEA's suppliers provide about 80 percent of its product line. Although individual suppliers are directly responsible for any harmful effects on the environment, IKEA understands its role as the purchaser for deciding which suppliers it will use. Many suppliers, particularly in Eastern Europe and Southeast Asia, have lower environmental standards than in Western Europe or North America. In IKEA's view, sourcing products in those countries provides an opportunity to advise suppliers of suitable technical solutions to reduce environmental impact. IKEA's responsibility includes providing information about IKEA's environmental policy, environmental action plans, and environmental requirements on products. IKEA's policy is to adopt and apply the strictest standards found anywhere in the world to each specific component in their entire product range. So rather than seeing low environmental standards in a country as an opportunity to avoid responsibility for its environmental impacts, IKEA takes this as an educational opportunity to bring a higher level of awareness and understanding to the particular situation.

IKEA now accepts that its role extends far beyond simply providing information to its suppliers. IKEA is working with a definite goal of reducing its environmental impact while maintaining low cost and value for money for its customers. To do this, IKEA works closely with its suppliers as illustrated in the four-step process developed by textiles. Wherever possible, suppliers are encouraged to practice active, preventive environmental work.

Until recently, each of IKEA's trading regions has developed its own method of working with suppliers with respect to the environment. Now they are synchronizing and coordinating these activities and one person has been made responsible for environmental coordination for IKEA Trading. The stair model for working with suppliers is being developed and will be applied to suppliers in all regions.

Currently, IKEA Trading Northern Europe has an environmental checklist with 10 questions about the supplier's environmental work. It has defined a number of prioritized areas to be given special attention by the supplier, such as surface treatment in all forms, degreasing processes, leather preparation, chemical use in the textile industry, and waste handling. IKEA Trading North America has included questions about the supplier's environmental status in the form of a checklist in the supplier assessment document that is filled out on new and existing supplies. IKEA Trading Asia Pacific has begun compiling a register of the laws and regulations governing their suppliers' operations. They are also carrying out a comprehensive study of the most important suppliers to verify that they fulfill all applicable laws and standards as well as IKEA's specific requirements. The results of the study will be stored in a database which will be updated as environmental improvements are made by the supplier.

IKEA Trading Southern Europe has started an environmental program called "4SEA": Supplier Environmental Assurance built around four points. The program is an environmental management system invented at IKEA and is not very different from the ISO 14000 approach except that it places more emphasis on the current situation and the needed steps than on documentation. The program is designed to assure that the supplier is aware of the environmental impact of its operations and is working for continual improvement. The four points are:

1. The supplier must establish an environmental policy that is relevant to its own organization and in line with that company's environmental ambitions. The supplier must also describe how the work is organized and who is responsible for aspects of the program.

2. The supplier must establish procedures and documentation for areas of its own operations that have an impact on the environment. This involves having systems for laws and regulations that concern the organization, approval from authorities, follow-up of emissions, incident reporting, requirements on sub-suppliers, etc.

3. The supplier must establish and document targets for reduced environmental impact from its operations, for example concerning energy consumption, waste, and emissions to the air and water. Targets must be quantified and measurable.

4. The supplier must establish documented procedures and instructions for handling incidents.

IKEA is encouraging its suppliers to institute environmental management systems in their operations, and many suppliers have already fulfilled the requirements according to ISO 14001, an international standard for environmental work; EMAS (Eco Management and Audit Scheme) which has been developed by the European Union; or BS7750, a British Standard. IKEA is not demanding that its suppliers be certified according to these standards but that they work toward continuous improvement.

The management for IKEA Trading Northern Europe has initiated regional meetings with all of its approximately 400 suppliers. The aim of these meetings is to communicate IKEA's views on the environmental issues facing industry and to learn about suppliers' views, experiences, and needs. A number of suppliers have expressed a desire for receiving help from IKEA in developing their environmental program, particularly with respect to environmental training. To address this need, Trading Northern Europe is offering its suppliers training based on IKEA's environmental training program, which is founded on The Natural Step.

4. Transport and Distribution

Transport is crucial to IKEA because it is a heavily transport-dependent company. In 1996, IKEA produced the booklet *Moves in the Right Direction* which makes an open and honest assessment of the environmental impact of transport. The booklet points out: "Of all society's present-day activities, transport has perhaps the greatest single impact on the environment. If we were to look at total impact, i.e., do a lifecycle analysis, we would have to include a multitude of factors in the calculation — from extraction of raw materials, construction of ships, cars, planes, roads, etc., to consumption of energy, emissions, and finally reuse and recycling of vehicles."

In fact, the complexity of transportation networks for a modern multinational corporation such as IKEA and their manifold impacts on the environment is quite extraordinary. Considering that IKEA has approximately 2,300 suppliers around the world manufacturing approximately 10,000 different products, with each product made of perhaps dozens of parts themselves made and shipped by dozens of sub-suppliers, the environmental ramifications are significant. And this is just from one company in a global economy of millions of suppliers, transporters, and users. It is easy to understand why decreasing the environmental impact of their transport needs is one of IKEA's fundamental goals.

Therefore, environmental considerations are now an integral part of IKEA's transport purchasing. According to Peter Olofsson, Freight Purchaser for IKEA Northern Europe, environmental impact is now one of the four criteria upon which transport decisions are made. The other three are capacity, flexibility, and cost. IKEA has outlined several priorities for action in the transport area:

1. Competence development of all co-workers directly and indirectly involved in transport or transport-related activities, through a specially designed internal training program covering transport methods and their environmental impacts.

2. Efficiency through better planning and planning systems to minimize the number of transports and to ensure that each is used optimally. Continuing development of packaging and aids to further reduce the transport volume.

3. Transport methods that increase the volume of goods transported by rail, including a combination of road–rail transport. IKEA is monitoring the development of new transport concepts, techniques, methods, and fuels, and actively supports and participates in research in these areas.

4. IKEA is formulating environmental requirements that are communicated to its carriers. These requirements are being made a condition for contracting and will be reviewed and updated annually in consultation with the carriers.

IKEA realizes that there are limits to what they can do to reduce their transport-related environmental impact. Beyond that they must depend upon their transport carriers who are also limited by existing transportation infrastructure, availability of alternative fuels, etc. These are areas where IKEA is building collaborative relationships to move the system in the right direction. Wherever possible, IKEA plans to use rail transport and combined road-rail transport. In the long-term, this requires influencing railway companies and public opinion about the economic and environmental benefits implicit in these choices.

IKEA is working in close co-operation with its carriers to discover ways to reduce the environmental impact of transport. The company has developed a program called "IKEA, Transport, and the Environment" to develop ideas with their carriers for making transportation more efficient. An IKEA "Environment

Day" was held regionally in Northern Europe in which nearly 100 European carriers participated. The first part of the day included presentations about why IKEA is now focusing on the environment in all aspects of its business using The Natural Step framework as the conceptual model. The second part consisted of collaborative work with the carriers to generate ideas about how IKEA and its carriers could work together in a more environmentally responsible way.

The transport staircase, which is under development, currently has the following steps: First, require environmental policies from all carriers; second, require an environmental action plan from all carriers; third, construct an environmental audit covering such items as policies, the level the carrier is at according to IKEA's environmental criteria, information on their action plan, equipment, tires, fuels, possibilities for rail or combi-transport etc.; and fourth, divide the carriers into A and B carriers based on a point system from the audit. Carriers wishing long-term contracts would have to quickly reach the A level.

5. Meeting the Customer

This goal is very much an internal process, which includes the environmental adaptation of all IKEA stores, training or retraining of co-workers, and communications with customers. All IKEA stores are conducting material balance inventories to determine the throughput of material and energy in their stores. All new IKEA stores are to be built with environmental criteria in mind. It is the policy in North America, for example, that every new store that is opened from now on will take environmental impact into account in the building design and construction. One of IKEA North America's goals is for that policy to be part of the investment proposal for every new store. As IKEA North America plans to add several stores and to renovate several more in the next few years, this policy has important ramifications for IKEA's investment and planning. To encourage stores to participate in this initiative and to make it more enjoyable, IKEA is considering instituting a friendly competition among stores, and perhaps even among countries.

In the U.S., IKEA is working with the Environmental Protection Agency on their Green Lights Program which encourages the use of energy-efficient lighting. IKEA has partnered with the EPA for about three years. Partners to the program agree to survey 100 percent of their facilities lighting systems and within five years of joining the program to upgrade 90 percent of that square footage to energy-efficient lighting, as long as the upgrade achieves a minimum internal rate of return of 20 percent and there is no compromise of lighting quality. IKEA U.S. has made excellent progress in the program. As of November 1998, they had reduced their kilowatt demand by 781 kw and their kilowatt hour usages by more than three million. The expected annual savings from lighting load reduction, air conditioning reductions, and reductions from lower lighting system maintenance costs is estimated to be more than $500,000, with a simple payback period for all projects of 1.9 years. Environmentally, IKEA in North America has avoided more than four million pounds of annual carbon dioxide emissions, over 17 million grams of annual sulphur dioxide emissions, and almost seven million grams of annual nitrogen oxide emissions equivalent to planting 982 trees, removing 482 cars from U.S. roadways, and preventing the combustion of 313,500 gallons of gasoline.

The goal for the future is to carry out lighting retrofits for three IKEA stores in the U.S. that have not yet been done and to ensure that future facilities within the U.S. are designed to include the most energy-efficient lighting systems possible.

IKEA's philosophy is to become known as an environmentally responsible company by actually being one. It does not intend to advertise itself as a "green" company and is particularly wary of any actions that can be misperceived as greenwashing. IKEA also has a long tradition of informing its customers about the contents of its products to facilitate the making of informed decisions in purchasing. IKEA is working to ensure that its products can withstand environmental scrutiny and that its co-workers can be the best ambassadors for the environment through education and communication of what IKEA is really doing for the environment. In addition, to further inform its customers, IKEA has recently developed *Green Steps,* an informative booklet on its environmental policy and actions. With customary IKEA understatement, the booklet will not be put in stands by the front door, but will be available for customers who ask for it, or who show interest in how IKEA is dealing with environmental issues.

IKEA's catalog is one of its most important tools of communicating with its customers. Once a source of considerable pride as the largest color publication in the world, IKEA began to receive considerable criticism for the environmental impact of the catalog. The company set out to create an environmental action plan for the catalog. The first step was to identify the environmental concerns involved and to figure out how to improve them. One of those issues was the use of chlorine bleach. By working in partnership with Swedish Greenpeace, IKEA identified a way to produce its catalog on totally chlorine-free paper starting in 1992. IKEA identified paper sources with the help of the Greenpeace network. During that first year, the company purchased most of the world's supply of totally chlorine-free paper and, by doing so, helped push demand for the product. By the second year, IKEA was able to find sufficient supply with no problem. Currently, the catalog contains some 10 to 20 percent recycled paper, which is considered to be the maximum range for that quality of paper. Other catalogs, such as the summer and winter brochures, are made from 100 percent recycled paper because they are not required to have the same durability as the main catalog. IKEA requires a guarantee from its suppliers that the paper in their catalogs is not made from old-growth forests.

In 1997, IKEA launched a campaign to provide Swedish customers with low-cost, low-energy light bulbs. Kamprad decided that he wanted to encourage people to change from the old kind of inefficient incandescent bulb to the modern low-energy, or compact, fluorescent bulb. These produce the same light level for just 20 percent of the energy consumption of the conventional bulbs. Eleven watts of electrical energy give the same light as 60 watts in an ordinary bulb. IKEA found a Chinese manufacturer for the bulb and was able to sell it at a price one-third that of other compact fluorescent bulbs on the market in Sweden — the equivalent of US $5 instead of $15. To encourage people in Sweden to try them, IKEA in 1997 gave away 532,000 compact lamps to Swedish households. Each household could receive one free bulb by redeeming a coupon at an IKEA store. It was estimated that if every Swedish household exchanged 20 of their bulbs, total Swedish energy consumption could be reduced by an amount equal to the production of one nuclear reactor's power. Considering that Sweden has a population of only nine million people compared to a North American population of roughly 300 million, one can calculate the enormous savings in electrical consumption, and therefore the lowered environmental impact, if the populace of North America converted to low-energy light bulbs.

Just the Beginning

There are many, many other green steps, both small and large, that IKEA has taken and plans to take. There is IKEA's experimentation with solar energy and its hopes to ultimately be able to build new stores at least in part powered by solar panels. There is the list of materials that IKEA has eliminated, or nearly eliminated, including lead, PVCs, cadmium, and chrome. There is IKEA's children's furniture line that meets a long list of environmental criteria. There is the new range of "a.i.r." sofas and armchairs filled with an inexhaustible, free, and environmentally friendly material: air, in terms of its materials and manufacturing the air sofa uses only one-sixth of the resources of a conventional sofa. There is the North American Recovery program and the Christmas tree recycling program. The list goes on and is growing.

Final Reflections

IKEA occupies a special place in the development of The Natural Step as an effective instrument for business. It was the first major corporation to engage with The Natural Step, that being in 1990. It has the longest continuous business relationship with The Natural Step of any corporation, now a continuous ten-year relationship. It has trained more of its employees in The Natural Step than any other corporation, i.e., approximately 30,000. Many of the most effective environmental management tools, methodologies, and concepts utilizing The Natural Step were pioneered at IKEA over the past decade and continue to be pioneered today. IKEA was the first company to bring the natural step framework to North America and to begin to link the strengths of organizational learning with The Natural Step framework for sustainability. Finally, IKEA has a culture of entrepreneurial innovation, risk taking, forgiveness of mistakes and learning from them as well as caring for all of its stakeholders, and has come to an understanding of the business relevance and importance of sustainability. This has been fertile soil to create an effective dialogue between The Natural Step and business.

Several factors have facilitated IKEA's process of integrating sustainability as a core value of its business. The foundation of this is the link between The Natural Step framework and the values of IKEA's founder, Ingvar Kamprad, who has always detested waste in any form. Furthermore, exciting product innovation has resulted from seeking to balance environmental criteria on one hand with a low cost structure on the other. The integration of sustainability as a core value also owes a great deal to the tremendous drive of a small group of dedicated and enthused individuals, most notably Anders Moberg, IKEA Group President. In addition, the enthusiasm and pride with which many co-workers throughout the company have embraced the inclusion of environmental concerns in their work has been very important. Still another significant factor is that IKEA focused its environmental lens on the heart of its business — product design and development — and on supplier relations through educating them about IKEA's sustainability vision, values, and plans.

In reflecting upon the ongoing ten year intellectual and commercial relationship between IKEA and The Natural Step, there appear to us to be at least five main benefits to the company.

First, The Natural Step has been very helpful to IKEA in creating awareness, understanding, and enthusiasm for environmental issues among IKEA's senior management, middle managers, and co-workers. The Natural Step provides a key part of the environmental education programs used to train all co-workers. It provides the scientific core of the three different types of environmental training programs offered in IKEA today (as described above).

Second, The Natural Step has given IKEA management and co-workers a means to understand their relationship as a company and as individuals, to the natural world, and how IKEA in its widespread operations affects, and is affected by, the natural environment. By embedding The Natural Step framework into IKEA's strategic and day-to-day operations, through environmental policies, environmental action plans, environmental training, and through making environmental factors a core consideration of investment, supplier, transport and product design and specification decisions, IKEA is approaching a more ecological worldview. In effect, in terms of its corporate identity as it relates to the natural world, it knows who it is, what it stands for, and why.

Third, with respect to the attacks of critics and the media, sometimes highly emotional, about the safety and environmental impacts of its products and operations, The Natural Step framework empowers and enables IKEA to analyze its products and operations and respond knowledgeably to criticism. IKEA does not claim to be environmentally pristine, far from it, but it at least has a much clearer understanding than most corporations of its inconsistencies and it has a step-by-step vision for their eventual solution.

Fourth, The Natural Step stimulates innovation and out-of-the-box thinking. It provides a framework for design innovation that empowers designers in all media to innovate for the betterment of profits, people, and planet. A recent example of how sustainability considerations stimulate innovation is the new "a.i.r." sofa from IKEA which exemplifies dematerialization in terms of volume of space to factor six.

Fifth, The Natural Step provides a rational, common language and mental model for IKEA and its suppliers to create a shared basis for understanding IKEA's environmental vision and enables them to better and more efficiently implement IKEA's purchasing policies. IKEA and its thousands of suppliers around the world comprise a very complex system of relationships, languages, and cultures. So far hundreds of IKEA suppliers in Northern Europe have received training in IKEA's Natural Step-influenced environmental policies.

Despite many advances in both sustainability thinking and action, co-workers at IKEA are noticeably humble and honest as they describe their ten-year environmental odyssey. They are the first to say how far IKEA still needs to go. Moving toward sustainability is recognized as a very long path, consisting of thousands and thousands of small green steps. Often it is a frustrating road when the pace of change does not seem to match the urgency that is felt by many people. However, by any standard, IKEA has made remarkable progress. Perhaps most importantly, the senior leadership of the company and a large body of co-workers understand the basic issues of sustainability and the reasons it is so relevant to IKEA's global operations, both today and in the future, and are motivated to continue IKEA's march towards a sustainable world — a world where IKEA will continue to pursue its mission to help provide a better everyday life for the majority of people.

CHAPTER 5

SCANDIC HOTELS:
"Interactive Values Creation"

We are changing from a society that uses resources to a society that saves resources. No company can avoid either taking environmental responsibility or focusing on environmental issues in all aspects of their operations.
Roland Nilsson — *CEO, Scandic Hotels*

I N 1992, SCANDIC HOTELS AB was a northern European chain of about 100 hotels in deep trouble. Realizing that major surgery was the only way to save the company, the owner fired the existing CEO and brought in one of Scandinavia's most respected businessmen, Roland Nilsson, to head the company. Today, Nilsson is CEO of one of Europe's most successful major hotel chains, what he calls *"the new Scandic,"* and he and his new team have performed one of the great turnarounds in the history of Scandinavian business. How Karl-Henrik Robèrt and The Natural Step helped Roland Nilsson and his team create the new Scandic is a fascinating and instructive story.

Interestingly, Scandic Hotels has American roots. The Scandic chain started life in 1963 as the Esso Motor Hotel chain, established by a subsidiary of the U.S. petroleum giant Exxon. The original intention of the chain was to bring the American concept of a motor hotel, or motel, to the Scandinavian motoring public. The concept enjoyed initial success and by 1973, the Esso Motor Hotel chain had become the largest hotel chain in Sweden. In 1983, Exxon decided to focus on its core activities and, as a result, sold the Esso Motor Hotel chain to a consortium operating as Scandic Hotels AB. In 1986, Scandic Hotels AB became a wholly-owned investment of one of the consortium partners, Förvaltnings AB Ratos, which is a Swedish investment holding company whose shares are listed on the Stockholm Stock Exchange.

By the early 1990s, the chain was fighting to survive. Most of the markets in which Scandic operated were experiencing a major recession that severely affected the hotel industry. This recession exposed a number of significant weaknesses in Scandic's operations and resulted in Scandic incurring huge losses during the period 1991-93 which almost caused bankruptcy. According to Kerstin Goransson, the current Executive Vice President and CFO, between 1990 and 1992 Scandic showed losses of approximately 350 million SEK (roughly US $50 million at the time).

After two years of administering corporate triage, dealing with the legacies of the past, Nilsson was ready to address the future of the company in an original and proactive way. With a very strong grasp of his customers, Nilsson decided that the way forward — the new Scandic — had to be based on a whole new set of core values, values based on a profound caring. The word in Swedish for this very deep caring is *omtanke*, and this became the company's central value. For the men and women of Scandic, *omtanke* translates as a *profound caring* for their customers, their co-workers, their shareholders, the communities in which they operate, and the natural environment.

To mark the transition from the old regime to the new Scandic, Nilsson in 1994 took his entire senior management group, over 100 people including all the hotel general managers, to neighboring Iceland for a five-day corporate retreat and workshop. To demonstrate his seriousness about the importance of the environment to the new Scandic, Nilsson provided Robèrt with one full day of the five to give all of Scandic's senior management an introductory training in The Natural Step. Initially sceptical, many hotel managers subsequently described the The Natural Step training by Robèrt as "life-changing" and "the most powerful presentation that they had ever attended." In retrospect, most executives now see that event as the turning point in the company. It signalled a new vision for the future.

From that inspiring beginning, Scandic devised a plan to train each of their more than 5,000 employees in the basic principles of sustainability using The Natural Step framework. Each hotel then created a local program of activities to make step-by-step improvements in environmental performance. To date, Scandic has documented over 2,000 individual measures and the company's overall environmental footprint has been substantially reduced.

Scandic Today

Energized by new values that touch the hearts of its employees and its customers and empowered by visionary leadership, Scandic is enjoying record profits and is expanding rapidly. In fact, the new Scandic is so successful and profitable that in December, 1996, the company successfully undertook an initial public offering of approximately US $100 million for expansion — inconceivable for the company only a short time before. Scandic is now the dominant player and clear market leader in the entire Scandinavian market of Denmark, Finland, Norway, and

Sweden and has become one of Europe's most successful hotel chains. After a major acquisition, consolidated revenues and operating income for the 12-month period ending December 31, 1997, were roughly US $700 million (SEK 5,038 billion) and US $31 million (SEK 226 million). Scandic now has more than 120 hotels, of which 109 are in the Nordic region, and about 6,600 employees, and operating profits are steadily increasing (See Figure 5.1).

Scandic operates full service hotels in the three and four star categories that typically are located either in city center locations or on the outskirts of cities and major towns with easy access to local airports and/or major road networks. It has more than 20 percent of the total room capacity in Sweden and is achieving a high and growing degree of market coverage in Finland, Norway, and Denmark. Scandic has the highest market penetration of city-center-located hotels in Sweden. It is now both the market leader and the price leader in its field.

Scandic is the first dedicated hotel operator to have its shares listed on the Stockholm Stock Exchange. Most listed hotel operators operate as property owners. Having strategically divested itself of ownership of its hotel properties, Scandic is able to focus its attention entirely on the management of its hotels. This means that Scandic ties up less capital relative to other hotel operators and can produce higher investment yields. Scandic has, to a large extent, negotiated leasing agreements with variable rent, thereby reducing its exposure to market turbulence.

To enable hotels to measure their progress, not only year-to-year but also in relation to one another, Scandic has developed a benchmarking system called "BINC" (Best in Class), which makes it possible to compare a number of parameters reflecting operational, financial, and quality performance. This benchmarking system has become an excellent platform for encouraging improvements and knowledge-sharing among the chain's hotels. At the core of all of Scandic's success is its focus on customer-centered values.

Interactive Values Creation

At the heart of Scandic's masterful turnaround is what CEO Roland Nilsson calls "interactive values creation." Nilsson is exceedingly customer focused. Prior to his taking the helm, Scandic did not have a set of unifying core values with which either its customers or its own employees could identify. According to Nilsson, it is fundamental to create values in common with the market. Nilsson gave considerable attention to developing his own explanatory model for why companies are successful. He concludes: "If you have strong values that are in common with your market, you create values in common together — you and your customer. That's unbeatable because it's not possible to copy that relationship."

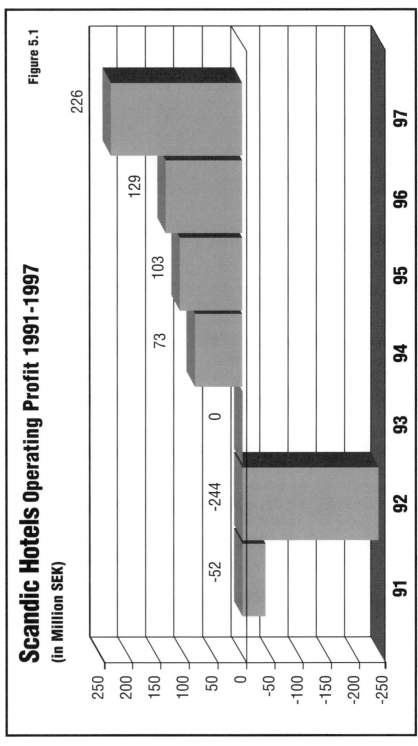

Scandic Hotels Operating Profit 1991-1997
(in Million SEK)

Figure 5.1

In the Scandinavian countries, *omtanke* captures the sense of these strong shared values. If *omtanke* could be translated into English, it would be analogous to "profound positive caring and attention". Nilsson describes *omtanke* as an essential core learning process in Scandic, "a way of maintaining the values in the company in a very solid way." On a very practical, day-to-day level, *omtanke* means that the atmosphere among co-workers should be open and honest; that co-workers should deal with one another with the highest integrity; and that they should each be responsible for their jobs and responsible toward each other. In addition, *omtanke* means taking care of the owners, the shareholders, so they will have a valuable return on their investment. *Omtanke* also applies to the wider context of society, which includes taking care of the environment. According to Nilsson, in the new Scandic, "environment can be seen as a thread throughout."

Ken Hopper, General Manager of one of Scandic's Stockholm hotels, draws the connection between interactive values creation and customer loyalty. He believes there is a shift in the market from hard to soft values and that emotional selling factors are becoming increasingly important. He comments: "This is very clear in Europe, and because of that, we believe that in the markets of tomorrow you need to address these emotional values. So by an interactive dialogue with your customer, you can create values shared between the two of you. And value sharing really ties you together and creates a very high customer loyalty."

In creating the vision for the new Scandic, Nilsson and his management team realized that one of the core values had to be environmental responsibility. According to Vice-President Gunnar Brandberg, Scandic could not avoid taking responsibility for the environment. When asked why, Brandberg responded, "The environment tends to set the rules for us. There's a limit to how much we can do in conflict with the rules of nature. Sooner or later, nature catches up and tells us what to do in a hard or soft way. It's better as a company to start from the beginning, or start earlier, than be forced to do something later either by law or by the environment itself."

Scandic executives observed that in its markets, a significant and growing number of customers were actively choosing products or companies that stood for environmental friendliness or that actively worked for a better environment. This tendency appears to be increasing and is considered a defining value of the future market, a market Scandic is, in turn, helping to define. By responding vigorously to these market signals and communicating their actions clearly to their customers, Scandic is reinforcing this value as something reasonable to expect from the hospitality industry. It is, in fact, setting an industry standard of ecological responsibility held in common with the people it serves. This is interactive values creation in action.

Nilsson believes that during the next decade there will be an increasing focus on the environment, that we are entering a transition period during which businesses are adapting to the integration of environmental issues as a natural part of business behavior. The integration of an environmental perspective throughout the business world will become as "natural as having good bookkeeping." Scandic's goal is to become one of the most environmentally friendly companies in the hotel industry, to take the lead and to continuously work to reduce the environmental impact of their business activities.

As is the case with most corporations, when the CEO first introduced the concept of making the environment a core value for the company, not all of his executive team agreed. Some were outright sceptical. Even some of the board members wondered whether this was an appropriate focus for Scandic. The company's Vice President and CFO, Kerstin Goransson, for example, says that she was cautious about it at the beginning. She "thought it would only cost money and nothing else." Tommy Hansson, then Sales Director, recalls he was not happy with Nilsson's idea about investing a lot of money in environmental concerns at the beginning, but has dramatically changed his mind. Today he asserts that Scandic is making profits out of this approach. He says: "At the beginning, I thought it was a tremendous amount of money to invest in new roles, time, education, and training. And I thought that we would be a little too far ahead of all the other companies. Fortunately Roland understood the trends, how to do these things much earlier than everyone else. If we had not made this strong investment, we would never have the lead we have today. So from the start I was negative mainly because I didn't believe it was profitable, but I was wrong." According to Nilsson's calculations, the environmental focus is an investment. If Scandic does not pay attention to environmental aspects, it will cost more in the long run. Nilsson remarks: "So we can accept a higher investment today, because it will lower the cost in the future. It hasn't cost us anything. No one can claim that this has cost us more money."

For example, Scandic was the first hotel chain in the world to invest in and install a completely environmentally benign and recyclable soap and shampoo system throughout the chain. Their customary hand soap weighed 15 g and was wrapped in a plastic covering. A guest staying for one night would use approximately 3 g of soap and the remainder would be thrown away. Today, this waste has been eliminated by the use of refillable containers, and the soap and shampoo used is biodegradable. Overall, soap and shampoo use has been reduced annually by 25 tons and refuse has been reduced by 8.5 tons. This investment continues to save the company money and helps protect the natural world at the same time.

Scandic and The Natural Step

Why was The Natural Step attractive to Scandic? According to Brandberg, it was because The Natural Step was not "the traditional environmentalist telling us what to do." Instead, The Natural Step helped Scandic set a course to sustainability and said "with this direction in mind, do what you can within your company." Brandberg adds that The Natural Step understands that a healthy, robust company can do more to help the environment.

In 1993, when Nilsson decided that concern for the environment needed to be a core unifying value for the company, Scandic contacted several organizations to learn more about environmental issues and how to integrate them into their business. Nilsson invited Robèrt to make a presentation to the management group late in 1993 to give them the opportunity to learn more about The Natural Step methodology. Brandberg recalls that Robèrt spoke for about one and one-half hours after which there was discussion and questions. He says, "that was enough to trigger everyone." He recalls that he left the room wondering whether it was already too late, or if there was truly something that Scandic, that industry, that society could do to change the current trends. He says: "I think that contributed to the degree of seriousness of the matter."

In the spring of 1994, when Nilsson took the entire senior management group to Iceland, environmental issues were a fundamental part of the agenda. Nilsson chose The Natural Step approach because he saw it provided a knowledge platform with which to proceed in the environmental realm. He asked Robèrt to introduce his general managers and executive group to the basic concepts. The impact was powerful and profound on general managers and the executive group alike. Hopper recalls: "We had a presentation from Karl-Henrik Robèrt. I sat there among these people and just said, 'What a concept! What a mission!'" Uni Astrum, then General Manager of the Scandic Hotel in Slussen, and now Director of Sales for the company, remarked that before she went to Iceland, she had given very little thought to the environment. After hearing Robèrt, she said: "Previously I didn't understand these things. It was absolutely new to me. For example, I never thought about water, how the water that we have now is the water that we've always had on this planet. There is no new water. And it's like that: Aha! Because then I understood that I have to care for the water, that I can't spend as much as I want to all the time when it's not even necessary. Then something happens in you, when you can take it into yourself. You know, when you've really bought into something, then you act accordingly."

According to Brandberg, "The more we learned from The Natural Step, the more the management group became involved in environmental matters. The more you learn, the more you realize how important it is for the future. It's as simple as that."

The management group returned from Iceland with a new awareness about the relationship of the natural environment to Scandic's business. The task remained to translate this awareness into action and to design a program that would express environmental values within the framework of *omtanke* for customers, employees, shareholders, and society. Nilsson made a number of important moves early on. First, he provided strong CEO leadership and support to integrating environmental values into all aspects of the company's operations. Second, he created an environmental policy based on The Natural Step. Third, he combined environmental management with purchasing and made the combined office a senior executive position. Fourth, he gave directions to create and implement a company-wide environmental education and action plan based on The Natural Step.

Ola Ivarsson was selected by Nilsson to head the new senior position of Group Purchasing and the Environment. One of Ivarsson's new jobs was to prepare a plan to roll out the environmental component of the new Scandic. At the core of Ivarsson's approach was the understanding that a successful environmental program needs to be integrated into the company's business strategy. This means that, to be successful, the environmental program and strategy must start in the business environment in which the company operates. In addition, the environment program needs the total support from the top. At Scandic, it had it. According to Ivarsson, "Particularly in the early stages of a sub-project or in the early stages of a training process, you need top support. Because these processes are so complicated and so intangible, it's a very different goal to set and to measure. It is difficult to prove whether this will be a profitable project in the end or not." Ivarson believes that if you run the environmental program at a less senior level than he holds, or if you don't try to integrate it into the marketing or investment strategy, it will fail. " In the end it will lose importance internally because it doesn't connect with the other activities that the company is doing."

Evolutionary Insight

Both Nilsson and Ivarsson recognized that Scandic needed to adopt the principles of natural cycles into its day-to-day work throughout the company with a vision of integrating the company's business with the cycles of nature. In other words, the company is part of nature and must recognize that fact in its operations or eventually suffer the consequences. The environment is not something "out there" to be dealt with — it is "in here" where we live and work.

Scandic chose The Natural Step as its compass to find its way toward being an ecologically sustainable corporation.

Scandic's *Environmental Guide* states: "The Compass is based on The Natural Step's four conditions to achieve a sustainable society. To meet the four System Conditions is a long-term goal, but the process can be started now. It is important for individuals as well as companies to take the right path and, step by step, start to fulfill the four conditions. Let the environmental compass lead you in the right direction."

Ivarsson acted to make environment considerations a normal part of the day-to-day thinking of managers and employees alike. The first strategy he developed was to draft minimum environmental standards for all Scandic's operations and to write a manual for all hotels to follow. The first order he gave was to find a way of collecting, analyzing, and putting together the environmental legislation and regulations from all the different countries where Scandic operated as well as good advice on how to deal with them. Because Scandic operated in more than 100 locations and, at that time, in nine countries, Ivarsson quickly came to the conclusion that this would be an impossible task. He decided the only way that Scandic would be successful in integrating environmental aspects into its business operations was to establish a mutual knowledge platform and language across Scandic from which all the hotels could run their own process, similar to the one experienced on the corporate level.

Ivarsson believes that the only way to launch a successful environmental program in an organization is, first, to provide a knowledge base for the whole organization; second, to build a common framework from which everyone can make their own decisions about local activity programs; and third, to document these activities, to fine tune them, and finally to set some minimum standards for operations. He summarizes his insights this way: "If you have a corporate program which is based on so much knowledge, in many cases novel knowledge, you need to create engagement and power by decentralized responsibility based on a mutual frame of reference which is created through mutual training sessions. You need a good language. We were searching for a good environmental language, a platform, some conditions. Then we found the four System Conditions of The Natural Step and decided that would be the platform."

Scandic looked at other knowledge platforms but decided they were too complicated. They wanted everyone throughout the Scandic organization to be able to participate in the education and implementation of the program. If you want to do that, Ivarsson asserts, you need to find a simple explanatory model that can be adopted into everyone's day-to-day situation. The Natural Step provided that model. Scandic set a goal to train all of its employees in environmental issues and thinking using The Natural Step framework. According to Ivarsson, although The Natural Step was the best explanatory model they had found, it still needed to be translated into Scandic's own operational day-to-day situation. "The beauty of the System Conditions is that this is possible. The success we had using the System Conditions was based on the translation we made, giving lots of examples of how we can adapt those System Conditions to our operations. Otherwise it would have been just a nice theory without practical value to most of our employees."

Scandic looks at its environmental policy as its guide to setting a good example in the hotel industry. The guide states: "The policy will primarily lead us to improved operations using natural resources. It is every employee's duty to pursue this policy in their daily work." Scandic has articulated the following specific actions to fulfill its policy:

- To the greatest extent, follow the principles of nature's cycle in our work and the business will successfully integrate with nature's cycles
- Follow the rules and norms in each environmental area and hopefully be one step ahead
- Develop products and services so that we use nature's resources as sparingly as possible
- Choose raw materials and recyclable packaging — products that do not fulfil these criteria should not be used
- Strive to use environmentally safe and recyclable energy sources and use a distribution system that puts less burden on the environment
- Reduce waste and promote waste reduction
- Choose, influence, and educate our suppliers to help us implement our environmental policy
- Develop an environmental network of enthusiastic representatives from each hotel
- Every year, review the results of our environmental policy and establish goals for future development

Scandic clearly realizes that its environmental goal, policy, and actions are connected to its own future prosperity. The company feels that the environmental program is an important step showing concern for the environment and equipping them to contribute to the development of society. It is also an important way of strengthening their competitiveness and shaping their long-term success. Several areas where Scandic believes it will benefit include

- Maintaining and strengthening their reputation both internally and externally

- Forming long-term customer relations through increasing consumer awareness of the environment
- Conserving energy and other resources
- Improving and developing the company's activity by anticipating changes in the market and in society

Education and Training

Scandic initially developed its environmental program in the spring of 1994. They began by training 15 trainers in The Natural Step framework. This group then worked together to design a training program specific to Scandic. Extensive materials were prepared for the trainers and networkers. For example, environmental coordinators received a handbook that included training in how to plan and run a meeting, how to delegate, and how to choose activities. According to Ivarsson, it is very important that the process be user-friendly. Scandic runs "a tight ship with everyone having many things to do." Providing assistance with as many details as possible reduces the pressure on the individual trainer. Based on The Natural Step, the training program Scandic developed is called "The Environmental Dialogue" and consists of four components:

An environmental guide. It is provided to each Scandic employee. The guide contains information, ideas, and tips to stimulate environmental thinking and action. It also contains a description of the Environmental Dialogue process. It outlines Scandic's vision to the year 2000, environmental goals, policy, and recent activities. It covers the basic principles behind The Natural Step framework including re-incorporating human activities into nature's cycles and the four System Conditions. The guide outlines eight environmental areas as a starting point for the individual hotel's environmental thinking and activities, and provides ideas for areas in which the hotel might make improvement:

- Customers and the environment. This is based on the idea that Scandic's task is to provide value and care for their guests, including care for the environment on which we all depend. Areas to look at include communication with the clients, first impressions of the hotel, dialogue with guests during their stay, co-operation with business partners, and the creation of environmentally friendly conference support and materials.
- The external environment of the hotel, such as the grounds. Areas to look at include less use of non-degradable substances, more composting, more indigenous natural landscaping, less energy intensive machinery.
- The internal environment of the hotel, such as construction, interior decor, paint, and office equipment. Areas to look at include construction

material and interior decor, and the creation of an environmentally friendly office.

- Food and beverage service, including food, drinking water, beer and wine. Areas to look at include using organic foods, reducing the transportation of food and beverage items, seeking organic beverages.
- Water and energy, with a focus on ways to conserve both.
- Packaging material and waste, with a focus on reducing packaging needs, recycling waste wherever possible, reducing unsorted waste.
- Laundry, dish washing and cleaning. Areas to look at include choosing biodegradable substances for laundry, saving on detergents, reducing cleaning substances with harmful chemicals.
- Transportation, including ways to reduce the environmental impact of staff transportation and to increase demand for alternative fuels.

An environmental meeting. It takes place about a week after co-workers receive the environmental guide. These meetings begin with an introduction to Scandic's environmental work after which co-workers work in groups of six to eight colleagues to explore ways to make environmental improvements in their hotel. These teams are cross-functional, bringing together people from different departments to work on a common framework of issues. At these one-day environmental meetings, employees discuss what they think could be done at their hotel and who would be responsible for following through with each idea. The workers in the hotel decide on the priority areas for their hotel based on the suggestions made in the environmental guide.

An environmental program. This is an action plan created through the group process at the environmental meeting. Several groups in each hotel work in parallel to generate suggestions on how the individual hotel could take steps to reduce its impact on the environment. These suggestions are coordinated through the hotel's environmental networker, who divides them into three categories: concrete activities that can be carried out immediately; ideas that need further investigation; and ideas that need investment consideration. Then the suggestions are discussed with the hotel manager and prioritized further. The environmental program is then distributed to all employees and made available to hotel guests. A copy is also sent to Scandic's environmental headquarters and included in the hotel's business plan.

An environmental barometer. This is a quarterly report containing a status report from each hotel with respect to meeting the goals set out in the environmental program.

In the first year of the Environmental Dialogue process, all of Scandic's 5,000 employees in eight countries participated. Each hotel made up an environmental program of activities to improve the environment. More than 1,500 measures, generated through the Environmental Dialogue, were implemented. Some of these measures were large and sweeping, others were small. Each was a step toward reducing Scandic's environmental impact and making Scandic more resource-efficient and effective. Since the first year, Scandic has implemented an additional 500 measures generated through the Dialogue, which have required more time or investment to implement.

Environmental training is a continuous process at Scandic as acquisitions add to the employee base or employee turnover brings on new employees. The responsibility for environmental activities and training remains at the individual hotel, but is coordinated at the Group level. The results continue to be monitored quarterly through the environmental barometer or index, which measures progress on prioritized activities.

Employee Participation

Involvement in the environmental aspects of Scandic's business begins at the top. It is a shared core value among the company's top management group, beginning with the CEO. The degree and level of involvement is conveyed by the fact that responsibility for the environmental program resides with a senior member of the executive group, and specifically in combination with the vital function of purchasing. Involvement also definitely extends to all general managers of hotels in the chain. Part of their job performance is evaluated with respect to environmental indicators. Scandic has also set up a sophisticated organizational support structure to promote and reinforce employee involvement in each hotel.

Similar to Scandic management's experience at the Iceland meeting, the environmental dialogue produced a powerful impact among employees as well. Throughout the organization comments are made that nothing before had so mobilized workers on every level. The environmental program is considered to be the most effective employee involvement program ever experienced. It unified all levels of the organization around the vision of the new Scandic and infused employees with enthusiasm and innovative spirit. For example, Ken Hopper remarks:

> I've been involved in Scandic for ten years. We've had all kinds of different campaigns or processes. Nothing has ever been close to creating as much excitement as this environmental campaign. It was just huge. You did not have anyone who didn't feel something. It was incredible that people got so involved in this that they are willing to make some sacrifices and put in some energy and effort to get involved. It brought people together in a way we've never ever been able to bring our staff

together before, and we haven't since. Nothing we've done has mobilized a force that's created such unison.

CFO Kerstin Goransson said that she was surprised by the power the environmental dialogue process had for the whole organization: "I have never ever seen anything else unifying 5000 people. I could never imagine the power of doing something like this that involved everyone. Everyone was engaged and involved. The engagement was total and that surprised me a lot."

To facilitate participation, Scandic set up a network of environmental coordinators, or networkers, in all of its hotels. Each of these individuals received special training. Scandic also established a group of environmental trainers whose role is to provide education and support for the hotels' environmental coordinators. Environmental coordinators are drawn from all levels of the organization. Their role is to work with each hotel general manager to coordinate various environmental tasks and to keep hotel employees informed on environmental issues. Environmental coordinators seek information about environmental issues and provide it to their colleagues. They coach the others at the hotel in both general and specific issues regarding how to integrate the environmental framework into daily tasks. They serve as a resource — seeking out and providing their colleagues with new information to address specific challenges that arise. They work with department heads to help them inform their staff about new developments.

To maintain an on-going level of interest and participation, environmental coordinators include environmental issues in daily, weekly, and monthly meetings at each hotel — which are the "production units" of a hotel chain. Involvement is also bolstered through friendly competitions between hotels with respect to meeting environmental goals, through achieving high scores on environmental indicators, and through being recognized individually and collectively for the tangible contribution to protecting the environment that is derived from Scandic's policies and actions. In addition, a large part of Scandic's environmental program is communicated by means of the company's intranet. It can be accessed by all employees in the Scandinavian languages, and in English in 1999.

Ivarsson believed that an important way to keep employee interest and engagement alive was to go beyond the basic training level and to generate new, more challenging programs about every two years. The program Scandic developed as a follow-up to its initial wave of training and programs, which is described in more detail in the following section, is called the "Resource Hunt." It's an exciting program that has promoted very high levels of participation, successfully integrated environmental aspects more fully into company operations, and generated significant cost savings for Scandic.

Integration: Actions and Results

Scandic has been very successful at integrating environmental considerations into all aspects of its day-to-day operations. The cornerstone for this success is a strong educational program based on The Natural Step that provides a common framework and language for all employees, and on-going mechanisms and programs that promote and reward employee involvement in environmentally-related thinking and initiatives.

Measurements and Indicators

Ivarsson contends that measurements are vitally important for all environment programs. He believes that the more an environmental manager in any company measures, the more improvement will be made. "Companies are based on measurement. They are based on monthly accounts. It's on top of people's minds all the time."

Scandic has learned through experience that what gets measured gets done. For environmental thinking and action to be integrated into daily business operations, it is essential to figure out what to measure and how to measure it; and it is fundamental that the measurement take place accurately and fairly and be communicated clearly to employees. Scandic has developed the following mechanisms for measurement:

Environmental Barometer. To establish a measurement system to track progress, Ivarsson asked: "How do you measure knowledge in this context, knowledge by so many people and such complex knowledge? So the only measurement I could construct was simply the number of activities that were specified in the local environmental plans and then the number that were actually achieved after six months and 12 months. And this we called the environmental barometer." This measurement was very broad, simply counting the number of activities each hotel said it was going to do and the number that actually got done. Ivarsson felt in the beginning that it might have no value at all. Eventually, however, he learned that it did have value "because even such a broad or inconsistent measurement challenged people and we published those figures hotel against hotel, country against country." This feedback helped to maintain and even raise interest in environmental aspects. It gave the company environmental policy credibility in the employees' eyes and reinforced the idea that environmental concern was not just being paid lip service to, but was actually a priority of the management group.

Environmental Index. In 1995, Scandic developed the quarterly environmental index. The index is a form of management-by-objective tool. Scandic has identified about 60 activities in nine areas in which hotels are to perform in relation to an ideal. Typical areas for the index include hotels having 25 percent of their light sockets filled with low energy bulbs, having bicycles avail-able for guests, and performing a thorough energy analysis of the building. This index, which is displayed for guests as well as employees, measures and communicates the fact that Scandic is making constant environmental improvements.

Resource Hunt. The environmental barometer was very basic. The environ-mental index was a bit more sophisticated. The third level of sophistication with respect to the integration of environmental aspects into Scandic's business operations is the program which they have named the "Resource Hunt".

After the Environmental Dialogue process had been in place for two years, Ivarsson felt it was time for the next wave of activity to keep interest and moti-vation alive. He was interested in designing a program that would set new and more detailed environmental objectives. Ivarsson felt it was time to pick an area where Scandic had been less successful in the past or to which they hadn't given sufficient attention. He concluded that the focus should be on resource effi-ciency (energy, water, and waste), sustainability, and dematerialization. Ivarsson explains:

> The Resource Hunt measurement system entails a very sophisticated computerized system. For example, each hotel registers its total ener-gy and water consumption, and unsorted waste, on a monthly basis. This information is keyed into a computer model developed by Scandic. They also key in climate and other factors as needed in order to make a true comparison of the percentage savings of energy and water and waste across all the hotels participating in the system. So now, for example, Scandic can track what the average water con-sumption is in relationship to guest nights. Finally, the Resource Hunt measurements are incorporated into Scandic's overall benchmarking system.

Scandic's rationale behind developing the Resource Hunt makes perfect busi-ness sense. If one looks at the prices for the use of different resources, one can see that fresh water, fossil fuel, and electricity in most of the countries where Scandic operates have increased over time in costs at a rate higher than the general inflation. If the company wants to gain higher cost efficiency, it needs to address these areas. For example, electricity prices in Germany are about 40 percent higher than in Sweden or Norway. In Denmark, water is about 50 or 60 percent more expensive than in Sweden. As Sweden is now part of the European Union, Scandic calculates that prices will move upward. Ivarsson remarks: "At the same time we know that in many other countries, the cost of these things is increasing, not only in Europe. So we believe that because of this sharp increase, if we address these issues and focus more clearly, it will give us a competitive advantage." CEO Roland Nilsson describes Scandic's philosophy this way:

> What it's all about, really, is to utilize the resources we have on this planet in the best way, and that is part of our vision. We say that we are turning from a resource over-consuming society to a resource-saving society and that the environment discussion is really about taking care of resources in a better way. If the water is polluted and destroyed, then the resource "water" is suddenly a limited resource. We are utilizing resources poorly and the price tag on utilizing resources is going up more and more. The way we utilize energy is going to be punished one way or another, through taxes or through cost increases. As long as we don't find new energy sources all the time, we are going to crash into the side of the funnel. But everybody still acts as if these resources were unlimited, and we will always find other sources. But they will hit the funnel. By focusing on these items — energy, water, and waste — we are creating competitive advantages. We are also saving the environment."

The Resource Hunt was initiated using the same methodology as the Environmental Dialogue. A new booklet was prepared for all employees, local seminars were organized in which every employee participated, and objectives were set in a local activity plan. Ken Hopper explains that the Resource Hunt is actually taking the environment more deeply into the heart of their business operation: "It's focusing partly on processes, and partly on our way of thinking, too." The Resource Hunt focuses on steps — large and small — that everyone in the hotel can take to reduce consumption of energy and water and the amount of unsorted waste. CFO Goransson estimates that the combined cost for the total Scandic group for water, energy, and waste is SEK 160 million (over US $20 million). Savings in this area go straight to the bottom line as increased profits.

In some cases, the steps require changes in such ordinary behavior as turning off lights or water when they are not needed, or specific purchasing decisions such as switching to low energy light bulbs. Sometimes the steps require greater investments. In the Scandic hotel in Uppsala, for example, water saving devices were installed on all the taps in hotel rooms. It cost about US $4,000 to cut water use in half without sacrificing guest comfort. Hopper estimates that it took about one year to pay back the investment to make this change. After that, the decision represents continual savings. Jan Peter Bergkvist, General Manager of a Scandic Hotel in Stockholm, emphasizes the importance of saving energy: "We all have kitchens in our hotels and energy is about 10 percent of the costs. If you lower energy consumption simply by turning off the stoves, closing the refrigerators, and turning off the lights, you lower costs."

The Resource Hunt's first year was a great success. The initial three-year goal for Scandic as a whole was to reduce energy and water consumption by 20 percent and unsorted waste by 30 percent. Scandic's 1997 Annual Report provides the results of the first 11 months of the Resource Hunt. Average energy consumption at Scandic's Nordic hotels was reduced by seven percent to 47kWh per guest per night, and water consumption was reduced by 4 percent to 235 litres per guest per night. To put these figures in perspective, the average consumption per hotel according to a German survey carried out nationwide in 1996 was 55 kWh and 275 litres per guest per night. Scandic's amount of unsorted waste at its Nordic hotels was reduced by 15 percent. The estimated financial benefits generated by the Resource Hunt were in excess of SEK 6 million in 1997, roughly US $800,000, which went straight to the bottom line.

The Resource Hunt has captured the enthusiasm of Scandic's employees. At every hotel we visited, the Resource Hunt was a topic of conversation. Perhaps one of the most visible aspects of the Resource Hunt is the way Scandic hotels are dealing with waste. At the Scandic Hotel in Bromma, waste is sorted into 13 different categories. By carefully sorting and handling waste, the hotel in 1996 cut their waste removal costs in half. At the Scandic Hotel in Slussen, a four-star city center hotel, the volume of waste generated is significant. Emil Gammeltoft, who handles shipping, receiving, and waste removal, explained that paper, such as magazines, contribute almost .5 ton per week of waste. Packages and boxes added another .5 ton. This hotel has made arrangements with a paper factory to take the used paper to make new paper. Gammeltoft estimated that one ton of paper represents 14 trees and that through recycling, the Scandic Hotel Slussen had saved the equivalent of 1,500 trees. The hotel also recycles food waste to be converted into energy. Gammeltoft estimates that about 4.2 tons of food a month go from his hotel to a factory where they are converted into biogas to heat homes. Altogether, Gammeltoft believes that only one half of one percent of all the waste annually generated by his hotel cannot be recycled. Since they began sorting waste, he estimates, the cost for removal has been reduced by more than 50 percent per year, down from 186,000 SEK (about US $25,000) to about 70,000 SEK (about US $9,000) a year. And Gammeltoft is not satisfied with that. He believes that the costs can be further reduced by rigorous negotiation. He is hoping to get the cost down to 40,000 SEK (about US $5,000) a year. He is constantly on the lookout for new ways to achieve his goal.

An employee reward system is associated with the Resource Hunt. Ken Hopper explains: "One of the smart things that we have built into this Resource Hunt is that we give money back to the staff in the form of a special fund where we receive x amount of kroner per employee. This money is to be used for a special celebration, or maybe we'll take a trip or do something so people can see that all of our hard work saved these resources and now we should celebrate." The results of the Resource Hunt are also included in Scandic's Best in Class benchmarking system. BINC results are posted prominently for employees in every hotel. The inclusion of these environmental indicators and the fact that a hotel's overall performance depends, in part, on environmental improvement, clearly conveys the degree to which environmental aspects are integrated into overall hotel management.

BINC

Using the BINC instrument, the company measures 18 different key ratios. It measures hard values, such as financial indicators; soft values, such as customer satisfaction and employee satisfaction; and environmental values, such as progress on water and energy conservation and reduction in unsorted waste. Some BINC indicators are measured each month, some quarterly, and some only once or twice a year. The results from the Resource Hunt measurement system — the measures of water, waste, and energy per guest night at each hotel — are also included in the BINC benchmarking. The results of BINC are posted in each hotel on a white board called the BINC board. Posting BINC results is a tool to keep all of the employees informed and involved in continual improvement in their hotels.

CFO Goransson points out that "the total idea of this Best in Class is that this will be a self-educating organization, that people should call each other to find out how another hotel has performed well." The expectation is that those hotels that are best in class can be good examples for other hotels and can encourage inquiry into steps they have taken to reach this goal. Thus, besides promoting information and involvement, the system encourages continual learning, networking, and improvement.

Supply Chain Relations

Another very significant area where environmental aspects are integrated into daily operations is purchasing. The very fact that Ivarsson's senior role combines both functional responsibilities — purchasing and environment — indicates the intention to integrate environmental thinking into the heart of Scandic's operations. Ivarsson points out that enormous opportunity exists for picking the "low hanging fruit" at the moment a company selects its suppliers and products. "Suppliers are very important because you can't be an expert on all different possibilities or the best environmental products, for example, in the area of chemicals. You need help from your suppliers. You need to find environmentally proactive suppliers who are willing to help you find good environmental products."

Scandic develops projects jointly with their suppliers to improve environmental performance to their mutual benefit. Ivarsson explains that Scandic always tries to find the good examples and to work with them. "Of course the basis for any cooperation must be a sound financial performance by the products. But what we do then is to set objectives for suppliers saying 'we dislike your environmental performance now, but we want you to adjust within a certain amount of time'".

Scandic asks for environmental policies from all its suppliers. With its big suppliers, Scandic goes much further: it examines more closely how the suppliers conduct the environmental aspects of their business. Ivarsson remarks: "In order for us to find the good ones, just having an environmental policy isn't enough, so the real reduction in environmental impact can only be achieved if you form partnerships with your main suppliers. That is where we have started to concentrate our work." Three examples illustrate this approach:

Henkel Ecolab. Henkel Ecolab of Germany supplies all of Scandic's dishwashing chemicals and laundry and cleaning chemicals. Henkel has developed a delivery system for these chemicals which is based on having hotel staff mix the chemicals at the hotel by a very easy process. The hotel is charged only for the chemicals that are actually used. This system drastically reduces the number of different chemicals Scandic uses and gives the hotel systematic control over the type and quantity of chemicals used. Furthermore, because the cleaning supplies are mixed at the hotel, the number of individual plastic bottles that the hotel uses are reduced because the cleaning solutions are mixed and placed in the same bottles day after day. This reduces both waste and costs.

Previously, Scandic used up to 15 different cleaning materials at its hotels. Now each hotel uses between two and four different formulas. Most preformulated cleaning solutions contain a significant amount of water, but the Henkel system delivers the chemicals in concentrated form. This reduces the weight and volume of transport required to deliver the cleaning products, which cuts down on the environmental impact associated with transportation.

In addition Scandic had developed a strategic partnership with Henkel Ecolab which makes it possible for Scandic to monitor the chemical throughput of their hotels so they can more accurately assess the environmental impact from their discharge of chemicals and reduce it accordingly. Henkel is now able to run a chemical monitoring system for Scandic throughout Europe because they are Scandic's sole supplier of chemicals. By combining the purchased volumes with the recipes, Scandic is able to measure the amount of sulphur, for example, that has been taken into a hotel and estimate what amount is discharged from the hotel. These types of strategic partnerships help Scandic to assess its actual material and chemical throughput and thus its impact on the environment.

Sophus Berendsen. Another example is Scandic's supplier and launderer of linen. Sophus Berendsen is the largest such supplier and launderer in Sweden, and Scandic is its largest customer. Once it understood the environmental impact that conventional laundry practices were having on the environment, Scandic gave Sophus Berendsen two years to come up with a laundering process that would not use chlorine or optical brighteners. At first Sophus Berendsen said this would not be possible because the bedsheets would look greyish. Scandic told them they would take the risk.

Peter Havéus, Managing Director of Sophus Berendsen, recounts that at that time, Sophus Berendsen had no understanding of the impact their business had on nature, nor were they educated in those matters. Scandic suggested that if Sophus Berendsen wanted to be a supplier in the future, they should become acquainted with The Natural Step. Then Sophus Berendsen could see what they could do to improve the environmental performance of their business and what Sophus Berendsen and Scandic could do together to develop new environmentally friendly systems.

Sophus Berendsen contacted The Natural Step and met several times with Robèrt. Havéus recalls: "When the managers and sales people met with The Natural Step and listened to the information, they understood that this is something really important. After that we didn't have any debate in the company about whether we would work with environmental questions or not." Sophus Berendsen developed its first environmental policy and instituted Natural Step training for all its employees based on the educational model developed at Scandic. After they instituted the training, Sophus Berendsen conducted an eco-balance analysis on each of its laundries to assess the environmental impact of their activities, including how much wastewater they produced, how much detergent, paper, and electricity they used, and how they could reduce their impact accordingly.

Their education by The Natural Step brought a powerful and unexpected realization to Sophus Berendsen. Havéus explains: "Everyone in the plants now understands that it is not just a company problem, it is a human problem. You can't simply leave it when you go home in the afternoon. It follows you home and it's with you 24 hours a day."

Sophus Berendsen realizes that this environmental focus has given them a competitive advantage. It was good timing. They were ahead of their competitors and plan to remain ahead of them in the future. Now Sophus Berendsen asks its suppliers for their environmental policies as well. According to Havéus, Sophus Berendsen does this "because we have a responsibility to our customers to ensure that we are using environmentally friendly suppliers." Havéus adds that even if their customers did not ask for environmental responsibility, Sophus Berendsen's "concern would remain because it is now important to us and to our employees."

Property Owners. As a general rule, Scandic does not own the properties of its hotels. This means that the property owners of the hotels are key suppliers. Scandic is actively seeking the cooperation of these property owners to provide opportunities for further environmental adaptation in new construction and the renovation of existing structures. According to Nilsson, it will take significant time and financial investment to influence the whole network of suppliers, including the property owners. He believes that these key suppliers "still have the mentality of the 1960s. They believe the environment is not their problem." Ultimately, Scandic is ready to change locations if property owners are unwilling to change. Nilsson reports: "We already warned one of the property owners that if they would not do anything to the property itself, then we would leave it, and we left. And they had to depreciate it, I think 60 percent of the capital, which was naturally very painful for them."

Innovation: The 97 Percent Recyclable Eco-Room

Scandic, like every quality hotel, must invest in constant renovation and refurbishing of its hotel rooms. The company recognized this to be an excellent opportunity to further reduce its environmental impact. Scandic is the first hotel chain in the world to introduce the innovation of a 97 percent recyclable hotel room. According to Ivarsson, the development of this innovative concept started when the new Scandic was being created, and part of the investment process had to be for new rooms. In the process, with the environment now part of their framework, someone asked, "Why couldn't Scandic develop an environmentally friendly room that was recyclable?" This meant that the rooms would be designed and built for their eventual disassembly, and that they would utilize ecologically benign components to the highest extent possible under current technology. The idea was an immediate hit. The rooms have proven to be very popular with Scandic's customers due to both their esthetic quality and their contribution to a healthier environment.

Scandic worked closely with its suppliers to design the room. Not only are the new rooms 97 percent recyclable or biodegradable, but each room replaces synthetic carpeting with natural wooden floors, provides furniture of Scandinavian wood, minimizes the amount of metal details, and utilizes soft furnishings made from pure cotton or wool. Everything is carefully labelled with its contents to facilitate dismantling and recycling in the future. Approximately 2,000 rooms are being refurbished each year with an estimated decrease per year of plastics by 90 tons, metals by 15 tons, and mercury by 50 percent. To date, approximately one-quarter of Scandic's capacity in the Nordic region has been converted to these new eco-rooms.

General Manager Jan Peter Bergkvist makes an important observation: "At the beginning, it looked like the recyclable rooms were going to be a bit more expensive. You had to put more money into them when you made them. But then, after a while, we realized that we had learned so much about how to produce this room, and that the room has a longer lifespan in terms of the equipment and the floor, that the costs are going down. Therefore, in the end, it is a cheaper room." In addition, Scandic developed another way to recycle old rooms. Rather than discarding used components, Scandic prolongs their lifecycle by selling components from its old rooms, such as fixtures, furniture, and so on, to companies in some of the newly emerging republics around the Baltic.

Scandic uses its interactive values creation process to educate guests and to communicate with them about the company's environmental concerns and expectations. Every Scandic hotel has an "environment corner" which is a public display of Scandic's environmental policy, goals, and achievements. The corner generally contains other environmental publications and announcements. Scandic's environmental policy and actions are also communicated through the in-house broadcast of information about the hotel on guest television; a booklet called *The EcoLogical Choice* that can be found in each hotel room; and notices in the bathrooms explaining Scandic's environmental vision and asking guest cooperation in conserving energy through reusing towels and sheets, and in recycling through the use of a specially designed waste basket with compartments for different types of waste.

Scandic also communicates the environmental aspects and integration of its business in its annual report, which contains a special section on its approach to the environment and a two-page report on environmental indicators.

Scandic's environmental policy states:

- No company can avoid taking environmental responsibility and focus on environmental aspects of their operation.
- Scandic shall therefore take the lead and constantly improve our contribution to less or no environmental damage.
- Our objective is to become one of the most environment friendly companies in the hotel industry and to operate in accordance with the conditions of nature.

Final Reflections

The company's actions speak even more eloquently than its words. Scandic has introduced well over 2,000 individual measures to improve environmental performance and reduce environmental impact in their hotels. Environmental aspects are integrated into business decisions and daily actions on every level of the company's operations. Scandic's restaurants, for example, are exploring the opportunities for becoming "Krav" certified, an ecological certification that indicates that certain menu items contain more than 70 percent certified organic ingredients. Some Scandic hotels are also cutting petro-based fuel consumption by using solar-driven lawn mowers or ethanol-fuelled cars. Scandic now has both the vision and the will to someday become a completely ecologically sustainable hotel operation.

When Scandic Hotels engaged with The Natural Step, it hit the decks running. Few companies before or since have engaged The Natural Step with such immediate commitment, intensity, and understanding, or on such a grand scale. Within the first year of Robèrt's one-day workshop with Scandic's entire senior management team, all 5,000 Scandic employees had received The Natural Step training and over 1,500 operational suggestions had not only been put forward by staff, but had actually been implemented. From the very beginning, CEO Roland Nilsson understood that The Natural Step was the knowledge platform that he needed for the new Scandic to drive forward with his vision of interactive values creation between his customers and his people.

Five years later, the relationship between Scandic and The Natural Step remains close, creative, and collaborative. A Natural Step-based sustainability is now as integral to Scandic's operations and worldview as any other core element, such as financial control or quality of service. It is fully embedded as a key part of the way Scandic does business. As a result, Scandic has derived numerous benefits:

First, in a turnaround situation, Roland Nilsson had to sharply break from the ineffective practices and attitudes of the past that were destroying the old Scandic. Conversely, he needed to create a strong positive vision of the future and positive values for the new Scandic. He needed this for both his staff and his customers. A focus on environmental sustainability created a key new distinction and The Natural Step provided a rational, science-based platform upon which to proceed.

Second, and running parallel to the first point, Nilsson recognized that the hospitality industry's battles of the future, as with the world of information technology, would be won with software and not much with hardware. It is the total experience at a hotel, based much more on intangibles than on bricks and mortar, that often draws guests in the first place and keeps them returning. By understanding the values of those guests, satisfying those values, and influencing them, Nilsson saw the basis of a profitable and enduring business relationship. He understood that the environment had become a key value to the majority of his guests. The Natural Step provides Scandic a very solid platform from which to engage in the environmental arena.

Third, by combining both of the environment and purchasing portfolios in the hands of Ola Ivarsson who has developed a very strong understanding of The Natural Step framework, Scandic ensures that almost all material and energy which flows into the corporation must pass a TNS-based sustainability review. In effect, the Environment Director is now the *resource gatekeeper* for the business. Ivarsson has aggressively introduced many eco-efficient, cost-saving initiatives which have had very favorable bottom line results for the corporation. As Roland Nilsson has said about the TNS training and programs, "It hasn't cost us anything. No one can claim that this has cost us more money." In fact, Ivarsson has the numbers to demonstrate just the opposite.

Fourth, The Natural Step has turned out to be the single best team building program that Scandic has ever discovered. It has improved the morale of employees substantially, and a new sense of purpose and mission has come alive within the company. As Nilsson says: "It was the first cooperative activity where they were really unified irrespective of where they worked in the company. I mean it was fantastic. Everybody loves taking care of the world."

Fifth, by so totally immersing themselves in the understanding and implementation of Natural Step-based sustainable development and by leveraging the favorable impact of this on Scandic's guests through the process of shared values, Scandic has soared past its competitors. For the first time in the Scandinavian hospitality industry, a hotel chain has successfully made environmental sustainability a real competitiveness issue. By integrating the TNS framework into the heart of its corporate strategy and practices, Scandic has seized the initiative in its markets and continues to win customers and market share from its competitors.

Scandic, like each of the other three case studies in this book, at first sight appears almost paradoxical. On the one hand, there is a clear culture of profound caring for all of its stakeholders, as shown by the core value *omtanke*, and there is a deep concern for, and understanding of, the environmental impact and implications of its operations. On the other hand, with all that concern and caring, the new Scandic is a ferocious competitor in every one of its markets. It is driving its competition to the wall and making one acquisition after another. It has not only become the lowest cost producer and the price leader in its markets, it is drawing more guests to its hotels than any of its competitors — and it keeps them coming back too. Like each of the other three companies studied here, Scandic has made one of the biggest perceptual breakthroughs possible in business today, and it has done so by entering a new paradigm: true ecological sustainability is not a cost to the company — it is a source of profits and real competitive advantage. At its present rate of expansion and profitability, Scandic will probably soon outgrow its home base in the Nordic countries and need to expand into the rest of Europe. From what we have seen, that would be a very good thing for its guests, the industry, and the natural world.

CHAPTER 6

INTERFACE, INC.: "The Next Industrial Revolution"

Interface will be environmentally sustainable. But our mission is larger. We will also be financially sustainable, for the simple reason that our corporation must survive and that we must assure the livelihood of our associates and the investment of all our stakeholders. We will be socially sustainable, respecting the communities in which we work, positively influencing all those whose lives we touch, and taking care not to deplete the human spirit on which we depend. . . Our sustainability goals — financial, social, and environmental — are inextricably bound together, which is why we make such a point out of doing well by doing good.
Ray C. Anderson — *Founder, Chairman, and CEO, Interface, Inc.*

TAKING A STAND. Ray Anderson has been taking a stand for what he believes in his entire adult life. It is the nature, and the mark, of the man. By bringing his whole self — his keen intellect, his intuition, and most assuredly his passion — to whatever he does, he led the company that he founded from a standing start in 1973 in just 23 years to the milestone $1 billion in annual sales in 1996. Along the way he changed the face of his industry. Today, he is in the process of influencing industry on a global scale with his vision of an economically, environmentally, and socially sustainable world and of the role and responsibility of business within it. "We accept our responsibility as a member of the industrial world," states Interface's founder, Chairman, and Chief Executive Officer, "to pursue the creation of new products — and processes — that recognize the sustainable limits of our environment. We're striving to be first in industrial ecology and to set an example for the world." How Anderson and the company that he created have both grown in vision, in depth, and in influence is a truly remarkable story.

In 1973, at the age of 38, Anderson took a stand and followed a dream. He left an executive position with a well-known US carpet manufacturer and risked his life-savings and the investments of good friends to found his own company. He planned to manufacture and distribute under license from a British company a new kind of carpeting, free-lay carpet tiles, which at that time was still just an emerging niche market in the United States.

In the early 1980s, Anderson took a stand for Interface to become the pre-eminent name in commercial interiors. In those days it seemed like an enormous stretch, an unlikely dream, with its much larger and well-established competitors dominating the market.

In 1993, Anderson took a stand for the survival and future success of Interface in the midst of a severe downturn in the economy and in the fortunes of his company by hiring Charlie Eitel, a competitor, to bring a different way of doing business to Interface. "The need for change was clear, having grown in urgency each year since our peak performances of 1989/90 as we were impacted by worldwide recession, downsizing throughout the corporate world (our biggest market segment), new and renewed competition, and a massive shift in market preference in both carpet tiles and interior fabrics," explains Anderson.

In 1994, Anderson took a stand for the Earth when he first made his declaration that Interface would become the world's first truly sustainable company and the world's first restorative company as well. He declared that Interface would become the first name in industrial ecology worldwide — through substance, not words.

In 1996, Anderson took a stand for the long-term sustainable prosperity of the whole United States, and by example the rest of the world, by accepting the role of CoChair of the President's Council on Sustainable Development.

In 1997, Anderson took a stand for the education in environmental sustainability and industrial ecology of future American leaders in engineering by committing Interface and himself to create and endow the Anderson-Interface Chair of Natural Systems in the Industrial and Systems Engineering (IsyE) School at his beloved alma mater, Georgia Tech, where he had graduated with a degree in Industrial Engineering. Furthermore, due to Anderson's persistent efforts as Chairman of the Georgia Tech Advisory Board, Sustainable Technology joined Biotechnology and Telecommunications Technology as one of the three major strategic areas of study for Georgia Tech in the 21st century.

Nowadays, approximately 100 times a year, Anderson takes a public stand for sustainability: financial, social, and environmental — you might even say at an existential level that Anderson has become the stand for sustainability — as he speaks about his vision for a sustainable world. Anderson describes environmental sustainability as "taking nothing from the Earth that is not renew-able and doing no harm to the biosphere." This is one of the guiding lights by which Interface is led and which The Natural Step is helping to define and to integrate within Interface's global operations.

Interface Today

Interface, a US $1.3 billion, Fortune 1000 company, is the world's largest pro-ducer of contract commercial carpet. It is a global manufacturer, marketer, installer, and servicer of products for the commercial and institutional interi-ors market. It is the worldwide leader in the modular carpet segment, which includes both carpet tile and two-meter roll goods. Interface markets products in more than 100 countries and produces in 29 manufacturing sites located in the United States, Canada, Northern Ireland, England, Holland, Australia, Thailand, and Greater China. The company manufactures and sells 40 percent of all the carpet tiles used worldwide in commercial buildings. Interface also produces commercial broadloom carpet, interior fabrics, chemicals, and archi-tectural products. It markets products under such established brand names as Interface and Heuga in modular carpet; Bentley Mills, Prince Street, and Firth in broadloom carpets; Guilford of Maine, Stevens Linen, Camborne, Toltec, and Intek in interior fabrics and upholstery products; Intersept in chemicals; and C-Tec and Intercell in raised/access flooring systems. Geographically, the company's principal markets are North America (70 percent of 1997 net sales), the United Kingdom and Western Europe (23 percent of 1997 net sales), and Asia Pacific (seven percent of 1997 net sales). Interface is currently developing opportunities in Greater China, Southeast Asia, South America, and Central, and Eastern Europe.

Interface's long-standing corporate strategy is to both diversify and inte-grate worldwide. It seeks diversification by developing internally or by acquir-ing related product lines and businesses in the commercial interiors field, and integration by identifying and developing synergies and operating efficiencies among its products and global businesses. Between 1982 and 1998, Interface acquired a total of 48 companies. Since 1993, its sales have nearly doubled, growing from $625 million in 1993 to $1.135 billion in 1997. Operating income has more than doubled, approaching $100 million in 1997. Net income has grown from $13.8 million in 1993 to more than $37.5 million in 1997 — an annual compound growth rate of 28 percent. In 1997, Interface achieved record revenues in the United States, and Europe showed growing strength (Figure 6.1.).

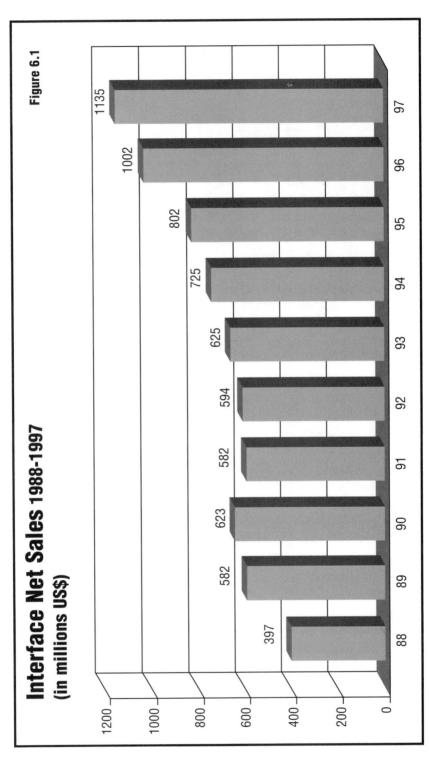

Figure 6.1

Interface Net Sales 1988-1997
(in millions US$)

Currently Interface employs more than 7,400 people worldwide, of which the majority are manufacturing personnel. In December 1997, and again in December 1998, *Fortune* magazine rated Interface one of the top 100 employers in the United States on the strength of the company's commitment to its employees. *Fortune* also named Interface one of the "10 Most Admired Companies" in its industry category. These are but two examples of the growing recognition and many awards that Interface has received for its internal revolution.

A New Tapestry

If we want to fully understand Interface today, it is helpful to view its story, particularly in the period between 1994 and 1998, as a tapestry. Many different threads were woven together to produce a rich and inspiring story. Some of these threads can be characterized by the following phrases heard repeatedly at Interface:

- "a spear in the chest"
- "putting people first"
- "playing to win"
- "doing well by doing good" and
- "the prototypical company of the 21st century."

Yet not all of these threads were connected from the outset, and it is only when they are woven together that their strength and interconnections are becoming clear. We believe that the tapestry which is emerging is richer, stronger, and more dynamic than any of the individual players at Interface anticipated or imagined. In order to assist our understanding of the company, we look first at each of these threads individually, and then we describe the tapestry which they create.

"A Spear in the Chest"

It was a time of significant transition. Anderson recalls: "I knew Charlie's approach was different, sometimes drastically different, but we needed change." Anderson's role had always been to be the man in charge, the one with the answers. He had created the company and sustained it, sometimes through sheer effort of will. He recalls that in the early days of Interface so much depended upon him. "When the company was so vulnerable, the market was small and there weren't all that many project orders out there to be had, you had to win. I mean, you just couldn't afford to lose. You just won or you died. If you don't get the next heartbeat, you don't live. And the next order was the next heartbeat." In the first two decades of the company, there were many, many times when Anderson felt that the next heartbeat depended solely on him.

When Eitel took the reins as President and Chief Operating Officer of Interface in 1997, Anderson began to ask himself whether he even had a role at

Interface anymore, and if so, what it should be. He decided that the new role was "defining the next heartbeat that will determine Interface's higher meaning. Where does Interface go from here?"

A second important element was that Joyce LaValle, at that time Regional Vice-President for Interface in Southern California, was working hard to land a prestigious contract with the Southern California Gas Company. LaValle had worked for Interface previously in her career and had returned after working for six years with another company. LaValle's daughter, Melissa Guildersleeve, was then running the solid and hazardous waste program for the northern half of the State of Washington. Melissa had heard Paul Hawken speak to the State of Washington Department of Ecology and had been so impressed with him that she sent her mother Hawken's book, *The Ecology of Commerce*. She told her mother that if LaValle was going to return to Interface she had to make a promise that she would "be responsible for all that carpet that goes in the landfill." LaValle read Hawken's book and found it "incredibly meaningful." To her, the Southern California Gas and Electric Company project represented an opportunity not only to be involved with a showcase project, but also to begin to fulfill her promise to her daughter.

John Picard was the environmental consultant on the Southern California Gas project and obviously an important influence on the choice of vendors. LaValle learned that he understood the benefits of using carpet tile with respect to longevity, but if Interface was to be considered for the job, at a minimum the carpet had to have recycled content. In addition, Picard challenged Interface to make the carpet a "product of service" rather than a product of material. By this he meant to challenge Interface to create a program whereby they would sell the services of carpet to the customer — design, texture, color, acoustics, and so on — but not the carpet itself. Interface would retain actual ownership of the carpet so that its entire lifecycle could be controlled by Interface, and eventually be processed and recycled into new carpet at the end of its first life, and of subsequent ones as well.

LaValle knew she could go to Interface's suppliers and ask for recycled content in the yarn, but the idea of a whole new way of buying seemed an impossible task. This would require strategic decisions from the top. LaValle recalled having read about products of service in Hawken's book, so at least she had a starting point. She arranged for Picard to meet with Anderson. Before they met, she needed to prepare Anderson. She recalls, "I needed him to read *The Ecology of Commerce*. I couldn't think of a better way. I didn't know how he felt about this subject, I'd never had this conversation with him." So LaValle gave her copy of *The Ecology of Commerce* to her boss, Gordon Whitener, with the request that he pass it on to Anderson.

Anderson recalls that LaValle wanted the carpet order for the Southern California Gas project because it would be a showcase project. He had received reports about Picard and the fact that he wanted an environmental product. Interface sent people out to work with LaValle to figure out what exactly Picard wanted. Interface could certainly include recycled content in the carpet. In addition, they had an innovative indoor air quality initiative underway and created a not-for-profit consortium called "EnviroSense," that provided improved microbial indoor air quality. They presented these market strengths to Picard but were told that it was not enough; Picard said, "Interface doesn't get it!" Anderson responded, "What in blazes is he talking about, Interface doesn't get it?" At about this time, Whitener passed Hawken's book on to Anderson.

At the same time, Interface was beginning to receive inquiries from customers regarding the environmental aspects of Interface's products. In 1994, Interface Research Corporation (IRC), the research arm of Interface, was charged with the task of coming up with the company's first environmental policy. To do this, IRC pulled together a task force. Jim Hartzfeld, Senior Vice-President of IRC, coordinated the initiative. In August, 1994, he brought together about 20 people from different companies, functions, and divisions within the Interface family. Anderson, as Chairman and CEO of the company, was asked if he would launch the task force by giving them his environmental vision.

Anderson didn't want to make that speech to the task force. He didn't have an environmental vision other than to comply with the law. As he was "sweating over that speech," *The Ecology of Commerce* landed on his desk. In Anderson's words, "Hawken's message was a spear in my chest that remains to this day. In preparing that kick-off speech, I went beyond mere compliance in a heartbeat. I wasn't halfway through the book before I had found the vision I was looking for, together with a powerful sense of urgency." In making the kickoff speech, Anderson incorporated many of Hawken's examples of what is happening to the ecosystem. He shared Hawken's central thesis: that business was both part of the problem and part of the solution. He concluded the speech by saying, "I believe that business is the only institution on Earth that has the ability to reverse this, and nobody's taking the lead. Someone has to take the lead! Why not us? Let's go for it!" Anderson offered the task force a vision: to make Interface the first name in industrial ecology, worldwide, through substance, not words. He gave them a mission: to convert Interface into a restorative enterprise. First Interface would reach sustainability, and then it would become restorative by putting back more than the company takes from the Earth by helping others achieve sustainability, even competitors.

Anderson kept his appointment with Picard. He walked into the meeting, held up Hawken's book and said, "I get it!" Together Anderson and Picard created the concept for the Evergreen Lease, converting carpet as a product of material into a product of service. Now known as Evergreen Service Contracts, the program provides an alternative to a conventional purchase of flooring needs. This program gives clients the option to lease the services (functionality, color, design, aesthetics) of a modular carpet system without taking ownership or liability for ongoing maintenance and the ultimate removal for reclamation or recycling at the end of its useful life. Under this "product of service" concept, Interface retains ownership of the installed carpet tiles, maintains them, and selectively replaces and recycles worn tiles.

LaValle was thrilled. She comments: "We did that job. And that job was a big deal. And four years later, it's still a big deal. It wasn't that large, but it was well publicized. The story that most interested people was this idea of creating a product of service." As systems thinkers, what we particularly like about this story is the interconnectedness — if not causality — between a young woman in Washington state reading Paul Hawken's book and following her instinct and the total re-invention of a Fortune 1000 company and a new meaning in life for its founder and Chief Executive Officer. Systems theory shows how all things are connected and that very small events can have enormous consequences: here, Interfaces's massive commitment to become the first name in industrial ecology and the prototypical company of the 21st century could be said to have been initiated by a young woman giving a book to her mother.

Not everyone within the company immediately jumped on Anderson's vision bandwagon. Even among the members of the original task force to whom he gave his first "spear-in-the-chest" speech, there was speculation about how serious the environmental direction would be. Some individuals from a more technical background immediately came to the conclusion that what Anderson was talking about was "the organizational equivalent to a perpetual motion machine." Some believed it was a passing fad that would simply go away if they ignored it.

In the months that followed the kick-off speech, Anderson clarified his new vision and began to communicate it to others. He gave other speeches patterned on the one given to the task force. Most were to audiences internal to Interface. He knew that this was a dramatic and revolutionary idea and that it would take time, persistence, and consistency on his part if others were going to share in it. Jim Hartzfeld was assigned the task to shepherd this new initiative in the organization. He says that Anderson did not impose this vision for the company on others, but provided a "continuous drumbeat" that communicated both the essence of the vision and the importance he gave to it.

"Putting People First" and "Playing to Win"

When Anderson delivered his vision to the task force, several other dramatic changes were taking place at Interface. Radical organizational, product strategy, and manufacturing changes were happening simultaneously. Everything was in motion. The leadership in the company was changing dramatically. Mass customization was being introduced. The industry was becoming more integrated and consolidated. The company was growing through acquisitions. All of this change created a feeling of crisis for some, and a feeling of excitement and possibilities for others.

At this time, Charlie Eitel introduced a new way for Interface's employees to interact with one another, a new way to view themselves, each other, and the company. The process, called "Playing to Win," had a powerful impact on the company, one which Hartzfeld believes "was absolutely fundamental for the organization to be able to accept this audacious challenge, to even think, well maybe we can do this." Playing to Win is a process designed by the Pecos River Learning Center. It's a three-day session that combines classroom-style learning with physically challenging outdoor activities. All Interface employees participate in this process.

Because of the importance of this type of learning and relating process to Interface's culture, the company established its own internal training organization, called One World Learning, licensed by Pecos River Learning to deliver the Playing to Win course throughout Interface. In addition, Interface installed three outdoor ropes courses around the world, near their corporate headquarters in the United States, in Australia, and at their European headquarters in the U.K.

The experiential learning and challenge provided by the Playing to Win approach was adapted by One World Learning into a service Interface provides to its customers called the "Why? Conference." Every summer, several hundred architects and designers attend this three-day experiential learning event.

Playing to Win underscores one of Interface's core values: putting people first. Eitel believes that no organization can survive over an extended period of time unless it genuinely focuses on people as its most important resource. Putting people first means developing a culture where people can experience a congruence of values at work and at home and where people have the opportunity to evolve shared values toward a higher purpose where their work has meaning. Eitel explains that he wants everyone at Interface to "have a sense of purpose and a sense of meaning. What we get back is a spirit and a culture that radiates through all our employees and our organization and creates a feeling that people are doing more with their lives besides being an economic unit of production."

In addition to providing the challenging experience of jumping off poles and playing to win, Interface's commitment to its people includes an appreciation of the challenging balance people must create between their home and work lives in an increasingly stressful world. This stress increases in times of corporate upheaval and change.

To support Interface associates through these times of change, Eitel made arrangements with J. Zink, a prominent family therapist, to become a resource for all Interface associates regardless of pay or position. Any Interface employee could speak with Zink by telephone and, in many cases, in person, to discuss any problem. Eitel believes that this move was not only unique to Interface but revolutionary in American business. He says: "Most people will agree, we're all moving at lightening speed in our daily lives, and the pressure to perform and produce results is taxing our physical and mental capabilities. This takes its toll on our families. It's so important to remember that we all have a breaking point and that we need help and support with life's challenges. Retaining the services of Dr. J. Zink was the best decision of my career." Eitel believes that it is easy to tell employees that you care, but providing them with the services of a nationally known family therapist at no cost to them clearly made that caring tangible.

In addition, another key element of putting people first is education for Interface associates. The company offers its employees numerous training and human development opportunities, including on-the-job general equivalency diploma programs, citizenship classes for people who have immigrated to the U.S., foreign language classes, and tuition reimbursement for higher education. The commitment to education is not restricted to North American or European factories but applies to Interface associates all over the world.

"Doing Well by Doing Good"

In the 1997 Interface annual report, Anderson states: "We can do well by doing good. And when that fact is understood in enough of the world's board rooms, the second industrial revolution will have begun in earnest."

"Doing well by doing good" is a phrase heard frequently at Interface offices and plants. According to Anderson, it means, first, that Interface wants to do well financially as a company, to be the most profitable company in its industry, setting a standard others must meet. Second, Interface wants to "do good" towards all of its stakeholders: its shareholders, employees, communities, customers, suppliers, and the environment. Anderson says: "As Interface is surrounded by these other communities and the environment itself, we want to nurture the linkages between us and them so that we weave one web, one global web that includes all of these stakeholders in our company. With Interface at the center and our common values at the center of Interface, people will look to us in our field of expertise and trust us. Trust us to do right by them and their clients." Eitel believes that once a company understands that it can do financially well, become even more profitable, by taking care of people and place, it makes it easier to make the necessary investments.

The combination of putting people first, playing to win and doing well by doing good has created a powerful *esprit de corps,* loyalty, and commitment to Interface among its associates. Anderson refers to this process as one of "unleashing the talent and energy of our people."

"The Prototypical Company of the 21st Century"

Interface has set the goal to become the world's first sustainable — and eventually restorative — enterprise. To Interface, sustainability means taking nothing from the Earth and doing nothing harmful to the Earth. Restorative means giving back to the Earth on balance. The 1995 annual report admits: "All of this is a tall order for a company that is 100 percent dependent on petrochemicals derived from oil and natural gas — finite, non-renewable resources — for its raw materials and the energy to drive its processes." Interface believes that sustainability is vital to achieving the resource efficiency that will be necessary for manufacturing companies "that hope to survive, much less flourish, in the 21st century." According to Michael Bertolucci, President of Interface Research Corporation, being restorative means that Interface must be financially successful and help others become more sustainable. "That is how we will maximize our impact and eliminate our footprint. We know we are not putting nylon back into the wellhead. We're not going to turn it back into oil and stick it in the ground." Instead, Interface intends to be so successful as a sustainable, and even a restorative, enterprise that it may serve as a role model for other companies on the road to sustainability.

The objective to become the prototypical company of the 21st century arises out of Anderson's environmental vision launched at the task force meeting in August of 1994. Interface Research Corporation became responsible for moving this initiative forward. They did so initially with an internal program called "EcoSense" that was designed to provide a way to measure progress in this journey to sustainability. At the same time, Eitel launched a process aimed at creating greater efficiencies called "War on Waste." This zero-waste ideology encourages Interface associates, first, to identify the measurable waste costs within the company that go into a product but do not add value to the customer, and second, to develop ways to eliminate those wastes and thus reduce costs. This war on waste is waged through a program called "QUEST," also started in 1994. QUEST stands for "Quality Utilizing Employee Suggestions and Teamwork," described in greater detail later in this chapter.

In 1994, Interface also established a team of external world-renowned experts in areas of environmental sustainability to advise the company. This team, originally known as the "Dream Team," now playfully referred to as "The Big Chihuahua," includes David Brower, Bill Browning, Paul Hawken, Amory Lovins, Hunter Lovins, Bill McDonough, John Picard, Jonathon Porritt, Daniel Quinn, and Ray Anderson.

In 1995, Interface created PLETSUS — Practices Leading to Sustainability. PLETSUS is a global clearinghouse for suggestions of steps that can be taken to move toward sustainability. Anderson also began giving public speeches outlining his vision for Interface, catapulting the vision to public attention.

The time was tumultuous. As Hartzfeld comments: "We had the audacity to absolutely change everything at once. That dislodged the inertia to change." Profound personal and organizational change was taking place. People throughout Interface were climbing and jumping off 25 foot poles as part of the "Play to Win" exercises. They were taking risks to discover what was possible.

Throughout this highly creative period of organized chaos, Anderson and Eitel learned to weave their own energies and strengths together into a powerful new force for change. Their emerging roles as the two senior officers of the company became more and more complementary. At first this was not clear to all associates, nor to the two leaders themselves. A battle for allegiance may even have developed in some people's minds in the early stages when Anderson first declared his sustainability vision. Anderson was talking about sustainability, while Eitel was talking about a war on waste. Anderson was pulling out of operational responsibilities, while Eitel was taking them on with tremendous success. Eitel was instituting the QUEST metric system and tying this to people's bonus compensation. Anderson's vision of sustainability was not being directly connected to performance measurements or rewards.

Then, in the midst of that weaving, in 1996 Anderson publicly committed Interface to introduce a new thread — The Natural Step — into the company. Today, two years later, Interface continues this weaving process, bringing together QUEST, EcoSense, and The Natural Step into one integrated and dynamic tapestry of sustainability.

Interface and The Natural Step

In 1996, Interface became the first American company to adopt The Natural Step. As Anderson explains, "The Natural Step has become a compass, a reference point, something to recognize and be consistent with." However, Interface's sustainability efforts were not driven by it.

Anderson first learned about The Natural Step through *The Ecology of Commerce* but gave it only passing interest until he met Hawken for the first time in July 1995. Anderson recalls: "It was then that he told me in greater detail about The Natural Step because in the interim year he had visited Karl-Henrik and had been taken with the whole notion of the four System Conditions."

In January, 1996, three Interface representatives participated in a study mission to Stockholm designed to explore and evaluate The Natural Step. One representative commented: "I couldn't help guide our company in a direction that wasn't based on some sound foundation, and I hadn't found anything that could do that until I connected with The Natural Step. When I participated in discussions that took us deep into sustainability, its elegance just became apparent."

Five months later, Interface, the Georgia Conservancy, and Georgia Tech co-sponsored bringing Robèrt to Atlanta. He spoke to 400 people at the Atlanta

Botanical Gardens and 290 scientists and engineers at Georgia Tech. It was during these events that Anderson made the commitment to introduce The Natural Step throughout Interface. In August of 1996, Interface organized an internal two-day intensive training on The Natural Step and began exploring how to begin integrating it with the other initiatives already underway. Interface decided to take all its employees through Natural Step training as the basis for understanding the workings of natural systems and the role of human activities. By the end of 1998, approximately one third, about 2,500, of Interface's more than 7,000 associates have participated in The Natural Step training.

Since 1997, One World Learning, the transformational training and education company created by Interface, has been charged with the task of developing and implementing The Natural Step training for all Interface associates worldwide. Several representatives from Interface and One World Learning have participated in each of the intensive advanced workshops organized each year by The Natural Step organization in the United States, and One World Learning created a six-hour environmental awareness course based on The Natural Step framework.

Because Interface has already had two major initiatives, QUEST and EcoSense, the core challenge now is to effectively integrate all three initiatives. The Natural Step provides two main benefits to Interface: core education for all employees about the way natural systems work and a compass to proceed on its journey towards sustainability.

Education and Training

The Natural Step curriculum developed for the six-hour workshop emphasizes experiential learning. Because of the diversity of educational levels of Interface associates, the workshops are tailored to specific participants and the language is simplified compared to the original scientific papers written by Robèrt and his colleagues. For example, in one workshop, the laws of thermodynamics are expressed this way: matter cannot be destroyed or created; and matter disperses. These laws are illustrated with exercises and examples. For example, "the fact that matter disperses" is illustrated by one drop of food coloring being dropped into a fishbowl.

The discussion of natural cycles is connected to Interface's vision of becoming a sustainable company. This provides an opportunity to discuss linear and cyclical processes and to relate them to the day-to-day operations of the given plant or function within the company. The four System Conditions are presented as in The Natural Step literature, and participants are encouraged to put them into their own words as a way of exploring what they mean.

This explanation serves as the starting point for dialogue that is followed by additional exercises to facilitate relating the four System Conditions to company operations, the resources used, the pollution that is created, and ways to move toward more sustainable processes and practices. Discussions about how to make work more sustainable then lead to brainstorming on how to apply The Natural Step at home.

At present, One World Learning is still experimenting with curriculum to find the best combination of experiential and traditional learning. David Black, President of One World Learning, remarks: "We decided to put together something that is palatable. We created a six-hour introduction to The Natural Step to take around the country. We made it very experientially based. We used videos. We gave out notebooks that weren't full so they could be working notebooks. We would do a task or ask a question, hand out something, and participants would fill it out. They'd build their own notebooks because we wanted them to think in terms that this doesn't end today, that's your notebook for the start of The Natural Step."

Currently, One World Learning is meeting a tremendous challenge: to ensure that all Interface employees, including those who join the company through acquisitions and new hires, have the Playing to Win experience. At the same time, One World Learning is charged with the task of introducing The Natural Step and helping integrate it with existing initiatives. In some places in Interface, such as Interface Europe, the introduction of The Natural Step preceded the creation of One World Learning. Interface Europe began by working directly with The Natural Step organization in the United Kingdom. Only now is that training approach being combined with the training provided by One World Learning.

Employee Participation

Interface's entire corporate culture is designed for participation. The Play to Win philosophy and exercises generate an *esprit de corps* that can be felt in every part of the corporation. Involvement works from the top down. As Charlie Eitel puts it: "True leaders cannot be absent from the action." Both Anderson and Eitel regularly speak and write both to internal and external audiences about the prominence of the company's sustainability vision in their thinking. Initiatives are clearly led from the top. Sustainability is clearly featured in the company's annual reports, and in 1997, Interface published its first *Sustainability Report,* perhaps the most comprehensive report of its kind ever created by a business corporation.

QUEST teams and the QUEST/Ecosense initiatives provide a fundamental set of mechanisms for employees to learn and become involved in the sustainability challenge. The QUEST/Ecosense task force alone is made up of more than 80 Interface associates from around the world who meet twice a year to share progress and ideas among the many environmental and waste-reduction teams they represent. There are more than 400 QUEST projects currently active within the company. Employee environmental awareness and involvement is increased through an EcoSense NetLetter accessible on the World Wide Web information kiosks, and an employee survey designed to monitor progress in employee environmental awareness. Associates are also encouraged to extend their involvement into their communities. They are active in restoring wildlife habitat around many Interface facilities, and in conservation and community awareness activities.

Integration: Action and Results

Because sustainability is a driving vision of the company, it is being integrated into every aspect of Interface's operations. It is now the way Interface does business. Anderson's vision of becoming the first name in industrial ecology indicates where Interface is going. The Natural Step provides a compass to indicate whether the company is on course to that destination. To obtain a thorough understanding of company progress, Interface performed a total corporate resource flow analysis, presented in the Interface *Sustainability Report*. In the report, the company provides a detailed analysis of the material and energy throughput of the company. According to Hartzfeld, who was involved in the coordination and compilation of the data, no one at Interface truly understood the company prior to seeing this picture of its material flows. The data came as a surprise even to Anderson: "We're in a business that is resource intensive. It just blew my mind when Jim Hartzfeld did the rough calculation that showed that for every dollar of sale we take one and a half pounds of materials from the Earth. The biggest single component of that would be burned up to produce the energy to convert the rest into product that would end up on somebody's floor, or be part of somebody's furniture system. That's just incredible to me!"

In a three-page foldout in its report, Interface presents its current material flows in the "take-make-waste" linear model that typifies industrial activity in the world today. The report goes into considerable detail regarding the types of materials used in each category of production, the kind of energy used, and the content of each category of waste. The report recognizes that the current industrial system assumes indefinite supplies of resources and infinite sinks in which to place our industrial wastes. According to this linear flow, what Interface takes from the Earth will end up as visible or invisible waste in landfills, in the air, and in the water unless the linear flow is converted into cyclical processes where material waste becomes a feedstock for other processes.

Recognizing that it, along with all industrial corporations, is part of the problem in an unsustainable system, Interface has made the commitment to act as a model for other companies to undertake such analyses of their processes and to make them public. Charlie Eitel points out that "in our *Sustainability Report* we just came forward and said, 'Here are our sins, here's what we've done.' Now we understand it, we've got a map to go by, and we've got a measuring system. Next we're going to do everything we can to change this. "

The Seven Fronts

An important challenge Interface and One World Learning are addressing is the integration of The Natural Step as the knowledge platform for understanding how natural systems work with the seven fronts that Interface had developed. The seven fronts are:

1. *Elimination of Waste.* The central focus for this front is QUEST, the campaign to eliminate the concept of waste from Interface operations.

2. *Benign Emissions.* Priority is given to the elimination of molecular wastes that have negative or toxic effects and are emitted into natural systems.

3. *Renewable Energy.* Focus is given to reducing the energy demands of Interface processes while substituting non-renewable sources with sustainable ones.

4. *Closure of the Loop.* This requires redesigning Interface's processes and products into cyclical flows.

5. *Resource-Efficient Transportation.* The focus is on finding ways to reduce the transportation of people and products in favor of transporting information. This includes plant location, logistics, information technology, video conferencing, email, and telecommuting.

6. *Sensitivity Hookup.* This involves the creation of a community within and around Interface that understands the functioning of natural systems and industrial society's impact on them.

7. *Redesign of Commerce.* Here the focus is on the delivery of service and value instead of on the delivery of material.

The *Sustainability Report* details Interface's progress on each of the seven fronts to sustainability. The information that follows is adapted from that report and summarizes the advances that Interface has already made on its journey.

1. Elimination of Waste. Interface's policy is to create zero waste. To achieve this goal, it is reexamining current sources of waste and creating programs to reduce and ultimately eliminate them. It is redesigning products and processes to reduce and simplify the quantity of resources used in production. The goal is to remanufacture waste into new resources which would then become technical "nutrients" for the next cycle of production. Interface facilities are implementing state-of-the-art technologies to monitor material, energy, and water consumption as well as waste creation. The company has developed ways to analyze waste streams and to give feedback on progress to employees.

With respect to product change, Interface's goal is to create more with less. Emphasis is given to redesigning products to reduce waste. Metric sizing, reduced standard face and backing weight, and decreased yarn usage contribute to reducing input of both material and energy. Interface's corporate office is coordinating a global monitoring program to develop best practices for product design to create more with less. Interface's subsidiaries are also implementing important process redesigns to produce the same high quality products with better methods and more efficient technologies. Broadloom and fabric manufacturers are working with Interface Research Corporation to develop technologies for dyewater treatment and reuse to reduce water and chemical consumption. Flooring Systems manufacturers are reducing scrap and excess by imposing more control over their production lines. Interface can document thousands of ways, large and small, in which their operations have reduced waste.

2. Benign Emissions. The *Sustainability Report* defines the problem around benign emissions as follows: "Though less visible, industry creates more molecular garbage than solid waste. Small concentrations of poisons, persistent man-made chemicals, greenhouse gases, and localized heating are affecting all living systems, accumulating in animal tissue, fouling water and air systems, affecting reproductive cycles, and changing our climate."

The solution Interface offers is that it will proceed toward eliminating all harmful releases into the ecosphere and will strive to create factories with no smokestacks, effluent pipes, or hazardous waste. Because it is difficult to safeguard against such releases, Interface plans to eliminate them at the source. Ultimately, the only substances emitted from their plants should be valuable products, such as carpet and fabric, and clean air and water.

Interface has identified 192 stacks as point sources for air pollution among its facilities in North America, Europe, and Asia. Each stack is being actively monitored and targeted for necessary modifications. Although all Interface companies are in compliance with environmental legislation, the goal is to eliminate the emission of molecular garbage altogether. In its manufacturing locations, Interface has found only 13 effluent pipes. Those Interface facilities that produce wastewater are working toward reducing and reusing the water and treating the effluent that is released into the environment. In addition, the company's goal is to eliminate all toxic elements of its products and manufacturing processes, mainly through product redesign and material reformulation. Interface has focused on indoor air quality for a decade with the creation of Intersept, an antimicrobial agent now being used in a variety of interior finishes, and through the co-founding and coordination of the EnviroSense Consortium, a forum of companies dedicated to improving indoor air quality.

3. Renewable Energy. Interface is focusing on improving production methods and equipment in order to consume less energy and to reduce demand. It is also pursuing renewable energy supplies including installing alternative technologies at its facilities and contracting with power companies to provide energy from renewable sources. Interface has signed a memorandum of understanding with the

EPA's Energy Star Buildings Program, committing the company to improving overall energy efficiency. Interface has joined E Source, a consortium of energy experts promoting energy efficiency in industry. Internally, a team of energy managers is using these resources to identify best practices. Numerous Interface manufacturing facilities and offices have already conducted lighting and machinery retrofits and installed motion sensors to reduce energy consumption. Research is being conducted into modifying formulas to decrease process energy requirements.

A key to Interface's conversion to renewable energy is the competitive availability of these energy sources. At present, fossil fuels receive large direct and indirect subsidies, but their cost does not reflect the pollution, acid rain, and climate change they cause. Renewable energy, on the other hand, receives scant support in the form of subsidies and is not given credit for being safer. All things considered, renewable energy is far less expensive. Until there are changes in policy and more efficient markets, Interface will reduce its overall energy demand and switch to available renewable energy resources in stages. Bertolucci reports that the company decided that every unit of energy that comes from a non-renewable source would be counted as waste and become a QUEST target. The goal is to be using only renewable energy sources.

4. Closure of the Loop. Most industrial systems are linear. Nature and living systems are cyclical. Interface is redesigning its processes and products to mimic nature in material flows where "waste equals food," that is, outputs from one process become inputs (industrial food) for others. Interface plans to reduce its use of raw materials and works to get the most value out of the materials used. This includes careful recycling of synthetic materials so that waste materials in society become valuable raw materials in industry. It also means keeping organic materials uncontaminated so they can return to their natural cycles. Interface is engaged in numerous research projects geared toward converting waste products into technical inputs — turning fiber into fiber, backing into backing — to truly recycle their components and avoid downcycling as much as possible. Downcycling is the conversion of high embodied energy products to low embodied energy uses, such as converting (that is, downcycling) the complex nylon molecules in the carpet face to be used as mere backing material.

Recycling, rather than downcycling, reduces the quantity of material that needs to be taken from the Earth and eventually goes to the landfill. It saves money and resources. Interface Research Corporation is working closely with its flooring companies to create technologies for recycling post-consumer carpet, re-extruding post-industrial fibers, and reusing PVC backing. All Interface companies are pressuring suppliers to increase recycled content for raw materials. Interface's ultimate vision is to create completely benign and renewable products that eliminate the company's dependence on petrochemicals. They are research-ing 100 percent natural fiber products made from industrial hemp, flax, and natural dyes. Interface Research Corporation is driving an effort to develop alternative backing systems.

5. Resource-Efficient Transportation. As Interface perceives it, transportation includes moving people, products, information, and resources. The company is striving to make its transportation in all of these areas more ecologically efficient by changing packages so they weigh less, manufacturing closer to the customer, and moving information instead of matter. To reduce transportation costs for people, Interface encourages and provides teleconferencing and video confer-encing technologies. Because all travel cannot be eliminated, Interface joined a "Trees for Travel" program that plants trees in the tropics to absorb carbon diox-ide in sufficient quantity to offset the emissions from air travel. It is estimated that on average every airborne mile generates a half pound of carbon dioxide per passenger. Each tree planted absorbs about 50 pounds of carbon dioxide per year after the first year. One ton of carbon dioxide is thus absorbed over a 40-year period leading to the calculation that one tree should be planted for every 4,000 passenger miles travelled. Interface Research Corporation is also experimenting with natural gas-powered fleet cars to reduce air emissions.

With respect to transporting products, Interface is increasing efficiency by shipping via transcontinental rail, locating manufacturing facilities closer to their customers, and reducing packaging and material requirements. Bentley Mills is replacing 34 propane-powered forklifts with electric lifts and handling equipment. Ultimately, the goal is to charge the electric machine batteries with solar power.

Interface is also maximizing the efficiency of information transfer by upgrading and standardizing the corporation with respect to new information technologies. A global network is being installed to encourage electronic com-munication instead of paper use. A global network of shared software, elec-tronic messaging, and internet access is being installed as all Interface internet sites are updated and expanded.

6. Sensitivity Hookup. Interface believes a major obstacle to sustainability is that most of society does not understand the basic principles of natural systems or the ways individual and collective human actions affect them. Their solution is to help all Interface associates and business partners gain a better understand-ing of these factors and their challenges not only to business, but to all of humanity. The sensitivity hookup for Interface includes teaching and imple-menting The Natural Step and Playing to Win philosophies and processes.

7. Redesign of Commerce. Interface's path to sustainability is one of redesign-ing the way business is conceived and done. It is a challenge Interface takes seriously. Interface continues to develop the Evergreen Service Contracts program as an example of the product of service concept. This is Interface's first attempt to transform a durable commercial product (carpet tiles) into a customer service. Others will follow. Interface has also invested more than $100 million in the creation of a U.S. based value-added services network called Re:Source Americas to focus on the delivery of the services of flooring products, not the products themselves. Re:Entry is a new initiative established by Re:Source Americas to provide reverse logistics — the reuse or recycling of used products. This is another step for Interface in creating a closed loop for its products so that they do not wind up in the landfill, but become feedstock for the conversion into new products.

Interface has also developed an approach to greening its supply chains. It has already held a meeting with 150 suppliers led by Anderson, Eitel, Bertolucci, and Hartzfeld. They conveyed to their suppliers the notion that Interface plans to be a successful, profitable, and exciting place that will also eliminate its footprint on the Earth. Eitel pointed out to suppliers that Interface depended upon them to make that happen and implied that only those with congruent values would remain Interface suppliers.

Redesigning commerce also extends to the way Interface designs its facilities. The Prince Street plant in Cartersville, Georgia, is a state-of-the-art facility that introduced new systems for energy efficiency and variable climate control for increased human comfort and productivity, waste reduction, water purification, and clean water restoration of natural aquifers. Prince Street incorporated the use of both recycled and non-toxic building materials in its construction. Interface views it as a platform for analyzing the financial feasibility of eco-friendly practices and construction. Similar innovations in construction and renovation are being applied in other Interface plant locations.

Interface and its subsidiaries are involved in a large number of organizations that promote social or environmental sustainability. The common thread is the mission of reinventing the way business is done. Interface is partnering with numerous organizations including The President's Council on Sustainable Development, The World Business Council for Sustainable Development, the U.S. Green Building Council, Business for Social Responsibility, the World Resources Institute, the Wildlife Habitat Council, and now The Natural Step.

QUEST/EcoSense

QUEST/EcoSense provide the primary mechanisms for moving forward on the long climb up the mountain of sustainability. Both programs were instituted in 1994, which became the baseline year for building metrics to chart progress. Since that time, through War on Waste, Interface has taken millions of dollars from its costs and estimates that by the end of 1998 the cumulative amount of savings will be about $76 million. The savings from QUEST are used to pay for early investments in other aspects of Interface's sustainability vision, many without such an early financial payback as QUEST.

As a program, QUEST is coordinated under the office of the chief financial officer. It is described as "part one of Interface's total waste elimination initiative." QUEST uses an index measurement system called Ecometrics, in which each facility is compared to its own historical baseline cost to measure progress to date.

EcoSense, also launched in 1994, is the mechanism which supports the vision that Anderson originally challenged the task force to help articulate. EcoSense is managed by Interface Research Corporation as a program to provide a way to measure progress on the journey to sustainability.

In 1996, the two programs were integrated. The QUEST and EcoSense task forces were merged into one, and 18 teams were formed with representatives from all Interface businesses worldwide. Each team was given a specified scope of investigation and implementation. Currently, there are more than 400 sustainability initiatives taking place throughout Interface. There are basic categories within which QUEST teams are created, and anyone is free to create a QUEST team at any time on any subject as long as it eliminates waste.

Integration Through Performance Bonuses

From the beginning, progress in QUEST and War on Waste was rewarded by connecting improvements to the employee remuneration bonus structure. Fifteen percent of an individual's bonus was directly related to the company achieving its QUEST targets. Interface Flooring Systems has even tied hourly employee's bonuses to the annual goals set by QUEST/EcoSense. In 1997, an EcoSense supplement program was developed to provide a roadmap for each facility to use in implementing sustainable practices. EcoSense supplement points are awarded upon successful implementation of sustainable practices in a facility. These points are used to supplement the QUEST Index used for bonus calculations. Activities for which EcoSense Supplement points are awarded include the following:

The Development of Effective Environmental Management Systems. Interface believes that external certification will signal to customers, suppliers, regulators, and others the company's commitment and diligence with respect to minimizing its impact on the environment. Points are awarded for achieving individual stages of the certification process for the two standards: the international ISO 14001 or the British BS7750. All of Interface's European manufacturing facilities have been awarded either ISO 14001 or BS 7750 certification. The Shelf Mills and Providence facilities were the world's first carpet manufacturing facilities to achieve registration with both BS7750 and ISO 14001. Interface Europe at Scherpenzeel was the first manufacturer in Holland to achieve approval of the Health and Safety Management System in the Dutch P190 standard. Interface

Flooring Systems facilities in the United States and Interface Asia-Pacific facilities in Australia and Thailand have all performed the initial ISO 14001 assessment. The Interface facility in Canada has received ISO 14001 certification.

Certification Under a Quality Management System. Points are awarded for achieving specific stages in the development of a certified quality management system, either ISO 9001 or ISO 9002.

Implementation of The Natural Step Training. Interface believes that understanding the principles by which natural systems exist and develop is vital to the company's journey to sustainability. Each employee should be exposed to these basic, scientifically founded principles that define how natural systems work in the long term. Points are cumulatively awarded for the achievement of specified levels of training. To maintain awarded points, the facility must train new employees in The Natural Step.

EcoMetrics. Interface is diligent about reporting. Its view is that without credible metrics, goals and progress cannot be established or measured. Interface has established four categories of EcoMetrics for which facilities can earn points by measuring

- material and energy flows
- materials that are recycled externally or internally
- elimination of emissions from all point sources and
- employee awareness and perceptions through surveys.

The Development, Implementation, and Internal Promotion of a Formal "Buy Recycled" Policy. Interface encourages purchasing products with recycled content.

Eco-Efficiency. Interface seeks to reward any effort that reduces the total amount of material and/or energy used to create products. These efforts increase the net value delivered to customers and reduce Interface's impact on the environment. Points are awarded for actual reductions in the amount of non-renewable material or energy used relative to products delivered to the market. Two sets of categories identify the areas where points can be earned:

1. Reductions in the use of non-renewable materials consumed in the manufacturing or packaging of products; implementation of non-renewable material reduction projects; reduction in total non-renewable energy use; and implementation of energy reduction projects.

2. Waste reduction including solid waste reduction, water emissions reduction, air emissions reduction, and emissions point source elimination.

In 1998, Interface introduced QUEST/EcoSense 2000 as a roadmap for the next three years. The program is designed to involve even more people than the previous initiatives. The program continues to combine waste reduction and environmental initiatives and adds another level of participation with the introduction of non-value-added activity elimination focused on identifying and eliminating all non-value-added fixed costs. The goal over the next three years is to remove 100 percent of the non-value-added activities from fixed costs and 50 percent of the waste cost from the product cost.

Non-value-added elimination is described as part two of Interface's total waste elimination (QUEST is part one). QUEST addresses non-value added variable and administrative costs in manufacturing areas. Non-value-added elimination addresses non-value-added activities and costs in fixed areas such as fixed manufacturing cost and sales, general, and administrative costs. A non-value-added activity is defined as any activity or cost that can be eliminated without deterioration in product or service attributes. As this is a new program, the baseline year for non-value-added elimination is 1997. Like QUEST, non-value-added elimination uses an index measurement system in which facilities are compared to their own historical baseline cost.

Final Reflections

If you have never experienced a billion-dollar industrial company whose employees believe that they are saving the world, it is quite an experience. In our exploration of Interface, we investigated seven different facilities: four factories in two countries, the major design studio, the main research facility, and the world headquarters. We were impressed with just how many employees really "get it" about why it is essential for industry to become sustainable and why it is in Interface's best interests to do so. Without exception they were sincerely proud of their company, their leaders, and themselves for the role they all play in making the planet a healthier and safer place to be. There is a dynamism and sense of mission at Interface that is palpable.

The company's intentional journey to sustainability is moving ahead rapidly, intensely, and comprehensively on eight different fronts simultaneously — their initial seven fronts and The Natural Step. There is no doubt that taking a stand for sustainability has fostered a total design revolution within Interface's products and manufacturing processes, and a cultural revolution of caring and purpose among its more than 7,000 employees.

Unlike with IKEA and Scandic Hotels, Interface's commitment to sustainability and implementation of environmental action plans did not originate with The Natural Step. For example, the QUEST War on Waste and the EcoSense environmental initiatives were well under way when Ray Anderson decided to bring The Natural Step into the mix. What benefit does The Natural Step bring to a company like Interface which already has more sophistication about environmental sustainability issues than most companies in North America?

For Interface, with just two years of experience so far, there appear to be four main benefits from using The Natural Step.

First, it provides a compass, a constant direction, a true north to all of the company's seven sustainability programs and the several hundred unique initiatives presently underway around the world.

Second, it provides an integrating framework and a common language to link those same programs and hundreds of initiatives. Without The Natural Step, there would be no common language, or common perspective, to the many different initiatives.

Third, it provides a systems-based environmental educational program to build a common understanding of the scientific principles underlying the company's many sustainability efforts. There is a 10-year history within the international body of knowledge represented by The Natural Step, which can be called upon for know-how and pedagogy for education and training initiatives.

Fourth, it provides the basis of a new mental model, a change in paradigm or worldview. This is particularly important to Interface because it is on the fast track of corporate culture change. To succeed in realizing its vision of being the first name in industrial ecology, the thousands of Interface associates around the globe require a common mental framework to transcend the conventional view of organization as machine, and to understand and embrace a model of ecological systems and industrial ecology. The Natural Step provides the science-based foundation for that new mental model.

Having introduced The Natural Step to about one-third of its workforce of more than 7,000 associates, Interface is faced with the challenge to engage those workers in meaningful follow-up so as to reinforce and keep alive the new worldview in the now more than 2,000 members of its workforce trained in The Natural Step. The company also needs to learn from its experiences with The Natural Step implementation to engage the remaining two-thirds of its workforce in the most effective manner. As one can see with IKEA and Scandic Hotels, when the workforce truly understands The Natural Step model and when upper management supports and harnesses the impulses for change arising from that understanding, great innovation in processes and products can be achieved. Given the commitment of Interface's senior management to the sustainability vision and given the company's outstanding record of achievement to date, there is every reason to believe that Interface will truly become the prototypical company of the 21st century.

CHAPTER 7

COLLINS PINE COMPANY:
"Journey to Sustainability"

*Collins Products is dedicated to utilizing the principles of The Natural Step
in its business practices. This is a commitment to the future of this company,
our employees, our families, our community, and the environment.
We believe that the integration of The Natural Step principles into our daily
business practices will provide us all with long-term environmental, social,
and financial benefits that we could not obtain by other methods.*
Collins Pine Company *Vision Statement for the
Collins Products Journey to Sustainability*

THE COLLINS FAMILY have been practicing sustainable development in their
business for generations — long before the phrase came into modern cur-
rency. For decades, the Collins family and their associates have understood
that the trio of a healthy forest ecosystem, jobs in the community, and profits
for the company were intertwined and formed an unbreakable web. Destroy or
overharvest the ecosystem and you destroy the chance of sustainable jobs and
sustainable profits. Today we speak of the same thing when we discuss the triple
bottom line of economics, society, and ecology. The Collins family have known
and worked with this formula for generations.

Pioneers in the Pacific Northwest timber industry, the Collins family made a
tradition of trail-blazing. This tradition lives on in the Collins Pine Company.
The company roots are traced to 1855 when Truman D. Collins and four partners bought 1600 acres of virgin white pine and a steam saw mill in northwest-
ern Pennsylvania. Five years later, Collins bought his partners out and, in 1888,
ventured westward to Washington State, purchasing timberland on the Cowlitz
River. In 1890, Truman's son, Everell, took over the management of the
Washington holdings, built Washington's first long timber mill and tripled production. Everell also built one of the first railroads in Washington, the Ostrander
Railway and Timber Company, and started a successful logging operation at

Silver Lake, Washington. They expanded their West Coast holdings further by purchasing 100,000 acres of timberland near Molalla, Oregon, and 67,800 acres in the Almanor basin in Northern California. In 1918, the company moved its headquarters to Portland, Oregon.

The Collins family, devout Methodists, considered themselves to be the stewards of their land and responsible to the communities that lived near their forest holdings and/or depended on them for their livelihood. The boom-bust cycle of the forest industry was often disruptive to these communities, which troubled the Collins family. In the late 1930s, Truman W. Collins, the founder's grandson, began to develop a vision of a new kind of forest operation, one that would ensure a perpetual supply of timber for a mill, mills that would never close, and stable, sustainable communities where jobs would be available in perpetuity. This sustained-yield forestry would promote healthy biodiverse forests, prosperous communities, and long-term profits for the company.

Truman launched his experiment in the Almanor forest, which had never before been cut. He hired leading forestry and biology experts to help create a management plan to ensure the health of the total forest ecosystem. The system was based on the U.S. Forest Service models being researched at that time. It used selective cutting, a practice that creates stands of uneven-aged trees similar to those found in natural forests. It leaves the healthiest and most vigorous trees and cuts those that are diseased or whose growth rates have peaked. The company developed a detailed classification system and conducted careful monitoring of overall forest growth to ensure that no more fiber would be taken out than was replaced naturally.

Since 1945, the Almanor forest has maintained 576 one-acre "growth inventory plots" that are carefully monitored. All trees in each plot over 12 inches in diameter are numbered. Once a decade these trees are measured to determine growth rates. From this data base, the company can estimate overall growth for the entire forest and plan the harvests accordingly. They cut, at most, the volume of timber that has grown during the preceding 10 years. Today, the Almanor forest is 94,000 acres. It has been logged continuously for five decades, yielding more than 1.7 billion board feet of timber. Yet this forest has a higher inventory of wood standing and growing than when logging began in 1943, much of it in mature trees. Under Collins Pine's philosophy, the company, in effect, reaps the interest on the growth of their forest while protecting the principal.

Throughout the company's 143-year history, the Collins family has maintained its ownership and an active interest. When Truman W. Collins died in 1964, his widow, Maribeth Collins, became Chair of the Board and continues to hold that position today. The company's values and philosophy reflect those of family members, past and present. The family is active in the community, staunchly support the work of the United Methodist Church, and engages in philanthropic work. In 1947, Truman and other members of the Everell Collins family created the Collins Foundation. This independent private foundation is dedicated to improving, enriching, and giving greater expression to the religious, educational, cultural, and scientific endeavors of the State of Oregon, and to improving the quality of life in the state. Maribeth Collins, President of The Collins Foundation, remains very active in the work of the foundation.

The Collins Pine Company management philosophy is that forests must be protected and appreciated for their own sake, as well as those who use them. Collins is committed to

- maintaining the health of the total forest ecosystem
- supporting the production of wood on a sustained and renewable basis and
- providing social and economic benefits to the surrounding areas and communities.

In 1993, the Collins Pine Company took another pioneering step. The Almanor forest became the first privately-owned forest in the United States to be comprehensively evaluated and independently certified by Scientific Certifications Systems in accordance with the strict rules of the Forest Stewardship Council. The Forest Stewardship Council is an independent, international, member-based organization that accredits certification bodies and promotes voluntary third-party certification. An interdisciplinary team including a forest economist, a logging and forest health specialist, a professional forester, a biologist, and the Scientific Certifications Systems project manager conducted three field investigations over a period of eight months and graded Collins' forest management in three areas: sustainability of timber resources, maintenance of the forest ecosystem, and socioeconomic benefits to the surrounding community. In these three categories, the Almanor forest scored out of a possible hundred points, 86, 81, and 89 respectively. The evaluators said they were "impressed with Collins Almanor forest management practices and the care taken for wildlife and the general forest ecosystem.

Collins' commitment to focusing on the *quality* of what remains after logging rather than simply the *quantity* of timber removed has impressed the team members. Similarly, the Evaluation Team was favorably impressed by the extent to which Collins has established and maintained a positive relationship with the local community, and by the relatively progressive policies it has established with respect to employee compensation, benefits, and workplace safety."

The Collins Pennsylvania forest, Kane Hardwood, became certified in 1994 and received a similar glowing report. In 1996, Collins Pine's achievements in sustainability were recognized with the Presidential Award for Sustainable

Development conferred by the President's Council on Sustainable Development. In March 1998, The Collins Lakeview Forest in Oregon and Northern California was also certified. This means that today all three of Collins' hardwood and soft-wood forests have received this respected third-party certification.

What does a sustainably managed forest look like? The Collins forests are bio-diverse, multilayered, canopied forests. They are self-sustaining forests containing more wood today than they did over 100 years ago. Collins Pine's Almanor for-est has never been clear-cut. Trees there range in age from new seedlings to trees more than 300 years old. The Collins forests support a diverse array of wildlife including bald eagles, black bears, wild turkeys, rubber boas, beavers, great blue heron rookeries, and endangered Goose Lake redband trout. The forests are enhanced by meadows, springs, creeks, rivers, and lakes. They are naturally healthy forests that do not use pesticides and fertilizers to promote growth.

They also differ in other respects from prevailing North American logging practices. There is more woody debris left on the forest floor after logging, allow-ing more nutrients to return to the soil. Abundant snags provide habitat for woodpeckers and other animals that require dead or dying trees. Logging roads are set well back from streams. Stands have a variety of species and ages in a for-est that reproduces itself without additional planting.

In 1996, Collins Pine Company expanded its forest operations to include the manufacturing of plywood, particleboard, and hardboard siding through the acquisition of a large three-mill complex from Weyerhaeuser in Klamath Falls, Oregon, one of the largest of its kind in North America. The plywood mill is producing the first fully certified plywood in North America and the particle-board plant introduced the first certified particleboard in August, 1998, in addi-tion to manufacturing its non-certified line of products. Because Collins cannot ensure that all of the raw material used at the mills comes from certified or well managed sources, management decided they needed to find another approach to ensuring the highest possible environmental sensitivity at the newly acquired plants to be consistent with their forest operations. Senior management of Collins Pine chose The Natural Step framework to accomplish this.

Collins Pine Today

Today, Collins Pine Company has nearly 300,000 acres of privately-held prime timberland that has been certified as sustainably managed. It is a $230-mil-lion/year enterprise with more than 1,000 employees. The Collins companies include the following busnesses:

The Collins Pine Company in Chester, California. The 94,000-acre Collins Almanor forest is located in the Sierra Nevada mountains of California. The timberlands were acquired in 1902 and have been managed on an uneven-age sustained yield basis from the beginning. Manufacturing began in 1943. The facilities include a sawmill, dry kilns, a planer, a re-manufacturing plant, and electric co-generation. The species of trees include ponderosa pine, hemfir, sugar pine, douglas fir, and incense cedar. The capacity is 70 millions of board feet (MMBF) annually.

Ostrander Resources in Lakeview, Oregon. This company consists of Freemont Sawmill plus the 78,000-acre Collins Lakeview forest located in southern Oregon and on the northern border of California. It is managed on an uneven-age sustained yield basis. Manufacturing began in 1945. Facilities include a sawmill, dry kilns, and a planer. Tree species include ponderosa pine, hemfir, lodgepole pine, and incense cedar. The capacity is 30 MMBF annually. Ostrander also owns 42 percent of Mull Drilling Company, a gas and oil exploration and production joint venture in Witchita, Kansas, that has 200 gas and oil wells in Kansas and Colorado.

Kane Hardwood in Kane, Pennsylvania. This 124,000-acre Collins Pennsylvania forest is situated in the Allegheny mountains of northern Pennsylvania. Operations began in 1855. The facilities include a sawmill, a pre-dryer, dry kilns, a planing mill, and a dimension plant. The species of trees include black cherry, soft maple, red oak, ash, hard maple, beech, yellow poplar, white oak, and basswood. The capacity of the forest is 20 MMBF annually for the sawmill; 4 MMBF annually for the dimension mill; and 14 MMBF annually for the kiln dry.

Collins Products LLC in Klamath Falls, Oregon. Collins Products, LLC consists of three plants: western softwood plywood with a capacity of 160 MMBF annually; hardboard siding, with a capacity of 130 MMBF annually; and particleboard, with a capacity of 120 MMBF annually.

Collins Resources International, Ltd. in Portland, Oregon. This company specializes in high grade lumber products for international markets using certified CollinsWood and non-certified wood.

Builders Supply. Collins also owns retail building material supply stores located in Chester, Paradise, and Oroville, California.

Certified Products. The Collins companies produce "CollinsWood," which is the registered name of a line of certified wood products, including hardwood lumber and veneer, softwood lumber, plywood, and particleboard. These products are now available throughout the world.

Enduring Values

Stewardship, integrity, quality, and customer service are the hallmarks of the Collins Pine Company and its affiliates. The responsible care of forest resources and the care for human and other biological communities are at the heart of the company's values. They believe that this is the only way to run a business, to survive both economically and ethically. The Collins companies set out the following guiding principles for their businesses:

- The importance of our products and services is our first priority.
- We are committed to continuous improvement in all aspects of our relations: the environment, the communities we live and work in, and our profitability and competitiveness.
- The mutual benefits of superior relationships with suppliers, customers, and other business and governmental agencies are recognized and will be maintained and improved upon.
- The conduct of our companies will be pursued in a manner that is socially responsible and commands respect for its integrity and its positive contributions to society.
- The dedication and involvement of all employees is essential to the attainment of our goals.

Collins Pine has been widely recognized for its vision and values. These are some of the prestigious honors it has recently:

- President Clinton's 1996 Presidential Award for Sustainable Development, presented by Vice-President Al Gore at the White House
- 1997 Green Cross Millennium Award for Corporate Environmental Leadership, presented by Global Green USA, which is affiliated with Green Cross International, founded by Mikhail Gorbachev
- 1997 Enterprise Awards for Best Business Practices for Building Strategic Alliances, presented by Arthur Andersen, US Bank, and *Oregon Business Magazine*
- 1997 Governor's Challenge of Change Awards for Excellence, presented by Governor Kitzhaber at the Oregon Economic Development Conference
- 1997 Founder of a New Northwest, presented by Sustainable Northwest;
- 1997 Honorable Mention, *Inc. Magazine* Marketing Masters Award mentioning the creation of the brand name CollinsWood, Collins' line of certified products.

The company has been featured in numerous articles and journals, including *The Washington Post, Inc. Magazine, The Christian Science Monitor,* the *Sierra* magazine, *Business Ethics, Daily Journal of Commerce, The Amicus Journal* of the Natural Resources Defense Council, and *The San Francisco Chronicle.* A case study of Collins Pine is included in *The Business of Sustainable Forestry* series of publications by Island Press. In 1998, James Quinn, President and CEO, was named "Man of the Year" by *Timber Processing* magazine and "Alumnus of the Year" in the School of Administration at JFK University in Orinda, California.

Certification and Beyond

Forest stewardship and sustainable management are not new practices to the Collins Pine Company. They pioneered the field because the family believed it was the right thing to do. In 1992, Wade Mosby, Vice-President of Marketing, returned from a trip to Europe where he had heard about a market innovation called GreenCross product certification. The markets in Europe were becoming more sensitive to environmental issues, particularly around products from rainforests and the need to promote and ensure sustainable forest management practices. It was clear that environmentally friendly wood products were becoming an important area of market differentiation, an issue that was very important to the company's strategy at that time. Jim Quinn, President and CEO, determined that since their Almanor Forest in California had already been carrying on sustainable practices for 50 years, they could get third-party credit for the work they were already doing.

Quinn's vision went further. The forest industry as a whole is often accused of environmental destruction, and "jobs versus environment" debates generally grab the headlines. Quinn remarks: "We wanted to create market differentiation, but we also wanted to be able to carry a story to the public that there are those in this industry that are doing a good job of forestry and protecting the environment." Certification seemed to be a natural step. The company had extensive experience and competence in sustainable yield management. Quinn says: "We already knew we were good. But if we go out and tell somebody we're good, it doesn't really mean anything. So if we stand up in a crowd of all the big companies and we say 'hey, we're the best, we're the environmental leaders as far as environmental forestry is concerned' that isn't going to do anything because everybody's out there saying that. So we decided if we're that good, we ought to be able to get others to say it for us, so that's why we went through certification."

The idea wasn't without resistance. Initially, the foresters didn't want to do the certification. Quinn believes that they didn't like the idea of having auditors looking over their shoulders at what they were doing. Mosby recalls: "When I told the forest manager, we had some strong words. He said, 'we're doing a good job, why do we need to be certified?' Later he became the biggest proponent we had in the company. And he became a member of the board of directors of the Forest Stewardship Council."

The Collins Company exercises control over its timberlands. However, only about half the material that goes through its saw mills comes from its own certified forests. Of that, only about 20 percent finds its way into the marketplace with the Collins trademark on it specifying it as certified. It is sold as a very focused product. Quinn remarks: "It carries our entire identity even though it is less than 20 percent. That's our banner product. That's our focus, our culture, everything we stand for."

When the Collins Pine Company purchased the Weyerhaeuser mills in Klamath Falls in 1996, they were faced with an interesting dilemma. Certified products are a minor part of what the mills produce. Collins can haul logs from their forests in California and Oregon that are certified, and make a certified plywood panel and particleboard from it. The hardboard siding operations present a different challenge. Collins buys shavings from sawmills and planer mills where the material is clean and of good quality, but Collins has no control over those resources. Quinn reflects: "Maybe 10 percent of what would go into those three plants comes from our resources that are certified sustainable. So where does the rest of it come from, and how do we keep from being hypocritical about being good in sustainability on our land and in our sawmills?"

Quinn was looking for a way to incorporate the new mills into the company's stewardship and sustainability ethic when he learned about The Natural Step. Quinn understood that Collins couldn't control all of the biological aspects of what others did with their own land. But it was possible to start focusing on those things they could control in the mills to make continuous improvements in their processes.

What was attractive about The Natural Step? Quinn remarks: "It's very difficult to be perfect, and I think that's one of the things that fascinated me about The Natural Step. There was nothing about it that said you had to go cold turkey. Everything was one step at a time. Everything was recognizing that you're trying to get somewhere but you don't have to just shut down and only run those things that are perfect. You focus on the journey to sustainability. So we embark upon a journey rather than trying to make an overnight change."

Collins Pine and The Natural Step

When Quinn learned about The Natural Step, he went directly to the source— Sweden — to learn more. He listened to what Robèrt had to say and found it to be consistent with the values and philosophy of the Collins family. Quinn recognized that the first and second System Conditions refer to many activities that are not sustainable and that will increasingly affect the competitors of the timber industry, such as cement, steel, and plastics. Those materials rely on non-renewable raw materials and use significant non-renewable energy in their production. Trees, however, are renewable. The real challenge, Quinn points out, is clarifying the difference between renewability and sustainability, which is found in the third System Condition. Quinn says: "A sustainable forest manager allows the trees to renew themselves. But that's only one part of it. The other side is that while you're managing the forest, you still have a conscious awareness of, and a focus on, biological systems and diversity such that you don't take all the trees out at once and deprive everything that lives there of their habitat. So you do a little bit at a time." The third element that appealed to him is looking after social and economic benefits, being conscious of the well-being of communities and future generations. Quinn saw that The Natural Step framework provided an excellent complement to the certification process of their timberlands, enabling all parts of the Collins Pine Company to share a cohesive vision of sustainable forest operations and production.

Quinn began by inviting The Natural Step organization in the United States to present the framework to top management. A one-day training session was also arranged for about 30 executives and staff from Collins' Portland and Klamath Falls facilities. After that, several members of the headquarters staff attended presentations and workshops about The Natural Step that had been organized in the Portland area under the auspices of The Northwest Earth Institute. Through these presentations and workshops, top management and key staff members developed familiarity with the basic principles and concepts behind The Natural Step.

Education and Training

The Collins Company decided to take a "train-the-trainers" approach. They designated environmental facilitators in their operations in Kane, Pennsylvania, and Klamath Falls, Oregon, and sent them to intensive training workshops organized by The Natural Step organization in the United States. Travis Wilson, Fiber Procurement Manager for Particleboard in Klamath Falls, participated in a training workshop held in Santa Fe, New Mexico, in the spring of 1997. Bill Watson, Dimension Mill Manager in Kane participated in a training workshop held in Boston, Massachusetts, in the fall of 1997. Each was charged with the task of developing an educational program based on The Natural Step framework to be implemented in their respective facilities. Quinn decided to focus first on the Klamath Falls mills to introduce The Natural Step training. However, all salaried employees in Kane have received initial training, with training of other employees planned for the spring of 1999. The Lakeview and Chester facilities will also participate in The Natural Step training in the near future.

When Wilson returned from the intensive training held in New Mexico in May 1997, he began by presenting a summary of what he had learned to the management group in Klamath Falls. He then began meeting regularly with Dale Slate, Vice President and General Manager of the Klamath Falls facilities, to explore how the training in the mills might be approached most effectively. Wilson recalls: "Dale and I started brainstorming about how we were going to lay this thing out, what we were going to do with it, how we were going to enlighten people. We were working from scratch, and we probably talked and met for a month off and on." In July 1997, a team of volunteer trainers was created from each of the four business areas, one from each mill (particleboard, hardboard siding and plywood) and one person from the common area (machine shop, truck shop, accounting/administrative office).

The team worked for several months developing training materials adapted specifically to Collins Pine and for the manufacturing facilities. It was a challenging task. Wilson recalls that when he returned from Santa Fe, he started to look at his material and notes and wondered, "How are we going to convey this kind of information to the general work force and have it mean anything or result in anything beneficial?" At first he hoped that no one would ask him about The Natural Step. Wilson remarks: "I had to think about it for a while. It was only through taking all that information and working for several months with this group of ours, putting together the presentation, that I really started getting an idea of what it was really all about. I mean, it was all in there, but I had to get it out to make sense of it. And we're still trying to make sense of it. It's not a simple task. There were no recipes."

One of the first steps in moving forward was selecting a name for the process. It was important that the process be owned by the employees in the facilities. They decided to call their initiative the "Journey to Sustainability," or "JTS". Next, the training materials were adapted to the Collins Products context. Wilson and his team illustrated points, using examples from the company and the industry. They integrated Collins Products company into the presentation and combined information about the Collins Company's philosophy with the framework provided by The Natural Step. At that point, most employees still did not know much about the company that had purchased their facilities from Weyerhaeuser. For that reason, it was important that the two-hour presentation contain information about the company and its history, beliefs, and values. About 15 minutes at the beginning of the training presentation was dedicated to talking about the history of Collins Pine and its decades of sustainable forest management. Says Wilson: "The most important part of the presentation was really not the scientific information or even the four System Conditions, it was that Collins Pine has done this for years. They've believed in this for years. It's not a fad, it's not something that's here today and gone tomorrow."

The material had to be considerably simplified without diluting its meaning. Wilson comments: "You can only go so far to simplify before you start to lose the real impact. You've still got to teach the science principles and the four System Conditions. That's the whole foundation."

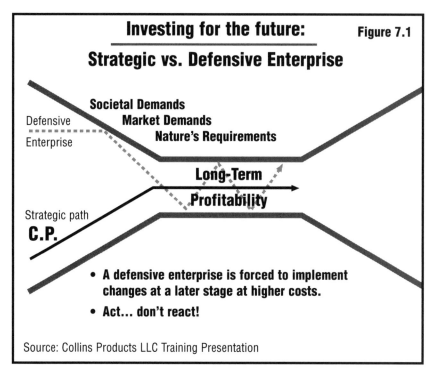

Investing for the future:
Figure 7.1
Strategic vs. Defensive Enterprise

Defensive
Enterprise

Societal Demands
Market Demands
Nature's Requirements

Long-Term
Profitability

Strategic path
C.P.

- A defensive enterprise is forced to implement changes at a later stage at higher costs.
- Act... don't react!

Source: Collins Products LLC Training Presentation

Wilson explains: "We put Collins Products in the slides. We talked about our presence in the funnel and how we'd like to become sustainable rather than contributing to closing the funnel down. We want to be part of opening it up, part of the solution. If nobody else joins us on this journey, we're still going. We talked about keeping ahead of the curve with regulations. You don't want to get caught in that trap of catch-up. We've got to stay ahead and change things before we have stricter laws or guidelines. We still have to make a profit. We still have to keep people employed and run the business. Yet hand in hand we want to do it correctly for the environment."

In September 1997, the Klamath Falls team put together a one-day training in The Natural Step for all salaried personnel assisted by a trainer associated with The Natural Step/US. In October, the team began training all facility personnel, each team member conducting the training in their respective areas.

Besides the challenge presented by adapting the material to both the Collins Company and the mill operations context, the training had to be condensed from the one-day eight-hour format to a short session of no more than two hours. This was necessary because the training had to take place during normal shift time which shut down plant operations staffed by over 500 employees. To date, all employees in the Klamath Falls facilities have received the initial

Natural Step training. Each team coordinator ensures that the same material is presented to all new employees.

Even as the core Journey to Sustainability team was putting together the initial two-hour presentations, consideration was given to follow-up training and creating opportunities to review the science and System Conditions. Wilson remarks: "You need to have time to digest all the information, take it back to your own setting, and make sense of it." The JTS team wanted to provide opportunities to reinforce the basic information and to connect it to progress being made in the Collins Company. By the end of 1998, all employees at Klamath Falls participated in a "rest stop on our journey" update and refresher workshop. The outline for the workshop included the following aspects:

A JTS training review featuring the "tree" with the four System Conditions on the trunk, with science as the root; a factory model with the four "Rs," and upstream perspective; and the funnel with examples of "hitting the wall" from Collins Products.

The JTS Structure (teams/mission/people) with an introduction to the JTS core team and other JTS teams, and slides of each team, missions, and the names of people involved.

The Year in Review, with impact numbers including two to three expenditure requests for capital with an impact assessment; operational projects with an impact assessment; and team projects with impact assessments highlighting information from the JTSE-Team (Energy Team), WE2T (Water Ecological Equilibrium Team), PET (Project Evaluation Team), Recycle Team, and Adopt-a-Highway Team.

The JTS Focus on the following six fronts with numbers and/or examples and goals:

1. Point source emissions
2. Zero waste water (all sources)
3. Elimination of waste to landfills
4. Maximization of renewable energy
5. Provision of community support and
6. Education and inspiration of employees.

A presentation of the JTS 1999 goals, including fully developing eco-indicators using the four System Conditions; getting a greater number of employees directly involved in JTS through one-on-one invitations; and creating the following new teams: the JAT (Journey Awareness Team), the CAT (Clean Air Team), and the PP & DT (Product Packaging and Design Team).

Employee Participation

The Journey to Sustailability teams and Klamath Falls management recognize that integrating environmental aspects into business operations in this major forest products manufacturing plant depends upon the involvement of employees. To increase workforce involvement, JTS teams were set up to address specific projects, such as water usage, energy consumption, recycling, and highway litter. New teams are being created to address product packaging and design, education, and emissions (clean air). Efforts are made to have each JTS team consist of one person from each plant and one person from the common area.

Team ideas are generated from conversations among employees and from interaction at environmental conferences and presentations Collins employees make to universities and other entities. For example, one new team being developed is the Journey Awareness Team. The purpose of this team is to provide education to employees about "personal sustainability" and to form eco-teams and making presentations in the community, especially to schools. The initiative for the team started when Connie Grenz, the new Director of Strategic Management Services, learned about the work of Vicki Robin, co-author of *Your Money or Your Life,* during the five-day intensive workshop in Chicago organized by The Natural Step/U.S. in May 1998. Grenz saw a fit between these ideas and others that she learned of during a meeting with Oregon Department of Environmental Quality staff who were working on an initiative for the schools in Portland.

Another new team is the Product Packaging and Design Team. Grenz proposed this team after studying a plant flow diagram of products/materials and energy that came into the plant, were processed by the plant, and produced products and waste. She noticed that the Product Evaluation Team was focused on materials coming into the plants, while a team focused on products to be designed and produced was lacking.

After a team name and mission is conceived of and approved by the JTS team, all employees are invited to volunteer for the team. A team is composed of one person from each mill and one from the common area, to make four members. One becomes the lead person. Employees usually meet twice a month on work time. They report to the JTS team prior to its meetings, also held twice a month, where updates and any requests for funds are reviewed and approved or sent back to the sub-team with a response. Occasionally, the JTS team meets more often when special presentations are made, such as a recent presentation to maintenance employees regarding the impact of using various towel products. Both management and hourly employees are involved in JTS training.

Dale Slate, Vice President and General Manager of Collins Products LLC, comments that their biggest challenge is maintaining interest. He says: "It is difficult to keep the interest up, and that is true with any project you take on. But with this one in particular it's just because of the nature of it. We need to keep people focused. We went through the training process. Everybody was trained but then two months later you get the feeling that nothing's going on. So how do we keep people interested and keep the process going? The only way you do that is to refocus and become personally involved not only here but at home. If it becomes part of your daily business life, it has to influence your personal life."

Wilson estimates that currently about eight percent of the workforce really understand the training. That eight percent consists of people who are directly involved in one way or another on committees or in projects related to the journey to sustainability. With the formation of new JTS teams, Wilson estimates the number of people actively involved in JTS teamwork will reach 10 percent. Because of the nature of the work at the plants, Slate believes that 10 percent is an optimal number for active involvement in JTS activities at any given time.

Feedback and information are key elements to stimulate involvement. The plants have created 10 Journey to Sustainability Information Centers throughout the mills to keep employees informed, solicit their suggestions, and track progress on the projects that are initiated. Klamath Falls is converting a small building into a JTS center. The building acts as headquarters for JTS activities, and JTS meetings are held there. The walls serve to post sustainability information, the four System Conditions, and other inspirational material. In the future, visitors to the plant may be invited to visit the center to learn more about Collins Products' sustainability initiatives.

To facilitate involvement, not only in Klamath Falls but also across all Collins Pine facilities, functions, and activities, Quinn created a full-time position in the fall of 1998 to further the industrial ecology of the Collins Pine companies. Connie Grenz, Collins Pine's Director of Strategic Management Services, is currently splitting her time between Klamath Falls and headquarters in Portland. The major tasks of this new position are to

- be the corporate coordinator for industrial ecology issues
- support innovative sustainable practices in all Collins companies
- ensure that all new projects, products, and services are evaluated for sustainability
- ensure that measures are integrated into the planning process to prevent or minimize potential environmental impacts
- expand employee training and motivation regarding The Natural Step principles
- develop corporate systems and procedures to ensure operations are consistent with the principles of sustainable development

- develop baseline data and indicators of sustainability for the Collins companies
- ensure the adoption of lifecycle management
- coordinate environmental policy and action plans
- support strategic partners in the implementation of sustainable practices
- develop ways to motivate assimilation of The Natural Step principles
- liaise with external organizations that support eco-industrial initiatives
- ensure consistent and accurate communication about the Collins companies' vision, values, and ecological practices.

An important element of Grenz's work is to gather, integrate, and disseminate new knowledge about the environmental aspects of the Collins companies' business operations, and to work with JTS and other teams to address these aspects effectively. Her position is critical to strengthening the involvement of the Collins workforce in these initiatives, particularly through developing metrics and mechanisms that provide meaningful feedback to managers and employees with respect to sustainability initiatives. Grenz notes: "Being able to leverage your skills to support education and innovation while promoting a common environmental focus within our operations is a dream job. It's a noble challenge. In industry, there is always a price on the bottom line associated with the products we make. But with the environment, we are dealing with a priceless natural commodity. So our goal must be clean production for clean air and clean water. *We must act as if we are a solely-owned subsidiary of the environment.*"

The involvement of the company's leaders has been both evident and important. Quinn is a very visible CEO. He often visits the Klamath Falls facilities and is outspoken about his vision for Collins Pine as a leader in sustainability. Dale Slate considers it essential to model the integration of The Natural Step principles into daily behavior. This applies to large decisions and small symbolic actions alike. For example, when the JTS energy team was initiated, Slate decided to be chair of the committee because it was likely to have an important impact on the facilities. Slate comments: "I wanted everybody to know that the emphasis was going to be there, so I wanted to head that up and get it started." In fact, one of the pipe fitters said that when others thought that this team would be a "flash in the pan," he declared that if Dale Slate was behind it, it would happen.

Collins Products LLC at Klamath Falls is just beginning this journey to sustainability. Slate recognizes that it is a long road. People have to take ownership to be involved. He says: "We started out with what we called the three 'R's': reduce, reuse, recycle. But we realized that what we really needed to do was to get everybody to refocus. Before we're going to get anything else to work, everybody has to refocus on how they are doing things. People are so used to doing it the way they've always done it. Getting them to refocus on how we're going to do it in the future is our biggest task."

Integration: Actions and Results

Although the Journey to Sustainability is still in the early stages at Collins Pine, several initiatives have been launched to promote the integration of sustainable practices into business operations. Following are some examples of these early initiatives:

Environmental Impact of Purchasing Decisions

In the Klamath Falls manufacturing facility, all new product purchasing requires an environmental evaluation, including an assessment of the resources used, the waste produced, and the potential effect on air, water, food, and housing of the items purchased. This particularly applies to capital projects. Klamath Falls has created a decision-making matrix for capital projects that includes a Natural Step analysis. Does the project decrease dependence on materials from the Earth's crust? Does it decrease dependence on compounds produced by society that can accumulate in nature? How does it impact the physical basis for productivity and biodiversity in nature? Does it increase the efficiency with which resources are used? The company uses an 11-item checklist to consider these impacts not only on Collins' operation, but upstream and downstream as well. Wilson comments: "It can't just be good for us, it has to be good for the environment in general."

Before a capital project is undertaken, the department evaluates it with a checklist. The JTS team reviews the checklist with the department manager or project sponsor to determine whether each item has been fully investigated. (for a sample of the form, see Figure 8.5, p. 161). Slate believes that this process has been very beneficial, in many cases helping managers sell their projects. The careful analysis adds additional economic advantages as well as meeting the environmental criteria Klamath Falls seeks. Slate comments: "The manager of particleboard was the first one to have to go through The Natural Step evaluation for a capital project. He said that the evaluation probably helped him more than anything else in putting better numbers together because the JTS team asked him some pretty hard questions. They asked him questions that he hadn't thought about. That JTS team is composed of people from all of the departments. So they were people that did not know a lot about the project, so they asked questions that people who were familiar with the project probably wouldn't have asked."

All new product purchases are now being reviewed by the JTS Product Evaluation Team (PET) to ensure that new and existing products purchased for the plant site meet or exceed the standards defined by the four System Conditions. To facilitate the process of purchasing sustainable products, the PET has developed a New Product Submittal Form, a short questionnaire that must be filled out by the purchaser and submitted to the team with a material safety data sheet if applicable (a form required by law for any materials that may pose health and safety risks for employees). This particularly applies to products containing harmful or potentially hazardous chemicals (for a sample of the product evaluation team form, see Figure 8.4, p. 161).

The product evaluation team is also initiating an inventory process of products used on site. For example, PET has also created a plant-wide listing of 1,050 material safety data sheets for the purpose of reviewing site material input of potentially hazardous elements. JTS area coordinators are using a 20-page list to review all the types of cleaners being used on site to see what can be eliminated or, when an element is in violation of the System Conditions, what substitutes are possible. Through this process, the product evaluation team has learned, for example, that seven different glass cleaners are presently used on-site. The goal is to reduce that number to one or two cleaners that have the most favorable impact on the environment.

The JTS team is also notifying all suppliers of Collins Products' Journey to Sustainability goals and has asked them to use biodegradable packing materials wherever possible as a first step toward working together to reduce impact on the environment.

Energy

The mission of the energy team (E-team) is to reduce total energy consumption on the plant site. Since March 1998, the particleboard E-team has initiated 59 work orders that will result in better use of energy resources. They break down as follows: 16 saving electricity, 38 saving steam or condensate, and 5 saving on water. Eleven of these work orders are currently in progress. Of the 48 that have been completed, the following two projects illustrate successful efforts in maximizing the efficient use of resources:

Maximizing Performance of Steam Traps. The energy team started preventive maintenance on 80 steam traps, which were inventoried as to their make, size, style, and operating status. Then they were taken apart, cleaned, and rebuilt. The new preventive maintenance procedure includes doing ultrasonic and thermal checks monthly. The team found that one-third of the traps were in disrepair, leading to inefficient losses of steam. Now the waste traps are recovering more than 90 percent of what was going to wastewater, at estimated savings of $25,000/year due to reduction in natural gas, electricity to pump water, and chemicals. In addition, employees are happier to see processes put in place to manage resources efficiently.

Insulation Repairs. The energy team started an ongoing process to repair and replace insulation on steam lines. This has provided an added convenience to plumbers assigned to mills.

Since March 1998, the hardboard facility has set up 39 work orders to address E-team concerns. Thirty are completed. They have installed automatic controls over lighting in the truck loading area to turn off lights during daylight hours. The projected energy savings are estimated to be more than 21 M kwh/yr or about $804/year. As the result of mini-audits, numerous leaks in insulation and steam traps have been repaired.

As a result of an energy team audit, approximately 24 work orders have been written in the plywood division. Most are complete. These projects are increasing efficiencies in eight electrical, two water, and 14 steam areas. The plywood mill is now taking condensate from the dryer for veneer and turning it back into flash steam and then using that flash steam for heating water that treats the blocks in the vaults. Previously, they used 12,000 to 18,000 Btu/hours of 300 lbs steam running for 24 hours. Savings for reduced powerhouse steam is estimated to be $152,000/year. In addition, in October 1998, 26 work orders were written for emission readings, fiber control activities, and ground water contaminant checks.

Efficient and Effective Use of Resources

Quinn comments that "we want to manage our resources appropriately and run a successful business off of that, but we think we shouldn't have to do it at the expense of the environment." Rather than truck away or let sit the unusable piles of fine, dark brown organic material that remain after trees are processed, Klamath Falls plans to spread the material for compost on a portion of the 800 acres of marginal farmland that Collins leases.

Another project Klamath Falls is undertaking is the recycling of sander-dust which is very fine powdery particle residuals from the production of particleboard. Previously, the plant was able to recover only about 30 percent of the sander dust and to recycle it into product. The remaining 70 percent were burned in a boiler to generate steam. Unfortunately, that required over-firing the boiler with natural gas because the sander dust didn't create sufficient thermal energy to completely combust. In addition, it created unwanted emissions. The boiler was out of compliance, and it would have cost between $500,000 and $750,000 to bring it into compliance. Instead, the plant has discovered how to recycle 100 percent of the sander dust for particleboard production. By shutting down the boiler, they reduced emissions by an estimated 543 tons/year and increased natural gas usage by 15 to 20 percent for the next two years, when they plan to have co-generation plant steam. Additionally, they are saving an estimated $525,000/year mainly due to reduced fiber purchase of about 14,000 bdt/year.

Quinn firmly believes that the thought processes stimulated by The Natural Step training helped to spur the innovative thinking on this project.

Another important capital project influenced by sustainability thinking was the replacement of six Pallmann generators with one Bliss Hammermill, resulting in savings of over 3 million kWh/year at approximately $118,000/year. In the process, they also were able to remove 18 Fenwall bottles (hazardous material) used for the fire suppression system.

The Klamath Falls facilities used to have a landfill that has now been taken out of use. Slate believes that having the landfill encouraged unsustainable behavior. Wilson agrees: "It's a real big deal to me on a daily basis because I have to make choices about where to put things that used to go into the landfill. I've got to either call around and find somebody who can use it or give it to somebody licensed to burn it as biomass."

Product Development

Collins Pine is seeking to develop its products by increasing its ability to produce third party-certified manufactured product including hardwood siding. To ensure the supply of certified raw materials for their products, Collins Pine has created another full-time position to locate certified sources. Larry Potts, former Vice-President and General Manager at the Chester, California, operation is now Vice-President of Sustainable Resource Development. In this role he is working to help other timberland owners enter into the independently verified sustainable forest management process. Potts is devoting all of his time to this position, promoting sustainability with the Collins Companies' suppliers as determined by criteria developed by the Forest Stewardship Council, wherever this makes strategic sense. This will enable Collins to procure a greater percent of material that can be used to produce certified wood products. Potts works with suppliers to support them in the certification process with a view toward ensuring an increased supply of certified raw material.

Recycling

As part of the goal toward zero waste, the JTS Recycling Team is heading the initiative to increase both awareness and practice of recycling in order to reduce the waste that goes to the community landfill. In 1998, the team set up three eight-yard cardboard recycling dumpsters for plywood, large signs to clearly identify all cardboard recycle boxes at all locations, and a process for all mills to track the number of loads taken for recycling. New signage was put in place for 13 office paper recycling stations. Pallets received with material from vendors were chipped for recycling. The hardboard plant began a process for returning packaging material to two vendors. Pallets returned to one vendor are equivalent to one truck load every six months. Eggcrates, cores, and pallets returned to the second vendor are equivalent to an estimated one truck load every nine months.

Water Conservation

With the leadership of the water ecological equilibrium team, Collins Products' goal is to eliminate water discharge to the river within five years. Toward that goal, the plywood plant is using discharge from their RF dryer to irrigate new landscaping in front of the mill. WE2T is tracing water lines to identify where meters may be installed to better measure water usage at the mills. "Water Facts" bulletins are being posted on JTS boards. In the particleboard and plywood plants, steam traps were evaluated and adjusted to minimize steam losses. In hardboard, performance modifications were set up to check all hydraulic system coolers and heat exchangers to maintain water flows and check valves at their prescribed levels. An inventory was made of all the air conditioners on site, revealing that some use a lot of cooling water.

In the hardboard siding plant, a five-ton-water-cooled air conditioner was replaced in the lathe operators control room, with an air-to-air model to test the feasibility of using the air-type model on site. The team held a water conservation contest, in which a prize was given for finding a leak in the sort yard, resulting in an estimated reduction of 525,000 gallons/year. During downtimes, unnecessary water flows are turned off throughout production. In particleboard, condensate from heat is returned by a steam-powered pump to the boilers instead of using new fresh makeup water, a process that reduces the need to retreat water and reduces water usage by about 2 million gallons/year.

Adopt-a-Highway

To contribute to the community and to keep the grounds near the plant sites clean of litter, a JTS team was established to coordinate participation in the adopt-a-highway program. The task of the team is to periodically pick up litter on three miles of road running along the plant site on Route 66. In 1998, 14 people were involved in picking up 50 bags worth of waste along six miles of roadside area.

In addition to these projects, at Klamath Falls the Journey to Sustainability is a regular agenda item in bi-weekly and monthly meetings. JTS project teams meet on average twice each month as does the core JTS Team. Progress in JTS projects is reported in operational reviews together with financial and other operational items. In this way, environmental aspects are becoming integrated with other daily operational considerations.

Final Reflections

In their forest operations, the Collins companies have been practitioners of sustainable development for decades. However, the purchase of the huge Klamath

Falls manufacturing complex presented a special set of challenges in every operational area. The mills doubled the size of Collins' business overnight, in terms of both revenues and number of employees. Integrating a workforce of this size into the Collins culture, its values, and its philosophy of sustainable operations presented a special challenge. It was in The Natural Step that CEO Jim Quinn recognized a knowledge platform to help in the necessary education and integration process. Although the company received its initial training in The Natural Step just one and a half years ago as of this writing, benefits to the company from The Natural Step are already apparent in at least three areas:

First, The Natural Step provides a means for Collins to express its philosophy and practice of environmental stewardship consistently in all of its operations, from forests to mills. The Natural Step is helping particularly to integrate and transform the pre-existing culture at the newly-acquired Klamath Falls manufacturing facilities into the culture of stewardship and sustainability already prevailing within the Collins companies. The Natural Step is helping the Collins workforce understand sustainability at the environmental, social, and financial levels, as well as its relevance to their day-to-day work.

Second, The Natural Step training and framework are promoting a more efficient use of resources both at the Klamath Falls manufacturing complex and at other Collins operations. Savings in resource use go directly to the financial bottom line. Journey to Sustainability teams have been established to reduce point source emissions, waste water, and waste to landfills as well as to improve energy efficiency and so on — in short, to operate the mills with higher efficiency, lower waste, and lower costs.

Third, The Natural Step analyses required for purchasing and capital project requests have stimulated innovative problem solving and out-of-the-box thinking. As noted above, The Natural Step framework applied to expenditure decisions has already resulted in verifiable cost savings in addition to reduced environmental impact.

As one comes to understand and appreciate the relationship of stewardship, care, and sustainability that the Collins companies have enjoyed with their forests and their workforce for generations, one cannot help but compare this to the boom-bust "take-make-waste" mentality that has been so characteristic of much of the forest-products industry in North America over the past two hundred years. The Collins family have quietly, responsibly, and profitably been stewarding their forests and their communities for merely 150 years. As it was literally a natural step to the adoption of TNS for their manufacturing operations, it seems likely that the Collins companies and The Natural Step will enjoy a sustaining relationship for many years to come.

PART THREE

THE EVOLUTIONARY JOURNEY

The most meaningful activity in which a human can be engaged is one that is directly related to human evolution. This is true because human beings now play an active and critical role not only in the process of their own evolution but in the survival and evolution of all living beings. Awareness of this places upon human beings a responsibility for their participation in and contribution to the process of evolution. If humankind would accept and acknowledge this responsibility and become creatively engaged in the process of metabiological evolution consciously, as well as unconsciously, a new reality would emerge, and a new age would be born.
Jonas Salk
Anatomy of Reality

CHAPTER 8

Transformation by Design: Lessons, Tools, and Methodologies

The implementation and institutionalization of design requires the establishment of a system that will bring about the change implied by the design. Designers should set forth a set of functions that the implementation systems should carry out. These functions include the definition and display of the system we designed, the contemplation of the implication of the implementation of design, and the definition of the implementation functions.
Bella H. Banathy — *Designing Social Systems in a Changing World*

THE CHALLENGE of operationalizing sustainability is common to every company that embarks upon the journey. For the first wave of pioneers, there is no clear map — they must become the map makers or, using another metaphor, the system designers. The companies presented in this book are among these pioneer designers of new human systems. The lessons they have learned, much of it with considerable effort, and the tools and methodologies they are using, represent significant learning and provide many valuable ideas that can be adapted to other companies.

Nine Key Lessons

In the course of research, we travelled to over 50 different industrial and commercial sites and spoke to hundreds of people across North America and Europe. From this research, we have drawn nine key lessons set out below and expanded upon in greater detail in this and the following two chapters. Although some of these insights seem very basic, it is surprising how few managers seem to understand them at a visceral level.

1. Moving a corporation toward sustainability means change, often fundamental change, in the corporation's culture. A proactive attitude toward change is the most effective approach.

2. Leadership is the cornerstone of any major change initiative. Endorsement and active support from the top signal that the initiatives required to make sustainability operational will be given the priority and the resources necessary to achieve the objective.

3. Conscious organizational learning is fundamental for success in making change. For any investigation into how to apply sustainability principles, a corporate culture that supports experimentation is a necessity. The company recognizes that most real learning happens by doing. In such an atmosphere, ideas are celebrated whether they lead to anticipated outcomes or not. All ideas are welcome. Mistakes are viewed as necessary to learning and are documented for knowledge to be gained from the effort.

4. The vision of sustainability for the company should be well articulated and aligned with the visions and values of individuals within the company. This provides the basis for developing a shared vision and aspirations that are sufficiently compelling to inspire commitment.

5. A common knowledge base about sustainability throughout the corporation accelerates involvement and innovation. This includes developing a new shared mental model of what sustainability means, why it is important, and how it relates to the business of the corporation. Extensive employee involvement reinforces learning, stimulates innovation, moves sustainability from theory to practice, and helps embed whole systems thinking into the corporate culture.

6. Feedback at every level of the process reinforces learning and involvement and helps move ideas into action. Measurement provides indispensable information required for further learning. Because measuring environmental performance is a relatively new field, it is often necessary to experiment with what is most appropriate to measure and what type of metrics to employ. A culture of experimentation plays an essential role.

7. From a whole-systems perspective, the company views itself as part of a larger system of relationships of influence that includes shareholders, employees, suppliers, customers, competitors, communities, and other stakeholders. Promoting the company's sustainability agenda throughout all of these relationships accelerates the move toward sustainability.

8. The move toward sustainability is an evolutionary shift. It fundamentally changes the structure of business practice from a linear configuration to a cyclical process in harmony with natural systems. Although this is a profound shift in a mental model, the process of actually moving from the company's current reality toward sustainability usually takes place in a step-by-step process that simultaneously seeks to safeguard corporate

financial sustainability as it moves toward ecological and social sustainability.

9. The Natural Step framework is not an end in itself — it is a means to move humankind toward a sustainable society in balance with the rest of the natural world. The four System Conditions provide the first order principles that any society and company must meet to be truly sustainable. However, they do not provide the vision of what that society or company will look like, nor do they prescribe the specific steps or decisions a society or company should take in order to get there. The Natural Step framework is most effective when used in conjunction with other tools and methodologies such as environmental management systems, lifecycle analyses, resource inventories, environmental audits, and design for environment practices.

Tools and Methodologies

A diverse range of instruments and practices is currently being used to move corporations toward sustainability. Those being used by the four companies described in Part Two are summarized in Figure 8.1. The table is set up as a matrix listing eight aspects that are important to change initiatives in a corporation: leadership, vision and strategy; training, education, and coaching; employee involvement; practical application and innovation; feedback and measurement; influence; and integration into all business functions. Each aspect is linked to a set of statements that identify the general focus or objectives to be addressed. Then tools and methodologies are listed to address those areas of focus or objectives. While Figure 8.1 provides a general overview of a wide variety of tools and methodologies, the following are examples of some specific tools for each aspect.

Leadership

One of the most common tools used internally for engaging the support of company leadership is awareness and education. This is accomplished through a variety of means. At IKEA, education began with the task force analysis of the relationship between the business, the market, and the natural environment at the instigation of the president or chief operating officer. This led to the compilation of information that was shared with the senior management group through presentations and workshops. At Scandic, awareness began with presentations and dialogue among the executive staff about the relationship of environmental issues to the "new Scandic," at the instigation of the chief executive officer. This was shared with all hotel general managers and executive staff at the Iceland meeting of all senior staff and operations managers. At Interface, awareness began when the chief executive officer was asked to provide his company

Aspect	Focus/Objective	Tools and Methodologies Figure 8.1
Leadership	CEO/COO support Top management group support Engage other internal leaders (managers, supervisors) Demonstrate leadership	Ask CEO for his/her environmental vision for the company Introduce top management to the business case for sustainability Provide education and coaching in sustainability for middle managers and supervisors Have the CEO and other top leaders communicate the importance of sustainability to the business through videos, annual reports, memoranda to employees, speeches
Vision and Strategy	Develop the vision of a sustainable company in a sustainable society	Back-casting using The Natural Step framework Intuitive audits Exercises clarifying the corporate vision and mission statement to ensure they are in harmony with the framework for sustainability Exercises to identify "low-hanging fruit" Exercises to identify high-leverage areas where a certain amount of input will be magnified significantly into output or value for the company Financial modelling based on the new vision and high-leverage initiatives Detailed resource flow audits of facilities, processes, products, and systems Environmental policy Environmental action plans
Training, Education, Coaching	Educate all employees Provide ongoing coaching to help embed principles into practice Provide specialized education in new areas of knowledge required to move toward sustainability	Adapt TNS training materials and language to specific industry/business context and to specific profile of workers Develop training program, often train the trainers or coaches within and throughout the company Clear, tailor-made user-friendly training materials for internal trainers, generally designed in conjunction with an experienced TNS trainer/coach Games and exercises Booklets for all employees Exercises to identify "low-hanging fruit" Videos and other materials produced both internally and externally Access to expertise and resources to identify and provide areas of more advanced education or to help coaches answer challenging questions Experimental/breakthrough learning exercises to encourage trust and risk taking
Employee Involvement	Leadership example Team building Get everyone to try to apply sustainability concepts Encourage suggestions Encourage continual learning Continually reinforce and regenerate the process	Leadership involvement made visible through marker events indicating the new direction for the company, through videos and other media, through participation on project teams, etc. Games and exercises that require teamwork to identify ways to reduce waste and resources used Teams to address specific issues or formed around specific sustainability projects Employee suggestion processes with clear follow-through Environmental coordinators, facilitators, trainers, coaches, networks that facilitate the flow of information, resources, ideas, etc. Friendly competitions among employees, business units, geographic units, etc. to achieve specific sustainability goals such as resource savings, waste savings, etc. Meetings, celebrations, workshops, advanced training

Aspect	Focus/Objective	Tools and Methodologies	Figure 8.1 cont.
Practical Application and Innovation	"Low-hanging fruit" Practical ideas for change	Establish a framework for sustainability as an important criterion of how each job gets done Develop mechanisms for reviewing suggestions and innovations Provide the resources to try new idea. Experiment Provide on-going coaching with respect to specific applications Develop mechanisms for sharing what is learned	
Feedback/ Measurement	Track, evaluate, build on successes Track, evaluate, learn from mistakes Acknowledge initiative and involvement through immediate feedback, by taking concrete actions, or by advising why actions can't be taken Measure results Make results visible Reward and acknowledge results	Develop baseline information Develop metrics (resource-flow inventories, industry-specific metrics) Documentation of experiments and learning to generate more learning, recorded problems, attempted solutions, results, knowledge gained, etc. Benchmark Post results Translate resource savings into both financial and environmental indicators Awards, recognition of team results, individual initiatives, company-wide achievements Communication through bulletins, websites, newsletters, etc.	
Influence	Employees Suppliers Customers Competitors Shareholders Communities Other stakeholders	Workshops for suppliers on the framework for sustainability and the company's new expectations Partnerships with suppliers to develop ecologically and economically sustainable solutions to specific problems Partnerships with community groups such as schools, civic organizations, business associations to communicate the sustainability vision Booklets for customers Labelling of products Workshops for clients and customers that communicate the company's vision and actions Partnerships with scientific groups, academia, environmental groups, etc. to strengthen knowledge base, increase access to information, communicate goals, develop shared objectives to accelerate the move toward sustainability Annual reports Sustainability reports Environmental reports Websites	
Integration into all Business Functions	Make sustainability a normal business consideration	Environmental management systems Make sustainability initiatives and progress a part of all regular business meetings Include sustainability criteria into financial reporting requirements, capital requests, purchasing decisions Include sustainability achievements into performance evaluation and bonus structures Incorporate sustainability goals into the business plan	

with an environmental vision. Serendipitously, when *The Ecology of Commerce* was passed on to him to prepare for a meeting with an important prospective client, he found his vision. Thereafter, engaging other company leaders was done through the chief executive officer's "persistent drumbeat" about the new vision he saw for Interface and with his persistent willingness to share his awareness and to educate others. In Collins Pine, the idea of extending sustainability to mill operations was initiated by the chief executive officer and then realized through presentations and dialogue with senior management. In three out of four companies — IKEA, Scandic, and Collins Pine — The Natural Step played an important role in structuring the information for the dialogue and presentations. At Interface, *The Ecology of Commerce* played a catalytic role. Here, The Natural Step was introduced after top management had already been engaged with a vision of sustainability by the chief executive officer.

Once the senior leadership is committed to the concept of sustainable development for the company, it is important to demonstrate and communicate this engagement to others. The tools used to do this include videos featuring messages from the chief executive officer, chief operating officer, or founder; direct communications with employees; speeches; annual reports; newsletters; and the sharing of media coverage with employees.

Vision and Strategy

Most companies invest time developing their vision and strategies. The distinction with respect to sustainability is asking the question: "What does a sustainable company look like?" More specifically, "What does this company look like if it is sustainable?" This is an area where The Natural Step makes a significant contribution through the process of combining the System Conditions with back-casting (described in more detail in Chapter 2).

This process is often accompanied by intuitive audits, that is, audits based on general experience rather than detailed quantitative analyses; exercises for aligning the corporate vision and mission statements with sustainability; exercises to identify "low-hanging fruit" for early cost savings; and exercises to identify high-leverage areas that can become platforms for future action. Such exercises are common to visioning and strategic planning. The difference with The Natural Step is the use of the four System Conditions as the core mental model. The intuitive visioning process is followed by more concrete strategic processes, such as financial modelling and detailed resource flow audits. The outcome of the process is generally the development of new tools, such as an environmental policy and an environmental action plan for the business. Samples of environmental policy statements are included in the case studies in Part Two. Environmental action plans can be drawn up for the organization as a whole and/or for individual units. For example, IKEA has developed an environmental action plan for the whole company. Each region, such as IKEA North America, is expected to develop a compatible environmental action plan. In the case of IKEA North America, this plan is integrated with the unit's business plan. In turn, each North American IKEA retail store develops its own environmental action plan. (Because of the length and diversity of such plans, it is not possible to include a sample in this volume.)

Training, Education, and Coaching

Building a knowledge base about sustainability in the organization is essential for a successful integration of sustainable development into business practices. The primary objectives are to educate all employees, to provide coaching to help embed sustainability principles into practice, and to provide specialized education in the new areas of knowledge required to move toward sustainability. The general tools used are training programs, curricula, training materials, and access to expertise and resources. All four companies instituted new training programs that adapt The Natural Step training materials and language to their specific industry and business. IKEA, Scandic, and Collins Pine are using a train-the-trainers model. Interface is conducting training through its own in-house training organization, One World Learning. Our case studies provide detailed information about each company's training program, including some of the specific language and tools they use. In each case, The Natural Step functions as a knowledge platform upon which to create the company's own education and training program for sustainability.

Employee Involvement

One of the fundamental challenges is to move sustainability from theory to practice. After everyone participates in the new training program, the tools employed to reinforce learning generally include processes to encourage employee suggestions for improvements; games and exercises like Scandic's Environmental Dialogue; team-building initiatives, such as Scandic's Resource Hunt, Interface's QUEST/EcoSense teams, and Collins Pine's Journey to Sustainability teams; and support networks such as IKEA's and Scandic's environmental coordinators' networks and Interface's QUEST/EcoSense network. Other tools include friendly competitions to meet sustainability goals among units, such as stores, mills, hotels, and subsidiary companies, as well as between countries; celebrations of achievements; and awards and recognition for individual and collective contributions to sustainability goals. These tools are described in our case studies.

Practical Application and Innovation

Involvement needs to be reinforced with practical application for changes to become embedded in day-to-day practice. The objectives for this aspect include taking advantage of the ideas to pluck "low-hanging fruit" that ripened during the education and involvement processes and encouraging the generation of practical ideas for change that lead in the direction of sustainability. If a company is going to encourage involvement through soliciting suggestions, effective mechanisms are necessary to review and act on those suggestions. IKEA ran into trouble when it first instituted its environmental training because it was not equipped to deal with the volume of suggestions generated. Scandic, on the other hand, created a process where suggestions generated during the environmental dialogue were prioritized immediately and became part of the individual hotel's environmental action plan. At Collins Pine, suggestions are referred to the main JTS coordinating team where it is determined how best to respond to, and incorporate, the suggestions. If an appropriate team does not exist yet, it is created. In all of the companies, resources are committed to implementing good ideas. Another important tool to assist in the practical application of sustainability principles is coaching and sharing what is learned. IKEA, Scandic, and Collins Pine have designated personnel who serve as in-house coaches to others. These coaches provide information and assistance as specific questions and issues arise. They often receive advanced or specialized training and are connected with relevant networks of information and expertise. If they do not have the answers themselves, they are authorized to find them. At Interface, Interface Research Corporation provides technical and information resources through the QUEST/EcoSense team structure (see the case studies for more detailed information).

Measurement and Feedback

Measurement and feedback are fundamental to embedding sustainability into business practices. In general, the objectives of metrics are to measure results and to make them visible; to track, evaluate, and learn from both successes and mistakes; and to reward results and encourage continued improvement. The challenge is to develop the appropriate metrics and base-line information. The tools used are similar to those that document other business areas. They include developing industry-specific metrics, benchmarking, conducting resource-flow inventories, translating resource savings and costs into both financial and environmental indicators, documenting both successes and failures that result from experimenting with specific applications, communicating results, and recognizing achievements.

Both Scandic and Interface have already developed very sophisticated eco-metrics: Interface with its QUEST program and QUEST/EcoSense 2000, and Scandic with its Resource Hunt, which is included in Scandic's BINC benchmarking system. The result of Scandic's environmental work is measured on a quarterly basis using, among other methods, an environmental index, which is a target-controlled benchmarking tool for measuring how a number of priority

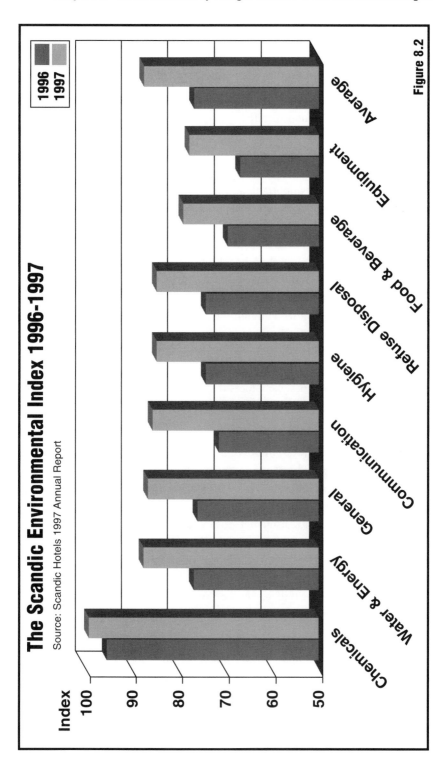

The Scandic Environmental Index 1996-1997

Source: Scandic Hotels 1997 Annual Report

Figure 8.2

environmental activities are progressing at each hotel. The Scandic Environmental Index for 1996/97 is presented in Figure 8.2. Sånga-Säby, another company using The Natural Step framework, is featured in Chapter 9. Working with the Stockholm House of Sustainable Economy, Sånga-Säby has developed sophisticated metrics to measure environmental progress based directly on the four System Conditions. A sample of the metrics is included as Figure 8.3 (for a full presentation of Sånga-Säby's detailed environmental report based on The Natural Step framework, refer to their website listed in the Resources section of this book, P. 212).

IKEA is developing important baseline information through resource-flow inventories of its stores and resource inventories of all of its product lines. These are important baselines for the stair model approach IKEA is applying to all its operations and suppliers. IKEA has developed a detailed manual on conducting a resource balance for a store that specifically relates the material balance analyses to the four System Conditions. Interface conducted a sophisticated resource-flow analysis that is presented in its *Sustainability Report* (see the Resources section for information on how to obtain the report). Collins Pine is just beginning to develop baseline information of the resource flows at the Klamath Falls mills.

Tools to provide feedback include posting results of achievements and measurements, recognizing results, and communicating with employees, shareholders, customers, and other stakeholders through bulletins, websites, newsletters, and other reports.

Influence

A company influences and is influenced by many stakeholders, including shareholders, employees, suppliers, customers, competitors, and communities. Tools used to influence stakeholders involve creating partnerships with suppliers to advance sustainability goals; partnerships with environmental organizations, scientific networks, and academia to increase knowledge and awareness; reports, such as annual, environmental, and sustainability reports; information materials for customers; and workshops for suppliers, customers, or communities to convey the company's sustainability goals and vision. The table (Figure 8.1) lists many of the tools these four companies use to communicate with and influence these stakeholders. Our case studies provide more detail.

Integration into All Business Functions

Ultimately, the goal is to make sustainability a normal, everyday business consideration as natural to good business practice as accurate financial accounting or quality control. Some of the tools to accomplish this involve making sustainability initiatives part of all regular business meetings; including sustainability criteria in financial reporting requirements, purchasing decisions, and capital requests; including sustainability achievements in employee performance evaluation and

Sånga-Säby: Environmental Report
Presentation of results

Figure 8.3

These tables show the key ratio results based on data for the entire year. The symbols show the trend from 1996 to 1997 and can be interpreted thus:

 Positive change from the previous year

 No change from the previous year (± 3% sensitivity)

 100% result over two or several years

 Negative change from the previous year

System condition 1: Substances from the Earth's crust must not systematically increase in nature!

Key Ratio	Numerator	Denominator	1994	1995	1996	Result	Target-98
Environm. vehicles, prop.	Biofuel-driven vehicles	All vehicles	0,8	1,00	1,00	↻	1,00
Heavy Metal, mercury	Hg in sludge, limit value mg/kg	Hg in sludge, mean value/yr	3,97	7,81	9,61	↗	9,50
Heavy Metal, cadmium	Cd in sludge, limit value mg/kg DS	Cd in sludge, mean value/yr	1,99	2,87	4,86	↗	4,80
Heavy Metal, lead	Pb in sludge, limit value mg/kg	Pb in sludge, mean value/yr	1,43	2,47	4,6	↗	4,60
Heavy Metal, chromium	Cr in sludge, limit value mg/kg	Cr in sludge, mean value/yr	4,76	8,33	6,15	↘	6,80
Heavy Metal, nickel	Ni in sludge, limit value mg/kg	Ni in sludge, mean value/yr	4,17	7,52	5,45	↘	6,00
Heavy Metal, copper	Cu in sludge, limit value mg/kg	Cu in sludge, mean value/yr	0,87	2	2,05	⇒	2,20
Heavy Metal, zinc	Zn in sludge, limit value mg/kg	Zn in sludge, mean value/yr	1,7	3,64	3,52	↘	3,70
Bioenergy margin	Renewable energy	Total energy consumption	0,03	0,94	1,00	↗	1,00
Biofuel margin	Biofuel for heating	Total biofuel for heating, litres	0,36	0,99	1,00	⇒	1,00

Product Evaluation Team (PET)

Figure 8.4

Goal, Product Standards, and Procedures
(excerpt)

Goal: To assure that new and existing products purchased for plantsite use, meet, or exceed the standards defined below in accordance with the procedures outlined below.

Product Standards: **Does this product:**(Refer to product MSDS if available)

	Reduce	**Same**	**Increase**
• Reduce (not increase) dependence on fossil fuels and mining?	❐	❐	❐
• Reduce (not increase) dependence on compounds produced by society that can accumulate in nature?	❐	❐	❐
• Reduce (not increase) dependence on activities which intrude on productive parts of nature, e.g long road transports; paving over green surfaces?	❐	❐	❐
• Increase the efficiency with which resources are used?	❐	❐	❐

Source: Collins Products LLC

bonus structures; incorporating sustainability goals into the business plan; and instituting environmental management systems.

In Scandic Hotels, the Resource Hunt is a regular agenda item in all department meetings. The Resource Hunt is also an integral part of the benchmarking system that measures the overall performance of each hotel. Thus the performance of the general manager and other hotel staff is based, in part, on environmental performance. At Collins Products in Klamath Falls, Journey to Sustainability progress is reported as a regular part of monthly staff meetings together with production and financial reporting. Collins Products has also developed processes to ensure that new purchase decisions are consistent with its sustainability vision. Figure 8.4 is an excerpt from the Product Evaluation Team's document on Product Standards and Procedures.

Figure 8.5

Collins Products
Expense Request Checklist

Project: _____

E.R. CHECK LIST

1. Will this project increase or decrease energy usage (i.e., electricity / steam) compared to the existing system? Explain.

2. Will this project require the use of chemicals? Y / N
   If yes, what type of chemicals, more or less than presently used, and how much per week, per month, per year?

3. Will this project require the use of consumable supplies (i.e., packaging)? Y/ N If yes, explain.

4. Will this project impact air emissions, point source or fugitive, indoor or outdoor? Y / N If yes, can it be measured? Y / N If yes, explain.

5. Will this project require the use of water in any way? Y / N
   If yes, explain.

6. Will this project create or increase any form of waste? Y / N
   If yes, explain.

7. How will this project impact the 3 Rs (REDUCE, REUSE, RECYCLE)?

8. Will this project impact the use of man made chemicals and compounds? Y / N If yes, explain.

9. Will this project increase our use of materials extracted from the earth's crust (i.e., metals)? Y / N

10. Can construction be altered to minimize our use of natural resources, minimize waste material and maximize the use of recycled materials? Y / N

11. Will this project result in an increase in board production? Y / N
    If yes, explain.

In addition, Collins Products is now applying the Natural Step System Conditions to all capital and maintenance project requests (see Figure 8.5 for an excerpt from this form). At Interface, 15 percent of the performance bonus is based on whether the company is meeting its sustainability goals.

Environmental management systems are an important tool for the integration of sustainability into business operations and are becoming a recognized standard indicating environmental responsibility. Because of the complexity and value of environmental management systems, Chapter 9 provides an in-depth look at how they relate to The Natural Step framework.

Advantages and Limitations of The Natural Step

To assess the advantages and limitations of The Natural Step to corporations, one must distinguish between The Natural Step framework and The Natural Step as an organization. The Natural Step framework, described in detail in Chapter 2, consists of back-casting, four principles of sustainability (the System Conditions), and a strategic step-by-step process by which companies move from their current reality toward sustainability. The Natural Step organization is an international network of non-profit organizations, generally constituted for the purpose of sustainability education, dialogue, and continual learning. The organization bases its work on science and uses The Natural Step framework in the development of educational programs and materials, scientific studies, dialogue about challenging or contentious issues, and practical applications at every level of society. The organization also studies the use of the framework in different sectors and other organizations, and the compatibility of the framework with other tools and methodologies designed for moving society toward a more sustainable future.

Advantages

In the course of our research, the major advantages expressed regarding The Natural Step organization are that it bases its methods on science, does not assign blame, sees business as a vital force in moving society toward sustainability, and seeks to support best practice to encourage learning and sharing of ideas. The Natural Step organization is nonprescriptive, nonconfrontational and nonjudgemental. Its methodology is a consensus process that seeks to bring all sectors of society into dialogue. In its methodology and implementation in corporations, practitioners of The Natural Step employ methodologies similar to those used within the quality movement, along with concepts from learning organization theory, both of which are familiar to and considered desirable by many business people. The Natural Step theory is intellectually open and evolving, inviting creative development of its core principles and all aspects of its praxis. There is an attitude within the organization of "learning by listening." Even when criticized, The Natural Step's prevailing attitude is to learn in each instance and, where necessary, to make modifications to the framework or practice.

The intellectual framework of The Natural Step provides several advantages and benefits to corporations. The System Conditions provide a comprehensive definition of an environmentally sustainable society that is based on scientific principles and is easily understood. This makes it an effective tool for decision-making, planning, and training. The framework is valid at any scale and activity. It can be used as an integrating framework to seamlessly tie together many different components of a system into one coherent whole, such as different and disparate environmental programs within an organization. It provides a shared mental framework that enables teams or groups of people to work toward a common goal despite diverse technical and professional languages or backgrounds. Using the framework to analyze important issues and to guide key business decisions helps a company avoid costly mistakes of focusing on short-term solutions that are unsustainable in the long term.

The framework encourages people to think "upstream" in cause and effect chains to the first-order principles of any system. By doing so, they are able to understand the causes of problems more easily and address problems more accurately. Analyses of detailed "downstream problems" then flow more logically. This supports problem-solving that tends not to create new problems for the future. It provides a common scientific basis for the creation of auditable measurements and indicators, such as resource efficiency within corporations, which become a measure of progress toward sustainability. The framework is not used as an alternative to other decision-supporting tools, such as lifecycle assessment, streamlined lifecycle assessment, design for environment, ecological footprint[1], factor four or factor ten, or environmental management systems. Rather, the framework is used to guide people using these specific tools toward a science-based vision of sustainability (see Chapter 9 for a discussion of TNS and environmental management systems).

When training in The Natural Step framework is given to all members of an organization, it creates a shared mental model that facilitates communication within the organization and establishes a common platform of knowledge upon which to build an effective environmental management system throughout the organization. When training in the framework is taken by both a corporation's suppliers and its customers, it stimulates a new level of communication as well as a new level of product, service, and process innovation among the players. It can function as a catalyst for a closer commercial relationship between parties. This has been demonstrated many times in Sweden where there is the most experience with The Natural Step.

The use of the framework is action-oriented and realistic. The methodology prompts people to begin immediately to move the organization toward sustainability while recognizing that decisions and actions must be consistent with good business practice in both the short- and long-term. The approach is predicated on taking one logical step at a time.

While corporations are often looking for answers to specific issues or questions, The Natural Step organization generally does not provide these answers. Rather, it provides a *framework for thinking* that helps clarify and identify the right questions with respect to sustainability and a way to map out the steps for formulating and testing solutions. This is an advantage because the problems and issues a corporation faces will vary over time; however, the first-order principles of sustainability remain unaltered. It is also an advantage for a company to master thinking within this framework in order to be able to apply it to emerging issues. The Natural Step organization does not have all the scientific or technical expertise in-house to address the many issues and questions that arise across industries. Rather, it continuously develops and works with networks of scientists, engineers, technicians, and other professionals who understand how to use The Natural Step framework and to apply it to specific issues that arise within an industry context. Access to this useful network is possible through The Natural Step organization.

Limitations

One of the major limitations of The Natural Step organization expressed by the companies was its early lack of experience with the corporate sector and corporate applications. The organization, founded by Robèrt, a cancer researcher, had a strong scientific foundation but very little experience with business. While the logic and non-judgemental approach of The Natural Step framework appealed to corporations, the translation of the framework into business applications had to take place in the laboratory of actual business operations. This meant that, applying the framework, companies like IKEA and Scandic Hotels quickly developed experience that far outweighed that of the Swedish Natural Step organization.

Another criticism is that The Natural Step organization has not gone far enough in its assistance to corporations. Although generally viewed as providing the best structure for framing and thinking about sustainable development, and being an excellent source of basic education about the relationship between human activities and the natural world, The Natural Step organization has not provided implementation strategies, tactics, or tools to corporations after the companies received general education in the framework. This has been a cause of some frustration to corporations as they must design their own environmental management system and implementation strategy.

Although this causes corporations to genuinely and seriously engage with the issues themselves, they frequently express a desire for implementation expertise that is only now being developed and provided within the The Natural Step network.

The Natural Step organization is relatively young. The first organization, established in Sweden in 1989, was not constituted to become an international network. In the early years, the Swedish Natural Step organization mainly responded to overwhelming demands from many organizations and sectors generated by the national awareness campaign that launched its existence. It quickly overextended its reach and resources and has gone through several reconfigurations with respect to focus and activities. As groups in other countries expressed interest in using the framework, the Swedish Natural Step organization became engaged in expanding internationally before it was clear what it was doing nationally. In North America, Natural Step organizations have only been in existence in the United States since 1995 and in Canada since 1997. They have begun only recently to build the capacity to provide valuable services to businesses. This has frustrated businesses that became interested in the framework but were unable to find the necessary support. Interface, for example, would have engaged with The Natural Step/U.S. much earlier, had the organization been able to provide the necessary services. Instead, Interface has advanced with its own sustainability agenda, and it is only now able to integrate The Natural Step framework into its overall efforts as The Natural Step/U.S. organization develops.

In the United States, The Natural Step/U.S. has focused on building awareness and providing basic training in The Natural Step framework. Sometimes those who receive this training become overzealous in their enthusiasm for their new-found framework and do not adequately acknowledge, or sometimes even understand, the powerful and necessary work being done in other quarters to further the movement toward sustainability, such as environmental management systems (EMS), environmental assessments or audits (EA), environmental performance indicators (EPI), life-cycle analysis (LCA), and design for environment (DfE). The Natural Step framework is not only complementary to many of these tools, it adds value to them. Natural Step teams have been set up internationally to study how best to integrate the framework with other tools. However, this development is still in the early stages and is being facilitated by the actual experience of companies that are applying the framework.

The Natural Step framework is also relatively new as a mental model for strategic decision-making and implementation in a corporate setting. There is still relatively little written material to assist corporations in using the framework, and there is limited, albeit growing, expertise outside of the corporations using it with respect to how one can most effectively work with the framework. The Swedish Natural Step organization has worked successfully with several industry sectors, such as energy, metallurgy, agriculture, and forestry, to convene multi-stakeholder dialogues around key issues in industry. In the United States and Canada, The Natural Step organizations are also beginning to offer the service of convening multi-stakeholder dialogues to address critical, difficult, or potentially contentious issues for industry and society, using its framework, consensus building techniques, and the scientific and technical networks developed by The Natural Step organizations internationally. Like the organization and the framework themselves, these activities are relatively young and their impact and results have not been evaluated or widely communicated.

The four System Conditions have been criticized as being too vague, too general, too orthodox, or too subject to interpretation to be useful in the "real" world. The challenge of every company studied was the application of the principles. The framework does not tell the company what to do — it provides the first-order principles that must be met for sustainability. The company must still make decisions based on the best information and best technology available. Complaints that the framework and The Natural Step as an organization do not provide sufficient access to information to make decisions is being addressed as The Natural Step organizations are developing networks of scientists and other technical experts who understand the framework and can work with companies on specific issues.

The fourth System Condition has been viewed as both a strength and a weakness of The Natural Step framework. In dealing with both "fairness" and "efficiency," it mixes the domains of ethics and science. Some critics of the framework state that it is "heartless" and incomplete because it does not take a stronger position on the moral or ethical dimension of sustainable development. Others have suggested that the System Conditions would be stronger and more acceptable to business if the fourth condition were dropped altogether, or at least the ethical reference. The response of The Natural Step organization is that unless the ethical, or social equity element of the fourth condition is met on a global basis, the other three System Conditions will, in a world whose population will be approaching 10 billion people in the 21st century, not be met either. We believe that the fourth System Condition will continue to be refined, as may all the others, as The Natural Step becomes increasingly well known and more people have an opportunity to consider and influence the further development of The Natural Step and its framework.

Despite its limitations, The Natural Step framework is considered by IKEA, Scandic Hotels, Interface, and Collins Pine to provide the best available organizing structure for understanding sustainability. They are each experimenting with ways to further use the framework and to strengthen its utility for strategic planning. Together with The Natural Step organizations, these and other companies are building a knowledge base of experience and applications that will make it easier for new companies to adopt The Natural Step framework and to accelerate their organizational learning about sustainability.

CHAPTER 9

A Compass for Environmental Management Systems

by Susan Burns[1]

*I wish I had known about The Natural Step earlier.
We were introduced to The Natural Step after we had already built
our environmental management system. The Natural Step helps the nuts
and bolts of the environmental management system make more sense.
I believe the The Natural Step framework can help build a
stronger and better overall system.*
Larry Chalfan — *former President and CEO
Oki Semiconductor Manufacturing*

THE NATURAL STEP FRAMEWORK is a strategic planning tool with implications for an organization at every level. The framework provides a clear vision and a scientifically rigorous definition of what it means to be environmentally sustainable. It acts as a compass that helps to determine if a company is in fact moving in the direction of sustainability. However, because the framework does not prescribe what specific steps to follow, a company will gain the most benefit by integrating it with an environmental management system. For many sustainability goals, a formal environmental management system is an effective vehicle for implementation.

An environmental management system is primarily a vehicle designed to help a company achieve and demonstrate improved environmental performance. It provides a set of procedures for implementing and monitoring environmentally relevant business practices. Used in conjunction with The Natural Step framework, it provides a clear vision of where the business is headed and a practical methodology for getting there. This chapter describes how and why The Natural Step framework enhances environmental management systems and explores the approaches various companies are taking when they combine a traditional environmental management system with Natural Step-style systems thinking.

Environmental Management Systems Today

Formal environmental management systems are gaining popularity around the world. With the globalization of the economy, many companies are upgrading their environmental management systems to conform to international standards, such as the Eco-Management and Audit Scheme (EMAS) in Europe or the ISO 14001 Environmental System Standard created by the International Standards Organization.

The ISO 14001 standard was published in the fall of 1996 and is part of the ISO 14000 series of environmental standards. The technical committee that drafted ISO 14001 (TC 207) included representatives from most of the industrialized countries in the world. More than 5,000 sites worldwide have been certified to the standard by independent ISO 14001 registrars, and many more are creating "ISO-conforming" environmental management systems without seeking certification.

A formal environmental management system can yield many benefits, including increased environmental compliance, reduced costs and liabilities, reduced impact on the environment, and competitive advantage. In addition, business customers are increasingly requiring that suppliers become certified according to one of the internationally recognized standards, or at the very least, institute a credible environmental management system.

Karl-Henrik Robèrt compares an environmental management system to a powerful sailboat. The boat comes with a detailed instruction manual describing where the stern and bow are, how to operate the sails, etc. Robèrt adds, however, that building an environmental management system without a strategic planning tool (like The Natural Step framework) is like having no compass or map to guide the boat. The metaphor can be taken further: a typical environmental management system may certainly support a company in sailing along the familiar coastline of regulatory compliance and incremental improvement based on present conditions extrapolated into a predictable future, but it may be of little use in the stormy waters of the global economy and increasing, changing, and uncertain ecological pressures.[2]

With The Natural Step framework providing a compass to steer a company in the direction of ecological sustainability, a company's environmental management system can move beyond goals like compliance and incremental improvement to support goals such as market leadership and improved competitiveness. The environmental management system can provide the steps that lead to new opportunities and reduced costs that strengthen the bottom line as well as create a sustainable, or even restorative, economy.[3] According to Bertil Rosquist, Environmental Manager at McDonald's of Sweden: "ISO doesn't tell you anything about goals. You can be quite a polluting company and still get certified if your management system meets the standards."

The ISO 14001 standard is a template, but a company need not be seeking ISO certification to apply the guidelines outlined in this chapter. Application of an environmental management system varies enormously across different countries' legal systems and across different accreditation/certification frameworks, but the fundamentals are essentially the same.

The management system outlined in ISO 14001 is cyclic. The cycle begins with setting an environmental policy. Next, a company plans how it will carry out that policy, and then the plans are implemented. Progress toward goals is continually checked and, when necessary, corrective action is taken. Periodically, the organization's top management reviews the efficacy of the programs and the continued relevance of the original policy and plan. At the end of each cycle, policy and programs are reviewed and revised as necessary, and a new cycle begins.[4] Each of the components of a formal ISO 14001 management system are outlined in Figures 9.1 and 9.2.

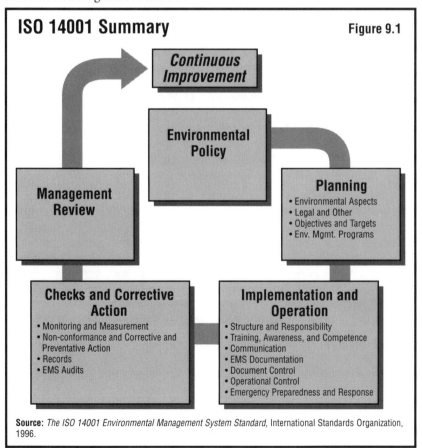

ISO 14001 Summary
Figure 9.1

Continuous Improvement

Environmental Policy

Management Review

Planning
- Environmental Aspects
- Legal and Other
- Objectives and Targets
- Env. Mgmt. Programs

Checks and Corrective Action
- Monitoring and Measurement
- Non-conformance and Corrective and Preventative Action
- Records
- EMS Audits

Implementation and Operation
- Structure and Responsibility
- Training, Awareness, and Competence
- Communication
- EMS Documentation
- Document Control
- Operational Control
- Emergency Preparedness and Response

Source: *The ISO 14001 Environmental Management System Standard*, International Standards Organization, 1996.

Figure 9.2

The ISO 14001 Environmental Management System

Environmental policy. Each iteration of an ISO 14001 cycle begins with top management setting or amending the environmental policy. At a minimum, a company's policy must express a commitment to compliance with environmental legislation and some form of continual improvement and prevention of pollution.

Planning. To facilitate ongoing evaluation of progress, a company must have procedures to identify environmental aspects and legal requirements and to determine which aspects have significant environmental impacts associated with them. Focusing on activities with significant environmental impacts, a company then sets objectives and measurable targets for improvement and designs programs to achieve those objectives and targets. The word "measurable" is important. For a company to be able to gauge progress, goals and targets must be measurable.

Implementation and operation. Once programs are designed, a company outlines a management structure and assigns roles and responsibilities to carry out the programs. Training needs are identified and employees are trained to ensure that they have the necessary awareness and competence to carry out their responsibilities. Procedures are established and maintained for communication regarding significant environmental impacts to relevant employees and to community members and interested stakeholders. The major components of the EMS must be documented and procedures must be established for controlling documents to ensure that they are up-to-date and can be located. Operational controls must be established and carried out for all activities that are associated with significant environmental impacts. In addition, the organization must establish and maintain procedures to mitigate environmental impacts associated with accidents and emergency situations.

Checks and corrective action. The organization must have documented procedures to monitor and measure activities that can have significant effects on the environment. They must also have procedures for handling and investigating nonconformance, taking action to mitigate effects caused as well as corrective and preventive action. Procedures must also be established and maintained to keep environmental records that demonstrate conformance with the requirements of the standard. Periodic audits are conducted to determine if the EMS conforms to the standard and has been properly implemented and maintained. The results of the audits must be provided to management.

Management review. At the end of each cycle, top management must evaluate the effectiveness and suitability of the EMS. Changes are made to improve the management system for the next round, and it starts again through the cycle.

Source: Adapted from Kranz & Burns, 1997.

There are many ways that The Natural Step framework can enhance an environmental management system. Jimmy Sjoblom, Environmental Manager of Sånga-Säby Hotel and Conference Center, notes: "By using the System Conditions, our ISO program is something we can use on the offence, rather than just guarding our back. The System Conditions tell us how far we can go, how far we can set our anchor. We are way beyond incremental improvements or defensive strategies. Defensive activities are not a constructive use of our resources." Bertil Rosquist of McDonalds of Sweden adds: "Since our whole environmental program is based on the System Conditions, incorporating The Natural Step into our ISO system will be no problem. In fact, ISO will solidify our goals even further."

Oki Semiconductor analyzed this ISO/TNS integration and identified at least 15 areas where the framework has added value to the process. In the ISO 14001 summary provided in Figure 9.1, the only areas where The Natural Step framework did not add value was in communication, environmental management system documentation, and document control under "Implementation and Operation." In every other area on the chart, The Natural Step framework improved the ISO process for Oki Semiconductor. Figure 9.3 is a summary of Oki Semiconductor's suggestions on how to integrate the two tools.

Integrating The Natural Step and ISO 14001 — Figure 9.3

1. Include Sustainability and TNS conditions in the company's environmental policy

2. Train all employees in the four system conditions, and include TNS in the induction process

3. Include TNS principles in the rating and ranking of environmental aspects
   - to help determine the significance of impacts on the environment
   - to help ensure objectives chosen are in accordance with sustainability
   - to help ensure resources expended will be balanced toward sustainability
   Use specific criteria from TNS for evaluation and ranking (in database)

4. Include TNS analyses in new materials, products, processes, and activities decisions
   - ensure new product/process system meeting agendas include TNS analyses
   - use ranking analysis sheets for thoroughness

5. Include confirmation of effective use of TNS analyses during internal audits
   - records confirming use must be defined and retained as objective evidence

6. Include a TNS activities review for effectiveness in Management Reviews
   - review the records as objective evidence, look for evidence of effectiveness

Source: Larry Chalfan, OKI Semiconductor.

173

Back-casting: How Strategic Planning for Sustainability Informs an Environmental Management System

Back-casting provides one of the most powerful tools for the strategic implementation of an environmental management system. Fundamental to The Natural Step framework as discussed in Chapter 2, back-casting is a method of strategic planning that aligns a company's long-term vision with the principles of sustainability. When back-casting, a company first analyzes its current situation in light of the funnel and the four System Conditions. It examines its current operations, products, and services to determine where it is most out of alignment with the principles of sustainability. For example, for System Condition One, it asks whether the company is dependent on materials from the Earth's crust that accumulate in nature. If so, are those materials used in a dissipative fashion? If so, is the company willing and able to phase out its dependence on this type of activity? This is done for each of the four System Conditions.

Next, the company envisions an ideal future in which it operates in accordance with the principles of sustainable society. This includes imagining how the marketplace of the future will view its products and services, and how its core competencies can be best positioned to service that market. This can be a tremendous source of creativity and innovation.

Finally, the company designs an action plan that will move it from its current reality to its long-term vision. It takes advantage of "low-hanging fruit", making sure that each short-term action serves as a platform for longer-term goals. This long-term strategic planning provides the direction for the environmental management system, which will then embed the strategic decisions made during back-casting.

The sustainability strategy embraced by Electrolux, the largest appliance manufacturer in the world, is an excellent example of this approach. In 1992, Electrolux formulated its vision and policy to guide its actions toward sustainability using The Natural Step framework. Electrolux states: "The vision presents images of our goals, the ideal situation that we constantly strive towards in our efforts to be a good neighbor in the global community. The basis of that is a thorough understanding of nature's limits and the sobering recognition of how our actions impact upon the environment. Our policy encompasses a holistic view of a product's entire lifecycle, from raw material handling and manufacturing to utilization to recycling." In Electrolux's view, an environmental management system offers a structure for its environmental work, a pathway to realizing its vision and policy. In 1995, Electrolux determined that all of its 150 production facilities worldwide would be ISO 14001 certified before the year 2000. The Electrolux 1997 environmental report credits collaboration with The Natural Step for inspiring their "holistic approach to environmental management."

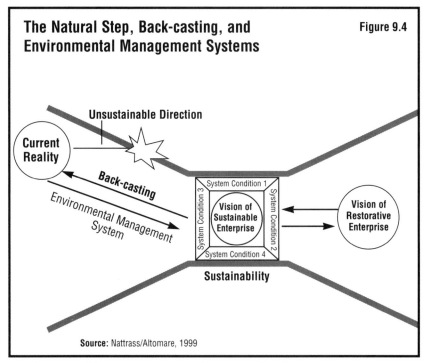

The Natural Step, Back-casting, and Environmental Management Systems

Figure 9.4

Unsustainable Direction

Current Reality

Back-casting

Environmental Management System

System Condition 3

System Condition 1

Vision of Sustainable Enterprise

System Condition 2

System Condition 4

Vision of Restorative Enterprise

Sustainability

Source: Nattrass/Altomare, 1999

This type of long-term strategic planning makes for a stronger environmental management system, especially when contrasted with the traditional forecasting approach of many companies. During forecasting, a company reviews its current impacts and sets targets that incrementally reduce its impacts year after year. This can lead to incremental improvements in environmental performance, but doesn't provide the type of leaps that are possible with seeing the whole picture. Companies that have a holistic picture and a strong vision of the future align multiple resources and departments toward this unified vision. If they don't have a holistic approach, a company's efforts could potentially move them along a number of different paths, without adding up to a coherent direction with significant improvements.

Advantages of Using The Natural Step Framework to Enhance an Environmental Management System

An environmental management system combined with a comprehensive sustainability vision supports a company's strategic goals and drives strategic decisions throughout the entire organization in a systematic way. Such an environmental management system will result in targets and objectives that take into account a global perspective and are keyed into the business's core strategy.

With ISO 14001 implementation, some companies stop at the plant boundary, assuming that certain issues are beyond the direct control of the facility being certified. The Natural Step framework can help expand and connect the environmental management system with other aspects of the business, and helps it to encompass as many domains of sustainability as possible. For example, a shared framework can help managers in product design, marketing, and manufacturing, to implement improvements more effectively throughout the entire product lifecycle.

The creation of an environmental management system, especially if one seeks certification, necessitates a serious commitment of company resources, particularly labor hours, to create the policies, procedures, and programs required, and to train employees in how to use the system. Especially if a company's current environmental management system is doing an adequate job of keeping the company in compliance, the investment in an enhanced system must be justified by significant new benefits to the company, and these ultimately must translate into increased profitability and enhanced competitive advantage. The Natural Step framework can help the environmental management system provide additional added value to the company.

Unfortunately, although our environmental problems are due to systemic errors in our relationship with nature, our regulatory system reacts to the downstream effects of these errors rather than addressing root causes. This keeps industry reacting to constantly changing environmental regulations rather than helping it get ahead of the game. A good example is the case of ozone-depleting chemicals. When chlorofluorocarbons (CFCs) were initially restricted by law, companies re-engineered their products and factories to accommodate hydrochlorofluorocarbons (HCFCs) instead; however, they are problematic as well. While they are less ozone-depleting than CFCs, they are persistent compounds, are greenhouse gases, and are toxic. HCFCs will eventually be phased out, necessitating companies to change course again. There is no doubt that benign substitutes can sometimes be difficult to find. Nevertheless, there are many opportunities for companies to avoid these costly course corrections by thinking systematically about long-term sustainability.

Some companies may encounter internal resistance to creating a formal environmental management system, especially if a company's experience with ISO 9000 certification (the international standard for quality management systems) was a negative one. A common sentiment among management and employees is, "Oh, no, not another program." Yet it is vitally important to have the majority of employees and senior management on board in order to build an effective system. Integrating the environmental management system with The Natural Step framework helps create this important buy-in because people can see how it supports the company's larger vision for the future as well as real business objectives. The Natural Step framework also provides coherence and meaning for employees by helping them understand the relationship between the system and their own personal values, leading to better participation.

How to Create an Environmental Management System with The Natural Step Compass

In a typical environmental management implementation, a company first sets its environmental policy, and then forms a cross-functional team made up of individuals from all areas of the facility. The team then completes a comprehensive review of the facility's environmental "aspects," or those activities that have the potential to interact with the environment.[5] It decides which of these aspects are significant, using a framework for decision-making of its own choosing. Significant aspects must be addressed by setting objectives and targets which can include such activities as:

- controlling the aspect, i.,e., inspecting a chemical storage area to ensure that no spills occur
- improving it, i.e., reducing energy use by 20 percent each year or
- studying it for action later on.

From here, the cross-functional team incorporates these objectives and targets into its programs, procedures, and work instructions, trains its employees on their role in the environmental management system and in these procedures and work instructions, and then maintains records to ensure that the procedures and work instructions are carried out. Periodic auditing is conducted to ensure that the system is functioning properly, and a periodic management review of the whole system leads to continuous improvement.

Although there are many ways that the framework can be integrated into an environmental management system, for purposes of this chapter, we have chosen several centrally important areas to explore in more detail. This exploration focuses on the following key steps for building an ISO environmental management system:

1. Setting an environmental policy
2. Creating an inventory of environmental aspects
3. Determining which aspects are significant
4. Setting objectives and targets
5. Measuring progress
6. Establishing training programs, awareness, and competence
7. Instituting a management review.

Setting an Environmental Policy

The Natural Step provides a framework for an environmental policy that is based on sustainability principles. The framework helps a company articulate a vision of the future that can be reflected in its environmental policy. It provides one additional benefit: the ISO standard requires that a company's policy incorporate a commitment to "pollution prevention." However, it does not provide a definition of pollution. Since the framework helps identify the root cause of environmental problems from a systems perspective, it can help to build a common definition of pollution among the members of the cross-functional team. Without this systems perspective, a company is left to rely on a definition of pollution that may vary from person to person, and from company to company.

Sånga-Säby is a Swedish hotel and conference center located in the countryside about an hour's drive outside of Stockholm. It is the first company in the hotel and restaurant industry to incorporate The Natural Step framework and be certified according to both ISO 14001 and EMAS. The company has utilized The Natural Step framework as a compass in all aspects of its environmental management system, starting with its environmental policy. In addition, as illustrated in Chapter 8, Sånga-Säby has been a pioneer in developing metrics based on The Natural Step System Conditions (see Figure 8.3).

Creating an Inventory of Environmental Aspects

Completing an inventory of environmental aspects is an important step in understanding how the company impacts the environment. The Natural Step model can help a cross-functional team to think about the way in which their operations impact the environment, and to see their operations in a global context. For example, companies may miss ways in which they impact the environment, other than those regulated by law. The Natural Step framework can help them identify all sources of potential impact to the environment, especially ones that may surprise the company down the road or that have a more global effect. Tom Chapman, former Vice-President for Corporate Communications of Mitsubishi Electric America, comments: "As we study how to combine TNS and ISO 14001, our approach is to use the TNS framework as a way to organize information about our environmental aspects. Before, the aspects were all just data, but using TNS has turned them into objectives. ISO 14001 is the 'what;' TNS provides the 'why.'"

Larry Chalfan adds: "Our idea of what aspects to include and what their impacts really were was very different after a year of studying The Natural Step. We now look more deeply at our impacts and ask very different questions." Charles McGlashan, a management consultant who uses the framework when designing environmental management systems, comments: "We used the The Natural Step framework when creating the aspects inventory at one of our client's automotive manufacturing plants. It really helped the cross-functional team understand and categorize the facility's impacts from a global perspective."

Determining which Aspects are Significant

When determining which aspects are significant (and are therefore the focus of the environmental management system) the The Natural Step compass adds significant value. Normally, a cross-functional team uses a framework of its own choosing using their best judgement about which aspects pose the highest risks. A common practice is to take a downstream approach to this process, looking at the local risks associated with emissions to air, soil, and water. This approach is adequate, but sells the environmental management system short.

Determining significance from the upstream perspective means that a company takes into account both the local and global environment, both short-term and long-term effects, activities that are not regulated today but may be in the future, and, most importantly, the company's long-term goals.

Referring to Strategic Goals for Guidance. One method for determining significance uses the results of the company's back-casting exercise. At the completion of this exercise, the company will have a good idea of the areas where it violates the System Conditions most severely, of its vision of itself in the future, and of some of the critical steps needed to get there. From this future vision, it can then set objectives and targets for the company as a whole. For example, if a company recognizes that its use of persistent compounds in its products and processes poses a significant risk (as seen through the lens of the TNS framework), it can set a corporate target of reducing its dependence on these materials. A facility can then automatically flag these aspects as significant and assign them a facility-specific target and objective in alignment with the company's long-term goals. IKEA has taken this approach by striving to eliminate all heavy metals and persistent compounds from its products company-wide. This type of comprehensive approach can only succeed with a commitment from the top levels of a company.

The Compass and the Aspects Inventory. Another way of incorporating the framework is to indicate, when building the aspects inventory, which aspects relate to which System Conditions. This can help a cross-functional team to think about impacts as they relate to the framework and to direct decisions on objectives and targets. The downside to this approach is that the exercise may be cumbersome, especially if a facility's aspects inventory is very detailed.

System Conditions as Indicators of Significance. System Condition One: John Holmberg, a physicist working closely with Robèrt to develop The Natural

Step model, derived a set of indicators for sustainable development.[6] These indicators can be used to help a company prioritize its environmental aspects. For example, how is one to determine the relative significance of the release of cadmium over that of mercury? We know that each is a violation of System Condition One, but their effects may not be equal. Holmberg's analysis explains that the material's relative abundance in nature compared with human-created flows will have an impact on its ultimate effect. For example, human-created flows of aluminum are relatively insignificant compared to aluminum's abundance in nature, whereas human-created flows of lead are 12 times those of naturally occurring flows, and human-induced copper flows are 24 times those of naturally occurring flows.

The following formula can be used to weigh the relative significance of a company's use of metals and minerals:

$$\frac{\text{Indicator of}}{\text{Significance}} = \frac{\text{Human-made quantity}}{\text{Abundance in Nature}} \text{ x Quantity used by the company}$$

This type of analysis can help a company determine which System Condition One aspects are most significant.

System Condition Two: Understanding System Condition Two can also help determine what aspects are significant. Companies may use a variety of methods to determine which materials produced by society are significant. Unfortunately, too many companies use the regulatory system as a guide. The downside to this approach is that a company will be reacting to changes in laws and regulations that are out of its control. Materials that are substituted can later be found to be problematic as well, forcing a company to change course again. Taking an upstream systems approach helps a company be proactive. Most companies need to do a material inventory to understand what materials will have to be reduced or eliminated to reduce their dependence on materials that are persistent, have a human-made presence in nature that is out of balance with natural flows, and are toxic.

Another important focus is substances for which the long-term effects are unknown. Endocrine disrupters provide an excellent example. As reported in *Our Stolen Future* by Theo Colborn, Dianne Dumanoski, and John Peterson Meyers,[7] endocrine disrupters are synthetic compounds found in plastics and other materials that tend to mimic hormones in the body. The body receives and utilizes them in very tiny amounts as if they were the hormones themselves. Endocrine disrupters are not regulated at the present time, but because they are suspected to have a role in infertility and certain cancers, they are currently being studied by the Environmental Protection Agency and other organizations. Chances are that they will be regulated in the future. The Natural Step compass reminds us that the time to think strategically about our use of such synthetic compounds is not when everything is known about a chemical, but when we know it is not in accordance with principles of sustainability.

System Condition Three: Companies in the mining, forestry, fishing, and agricultural industries have obvious System Condition Three impacts. For many manufacturing facilities, their direct impact on the productive capacity of the biosphere may be less directly visible, but no less important. For example, there are two areas in which an understanding of System Condition Three may help frame a facility's impacts. The first is the company's raw material use, such as water and paper, and the second is the impact of the physical building on the local environment. For the latter, a company may wish to consider landscaping issues or to examine the transportation issues associated with its workforce getting to and from work and with its goods and services being moved around. IKEA, Scandic Hotels, Collins Pine, and Interface all consider transportation to be one of the most important issues for society in general, and their companies in particular, to address. This is true not only because of the contribution transport makes to molecular garbage through the burning of fossil fuels (System Condition One) but also because of the increasing destruction of natural environments through the encroachment of roads and highways.

System Condition Four: Inefficiencies in energy use, material use, and the transportation of raw materials or the final product may be considered System Condition Four impacts. In addition, a company's impact on communities both local and global and the extent to which its products and services meet human needs are addressed here.

Setting Objectives and Targets

The process of setting objectives and targets is one of the areas where the framework adds the most value. Objectives and targets that are in alignment with a company's long-term vision can make an environmental management system a powerful tool. Too often, a company's targets are set to minimize short-term risks. It is preferable that objectives and targets be based on longer-term objectives set in a business context. These objectives and targets then provide a structure for balancing and integrating both business and ecological concerns.

As Figure 9.5 shows, Mitsubishi Electric America is an example of a company that integrates its business objectives in its environmental management system. Their overarching corporate environmental objectives and targets are integrated at the plant level, with the individual plants setting additional objectives and targets as well.

Figure 9.5

Mitsubishi Electric America
Corporate Environmental Targets

Facility Level:
- Reduce energy use by 25% below FY 1990 level by FY 2000
- Reduce waste disposal by 30% below FY 1995 level by FY 2000
- Reduce tree-based paper use and purchase by 75% (Factor 4) by the end of FY 1999 and by 90% (Factor 10) by the end of FY 2000
- Eliminate the use of old growth/primary forest products by FY 1998
- Eliminate the use of chlorinated solvents in open systems by the end of FY 2000

Product Level:
- Increase the use of recycled materials (excluding metals) in products by 30% above FY 1995 levels by FY 2000
- Reduce packaging materials by 20% below FY 1995 level by the end of FY 2000

Measuring Progress

Companies use a variety of indicators to measure environmental performance. Designing good environmental performance indicators is vital because what gets measured tends to gets managed. It is important to ensure that a company is measuring the things that matter, not just collecting data.

The State of the Art. Unfortunately, most companies still use an end-of-pipe approach to measurement. They measure such items as emissions, pollution, and tons of hazardous waste generated. They also measure compliance statistics. Limiting measurement to only these types of environmental performance indicators limits the effectiveness of an environmental management system because these types of data are normally seen by management as something peripheral rather than crucial to the mission of the business.

A Systems Approach. While some of the traditional environmental performance indicators are important (and many are relatively easy to measure and report), a new class is emerging. New environmental performance indicators tend to be normalized (compared to dollars in sales or number of units produced) so that they can be used by managers to run the business better. They emphasize sustainability and are integrated with profitability measures. They use an integrated systems approach and take into account global effects, material inputs (not just pollution), the entire product lifecycle, and business goals. Following are examples from three companies:

Electrolux. Electrolux's effective use of this approach is an inspiring example. In its 1997 annual environmental report, the company articulates the following environmental performance indicators that show its systemic approach (for more detailed information, see the Electrolux website listed in the Resources section of this book).

Figure 9.6

Electrolux Environmental Indicators

Facility Level:
- Energy cost per added value* (%)
- Energy consumption per added value (kwh/$)
- Carbon dioxide emission/added value (kg/$)
- Water consumption/added value* (cubic meters/$)
- Energy consumption per square meter of heated surface area™ (kwh/m2)
- Direct material efficiency (kg product/kg raw material used)
- * added value is defined as the difference between total manufacturing costs and direct material costs

Corporate Level:
- Share of total sales represented by environmentally leading products
- Average annual environmental improvement of product range
- Increase in recyclability of products
- Environmental improvement of manufacturing facilities

Interface. When Ray Anderson began shaping Interface's vision of sustainability, he asked about the total quantity of material moving through the company. How much material from the Earth's crust is removed each year due to Interface's operations? How much is deposited in landfills each year? He calculated that the company is responsible for 1.2 billion pounds of petroleum being extracted from the Earth's crust each year. Only one-third is used for the materials in carpet; two-thirds is the energy it takes to make the carpet. Over 250 million pounds of carpet are produced each year in the United States. With an average life of 15 years, most of this material goes to landfills. Quantifying these flows can be a very powerful experience; it motivates people because they can begin to see the whole picture.

An important indicator for Interface is pounds-of-petroleum/dollar sales. Interface's vision is to eventually make all carpet from recycled materials and to use totally renewable energy sources. If their strategy succeeds, the indicator will approach zero. Since starting its journey to sustainability, Interface has watched this indicator fall as sales have risen.

Sånga-Säby. After conducting a thorough review of all of its environmental impacts, Sånga-Säby designed a comprehensive set of environmental performance indicators based on the System Conditions. In its 1997 environmental report, 1995, 1996, and 1997 results are included together with 1998 targets. This impressive document represents the most complete use to date of the four System Conditions as the foundation of environmental performance indicators (an example of these indicators can be found in Chapter 8).

Establishing Training Programs, Awareness, and Competence

One of The Natural Step's most powerful areas of influence is in employee training. As Chalfan points out: "We tried to get people's hearts and minds engaged when starting our ISO 14001 program. During employee training, I reviewed the environmental situation, connecting it to our lives and the lives of our children and grandchildren. I explained, however, that I had faith that it could change, if we all do our part."

This broader perspective helps employees understand their own and their company's role in creating a sustainable future and often leads to a heartfelt commitment to the environmental program. This can be contrasted to many employee training programs that focus on regulatory compliance as something they "have" to do because "it's the law." The Natural Step training creates a framework for employees' ideas to help a company reach its goals during their day-to-day work lives. TNS training also helps employees apply ecological insights in their personal lives in satisfying ways.

Employees' understanding of their responsibilities and the consequences of their departure from established work procedures is a necessary component of a well-functioning environmental management system, and it is something that auditors will look for during certification. Connecting the company's potential environmental impacts to the global environment using the The Natural Step framework helps explain the rationale for specific work procedures.

Instituting a Management Review

The last step in the environmental management system cycle is the periodic management review. Management reviews the company's progress toward meeting its objectives and targets, the results of environmental management system audits to determine whether the system is functioning effectively, and the company's inventory of aspects; then plans are made for the next cycle. The Natural

Step framework enhances this process by illuminating the vision that a company can work toward, year after year. The Natural Step framework can not only enhance management's strategic planning sessions so that the environmental management system is seen in the context of the company's back-casting, action plans, and business climate, but also determine the impact of ecological trends on the business.

Conclusion

Environmental management systems are gaining popularity around the world. They provide structure for the integration of environmental issues into management and day-to-day operations. But they don't provide the vision that guides a company on the voyage to sustainability. Nor do they provide the understanding of what constitutes a sustainable direction. The Natural Step framework provides the compass to navigate these new waters. Once the vision and direction is set, an environmental management system is a valuable vessel for making the journey, operationalizing the vision and documenting progress.

CHAPTER 10

The Evolutionary Corporation

We are forced to choose, for the processes we have initiated in our lifetime cannot continue in the lifetime of our children. Whatever we do either creates the framework for continuing the supreme adventure of life and consciousness on this planet or sets the stage for its termination.
The choice before us is urgent and important:
it can neither be postponed nor ignored.
Ervin Laszlo — *The CHOICE: Evolution or Extinction*

THE METAPHOR OF THE EVOLUTIONARY CORPORATION is grounded on the belief that real transformation at both the individual and the organizational level is possible. In fact, as Ralph Metzner points out in *The Unfolding Self,* it is said that human transformation was the only miracle that the Buddha recognized as such.[1] All of the great religions have at their heart the possibility of the transformation, that is to say, the evolution of the individual human being. The assumption of human evolution also is the foundation of much of modern psychotherapy. However, as our individual lives usually demonstrate, and world literature illustrates in many examples, while change may be possible, and most certainly desirable, it is rarely easy.

In the design of an effective program of either personal or corporate transformation, one of the factors most critical to success is to develop a positive vision of the new state that you are moving toward, rather than fixating on the familiar — even destructive — ways of the past. This is why visioning has become so important to organizational design praxis. It is also the essence of the back-casting process of The Natural Step, whereby first of all a desired future state is defined: then one steps back from the future to the present, creating one's future path in so doing. Collectively we owe an enormous debt of gratitude to the four companies featured in this book and to the many other companies on similar paths. They are actually in the process of designing and discovering the future of the industrial enterprise; or, as Interface puts it, they are in the process of becoming "the prototypical company of the 21st century." Because of their pioneering steps, we can more easily create our own vision of what a sustainable enterprise would look like for us . Each will be different, just as all companies today are different. Yet to be fully sustainable, there will be core principles with which they are aligned. These include the four System Conditions of The Natural Step.

If there is to be a benign future for our grandchildren and their grandchildren as well as for the myriad other life forms on this planet, the future of the industrial enterprise must include ecological sustainability as surely as it now includes financial sustainability and growing social sustainability. Ecological factors will be integral to the business worldview of the 21st century. Men and women in business must become conscious of the evolutionary role that business plays in the future of this planet. They also need to take responsibility for that role. They need to help create the sustainable corporation — the evolutionary corporation. In fact, one of the great strengths of The Natural Step is the fact that it brings an evolutionary perspective to the sustainability discussion.

What are the characteristics of evolutionary corporations? They

- operate with a keen perception of the growing evolutionary force that human systems have become on a global scale

- take responsibility for the role industry plays as a major part of that evolutionary force

- engage in the purposeful design and redesign of products, services, processes, and systems to create a future that includes prosperity, a high quality of life, and the healthy co-evolution of human and natural systems

- work toward a positive future for shareholders, employees, customers, suppliers, communities, the global community, and the natural environment that provides the vital services which all these other systems need to survive

- extend the concept of a positive future to the well-being of future generations

An evolutionary corporation consciously operates with a growing understanding of the dynamics of the natural systems within which it is embedded and aligns its actions with those systems. It consciously chooses strategies consistent with vital evolutionary choices for all the systems with which it is connected and upon which it depends. Based on the case studies in Part Two, several characteristics of an evolutionary corporation can be identified: strong core values embracing sustainability, a commitment to learning, a whole systems worldview, an expanded sense of responsibility and accountability, robustness, evolutionary consciousness and conscious evolution, and a recognition of the benefits of sustainability to business.

Strong Core Values Embracing Sustainability

Values are the very foundation of corporate culture; they permeate the company's vision and guide decisions and actions from long-term planning to employees' day-to-day behavior. Core values can motivate people, engage them, and provide a source of self-esteem and pride in belonging to the company. They provide the rules of conduct and moral framework that guide a company's decisions and actions. They define that for which the company stands.

As John Elkington points out in *Cannibals With Forks*, the new agenda for business will increasingly revolve around values and ethics. Successful companies will need to become better at identifying, understanding, and responding to the values of those with whom they work and whom they serve. They will need to find out how they are viewed by stakeholders and to predict what those stakeholders' expectations are likely to be in the future. Scandic Hotels, with its understanding and practice of "interactive values creation," is a leading example of this. From an evolutionary perspective, strong core values provide the foundation of the world we want to create. Architect William McDonough reminds us that design is the manifestation of intention. Intention is built on our values. These four companies have core values of financial success and environmental sustainability. They also realize that although their commercial success must often come at the expense of their competitors, it cannot continue to come at the expense of the natural environment or future generations. In evolutionary terms, if short-term financial success leads to eventual extinction or severe diminishment of future development, it is no success at all.

A Commitment to Learning

All four companies are learning organizations exhibiting

- shared vision, compelling aspirations, and a culture built on shared transcendent human values
- shared mental models about how the world works
- the capacity to embrace change and to be flexible, resilient, and inventive
- engagement, trust, and team learning, including practices that encourage generative and strategic conversation and coordinated action
- systems thinking, particularly an appreciation of whole systems thinking and acting.

A Whole Systems Perspective

The challenge of complex human systems is that they are unbounded. That is, each complex problem tends to be related to every other problem. There are few clear boundaries of cause and effect. Factors that are assumed to be part of a problem tend to be inextricably linked to many other factors. Each apparent solution to a problem may aggravate or interfere with other problems. None of these problems can be addressed through the linear, bounded thinking of the past. To paraphrase Einstein, our current problems cannot be solved with the same system of thought that created them.

A whole systems perspective requires that corporations integrate the dynamics of natural systems into their decision-making and operations. A whole systems perspective reveals the connections between the company and all of the environments that influence it and that it influences, including the economic, social, and natural environment, whether the company's impact is immediate (such as hazardous emissions) or more remote (such as the ultimate disposal of its products at the end of their use). The whole systems perspective also implies an evolutionary time dimension as the company recognizes that its actions or its failures to act influence the possibilities for the interconnected systems to evolve and flourish over time.

Because every company is a system embedded in other systems, in order to consciously influence the trajectory of its individual, societal, or the natural/human systems evolution, it must work in coordination with other subsystems to effect change in the larger systems. To do this, all of these companies are working with networks of other companies and organizations to achieve triple bottom line sustainability.

An Expanded Sense of Responsibility and Accountability

Accountability to shareholders is a fundamental aspect of business and has traditionally been viewed as the primary measurement of corporate success. In recent years, this narrow scope of corporate responsibility and accountability has been questioned and expanded by law and public opinion to include a growing array of stakeholders, including employees, customers, suppliers, the communities affected by corporate operations, and the natural environment. The four companies studied are beginning to take what we call evolutionary and systemic responsibility, that is, responsibility for the damage they do or the contributions they make to the health and well-being of the various systems with which they interconnect. If we think back to The Natural Step perspective of the funnel (see Figure 2.2), this includes taking responsibility for the degree to which possibilities — societal and ecological — are being opened rather than more constrained for future generations.

Robustness

Financial strength, competitiveness, employee loyalty and competence, and external recognition are key elements of robustness. As the case studies show, all four companies are leaders in their fields with strong financial performances. All four are growing. They demonstrate high levels of employee loyalty, empowerment, and creativity. Each has received external recognition for their leadership both in the market and in their journeys to sustainability. They are focused on competitiveness and profitability today while positioning themselves to be competitive in the future.

In evolutionary terms, companies that are to influence their own evolution and that of their industries and societies must not only survive, they must prosper. Their prosperity provides them with the ability to experiment, innovate, and invest in new ways of doing business that are consistent with financial, social, and ecological sustainability. Their competitiveness gives them the strength to influence the way business is done in their industries. As they achieve environmental gains that others in their field still claim are impossible, the pressure to change increases on their competitors. Leadership and recognition enable the evolutionary corporation to influence the choices of consumers, policy makers, competitors, suppliers, and other businesses and organizations.

Evolutionary Consciousness and Conscious Evolution

The four companies studied in this volume are developing an evolutionary consciousness. They are beginning to understand that the raw materials, energy, natural cycles, human resources, and other components of their success and wealth are based on billions of years of evolutionary processes. Their current activities, in turn, not only form the basis for the future evolution of their specific company, they also have the potential to influence the future evolution of societal and natural systems. Evolutionary consciousness demands that every human system, whether it is a corporation, a family, a community, or a nation, take responsibility for designing or redesigning its system to safeguard the ecological balance that took billions of years to create and that human systems are changing in the course of decades.

Evolutionary consciousness empowers us to engage in conscious evolution: using the creative power of our minds to collaborate consciously with the evolutionary process to guide our systems and our society toward the fulfillment of their potential. In business, conscious evolution begins with an understanding of the current impact on other systems that a company depends on or affects. It is operationalized particularly through the way key issues are defined within the organization, the framework used to guide decisions, and the way systems, products, processes, and services are designed. For most companies, this requires a new way of thinking and elevated creativity and innovation on all levels of the organization. That is the lifeblood of an evolutionary corporation. The Natural Step System Conditions and framework constitute useful conceptual tools to stimulate the process of creativity and evolutionary systems design.

A Recognition of the Benefits of Sustainability to Business

Evolutionary corporations understand that society must become ecologically and socially as well as economically sustainable, and that business plays a major role in this evolutionary process. They further recognize that sustainable development — the path to a sustainable society — provides important benefits. Some of these benefits and rewards are discussed below (see also the "Final Reflections" sections at the end of each of the four case studies, which summarize many of the principal benefits each of those companies derives from engaging with The Natural Step).

Ethics

According to Mats Lederhausen, the CEO of McDonald's of Sweden, a very unique franchise now considered to be one of the three most environmentally conscious companies in Sweden, the most compelling reason for any company to make sustainability a core corporate value is "because it's the right thing to do." When a 1997 survey of Canadian and American executives conducted by The Society of Management Accountants of Canada asked business leaders why their companies practised sustainable development, the most important reason given, after compliance with legal requirements, was "because it's the right thing to do." A report produced for the Ministry of the Environment of Canada declares: "Any business leader with a commitment to good corporate governance will recognize value in pursuing sustainable development because 'it is the right thing to do.'" [2] Other reasons to support this moral imperative are cited in Table 10.1.

The Bottom Line

When costs are reduced, the benefit goes directly to the bottom line. The four companies in this study report significant cost savings as a result of sustainability initiatives. These savings derive from instituting reduced-waste or zero-waste programs as well as from reducing raw material used per unit of production and reducing operational resource needs such as energy and water. Interface, for example, has realized approximately $75 million of savings in the first four years of its QUEST program. In addition, its innovative carpet designs, prompted by sustainability criteria, show real promise of significantly reducing the required quantity of input per unit of output. At Collins Pine, The Natural Step approach prompted an innovative alternative to burning sander dust by recycling the dust back into production. This saved an estimated $500,000 to $750,000 in replacement costs for just one burner and an estimated $525,000 per year in raw material costs. Scandic Hotel's Resource Hunt is reducing demand, and consequently costs, for energy, water, and handling of unsorted trash at a time when these resources and services are expected to increase in

Why Companies Practice Sustainable Development

Table 10.1

Issue and Stakeholders	Explanation
Better relations with residents of local communities	The cost of poor public relations with residents of local communities can be substantial if it results in resistance to new project start-ups, facility expansions, or ongoing developments.
Increase eco-efficiency of operations – Stakeholders: shareholders, customers, environment	The term "eco-efficiency" is a contraction of ecological and economic efficiency. It advocates *doing more with less.* Companies benefit from eco-efficiency by reducing the energy and material requirements of production.
Promote industry-wide self-regulation/affect legislation – Stakeholders: industry, government, the public	When industry and government combine expertise, practical and cost-effective self-regulatory programs and/or legislation will often emerge. It serves the public's best interest when industry and government develop programs cooperatively.
Enhance due diligence protection – Stakeholders: corporate executives	During 1990-1995, a record number of Canadian corporate executives were convicted of environmental offenses (2.5 executives/year). Total annual environmental fines in excess of $1 million are not uncommon in the resource sector.
Address value chain – Stakeholders: customers, suppliers, etc.	Customers are increasingly concerned about corporate practices harming the environment. ISO and the International Chamber of Commerce have developed objective criteria to assess environmental product claims.
Address media and activist pressures – Stakeholders: media and activists	Organizations such as American Rivers, Greenpeace, Friends of the Earth, Nature Conservancy, and the Sierra Club can affect public perceptions of business, thus affecting start-up of operations.
Corporate commitment to stewardship practices – Stakeholders: employees	Any corporate sustainable development program must have the support of all employees, from the boardroom to the shop floor. Employees who are "committed" to a corporate cause will work more diligently to "realize a vision."
Lower insurance premiums – Stakeholders: insurance companies	Although few companies currently carry environmental insurance (i.e., many major companies are self-insured), insurance companies are including sustainable development initiatives in the underwriting process.
Lower bank loan rates – Stakeholders: banks	Most major banks employ senior environmental managers to assess the cumulative environmental risk associated with the lending of money for mortgage holdings, land acquisitions, etc. Interest rates are adjusted to reflect risk.
Facilitate inclusion in ethical mutual fund/investment port-folios – Stakeholders: shareholders	An increasing number of mutual funds and investment port-folios use "ethical" screens. Corporate sustainable development can facilitate a company's inclusion in ethical portfolios, thus affecting a positive impact on share price.
Moral commitment to stewardship practices – Stakeholders: environment, economy, society	Although "traditional" business drivers (i.e., the creation of shareholder value) are central to the adoption of sustainable business practices, corporate leaders also reference a personal commitment to stewardship practices.

Source: Sustainable Systems Associates, Ltd.

cost, in some cases at a rate higher than inflation. IKEA North America has identified important energy savings in the Green Lights program. The expected annual savings from various components of just that single program are more than $500,000.

These cost savings are only part of the story. As employees become engaged in sustainability efforts, they become more conscientious, creative, aware, and interested in how they use resources and thereby contribute to reducing the aggregate impact of the company on the environment. This creates leaner production and operations and often leads to innovations that improve both operational and environmental performance.

Workforce Impact

The August 1998 issue of *Fast Company* magazine reports on a year-long survey conducted by a team from McKinsey & Co. involving 77 companies and almost 6,000 managers and executives. The article predicts that over the next 20 years the most important corporate resource will be talent: "smart, sophisticated business people who are technologically literate, globally astute, and operationally agile."[3] The *Fast Company* article goes on to report that as the demand for this talent increases, the supply will be decreasing, setting the stage for a "talent war." The most talented people will be looking for employers that are high performance companies, provide an environment in which they are challenged to excel, and have an inspiring vision.

A 1998 paper by Bob Willard of IBM Canada features a study done by Tom Terez entitled "Meaning At Work," conducted in early 1997 through 15 focus groups and extensive one-on-one interviews. Terez was in contact with more than 100 people whose collective work experience exceeded 2,000 years. The study synthesized all the factors contributing to people's meaningful work experience into "22 meaning keys" and synthesized that information further into six major themes. Some of the most interesting ones with respect to our findings are purpose — the sense that what a person does as an individual, and what the organization does collectively, truly make a difference; the lack of emphasis on money — people do not cite incentives or high pay as key ingredients of the meaningful workplace, even though they do distinguish between "fair pay" and "high pay;" and meaningfulness — there is almost a desperate eagerness to talk about meaning in the workplace.

Willard concludes: "Certainly fair compensation is an important dimension of ensuring people want to work for a particular company. However, given similar compensation plans, the McKinsey and Terez studies show that good people also want to work for a company whose values and purpose they respect."[4]

An extremely high level of employee enthusiasm and morale, resulting in lower turnover of staff, is found at the four companies studied in this book. Both Interface and Scandic Hotels, for example, have been rated among the most desirable place to work in their respective countries; in each case, this occurred after sustainability become a core value. During confidential interviews at Interface, where we determined the location to be visited and the interview subjects, we were impressed by the number of people who made comments like "This is my dream job" or "I love this company" or "I really look forward to coming to work in the morning." In every company, hourly employees and management alike expressed great pride that their company had a higher purpose than "just making money." This translated into feelings that their jobs also had a higher purpose and that their contribution was important.

Competitive advantages

Attracting and retaining the best employees clearly provides an important competitive advantage for companies. According to Charlie Eitel, the people and culture at Interface provide distinct advantages to that company over its competition. Eitel expressed it this way: "We'll give our competitors our whole playbook — but they can't execute it! I'll tell you every play I'm going to run against you but you can't beat me! Do you know why? You don't have my people; you don't have my process; you don't have my discipline; and you don't have my culture!"

In addition to being more attractive to talented employees, the companies studied showed improved competitiveness in several other areas as well.

Product Innovation. For the proactive company, the often rigorous new criteria that arise out of the challenge to produce and deliver goods and services more sustainably are powerful drivers of innovation. Interface, for example, is innovating new flooring designs at an extraordinary rate, and Interface Research Corporation is intent on discovering how to "close the loop" with respect to the entire lifecycle of its products. Among many other things, they are exploring the options for true recycling of carpet and for producing carpet with competitive qualities made from biodegradable materials such as cotton, flax, and hemp; also, they are producing the first "solar-made carpet," made from all renewable, non-hydrocarbon based power sources. Interface knows that one of its most important markets, the commercial interiors architects, designers, and specifiers, are very interested in environmentally friendly interiors. The company is determined to innovate the products and services that respond to ecological interest *and* to exceed the competition in every other factor as well.

At Scandic Hotels, the ecological hotel room is an excellent example of an innovation that provides important financial savings in the long run and a superb "communication-of-values" function immediately. The message conveyed to guests is that Scandic cares about their well-beings, that these environmental rooms are both healthy and comfortable rooms to stay in, and that Scandic is contributing to safeguarding the natural environment. The competition is left with the task of catching up while Scandic forges ahead with new ideas and services.

IKEA is innovating both with respect to specific new products, such as the "a.i.r." sofa and the children's line of furniture which has strict environmental standards. Innovation at IKEA extends to the entire product line which is now being evaluated along environmental criteria. For example, IKEA is experimenting with the production of furniture that wastes less wood than conventional practices by using high-grade wood for surfaces that are visible, and lower grade wood, or wood previously discarded, for the portions of the product that are not visible. This both saves money and reduces environmental impact. As IKEA proceeds with its materials inventory on all its product lines, it will likely introduce numerous innovations that keep prices low for customers and reduce the environmental impacts of IKEA products — a combination that translates into real competitiveness in IKEA's major markets.

Collins Pine is constantly innovating products in their CollinsWood line. They already produce certified sustainable plywood and particleboard. They are also innovating a service to their suppliers to help them achieve certification as well. Because Collins cannot increase the amount of fiber it takes from its forest lands and still log sustainably, it is important for them to ensure an adequate supply to build this market. This will further increase the overall market requirements for sustainably harvested timber.

Low-Cost and High Efficiency Production. When a company embarks upon the journey to sustainability, one of the first things it generally does is become aware of the true demands its operations make on the natural environment. This includes cataloging and analyzing its material and energy flows, the lifecycle environmental impacts of its products, and the resource requirements of its operations. This often includes everything from the kind of cups used for coffee in the office to major capital equipment and raw material requirements. The microscopic awareness this process brings to business operations from the shop floor to the executive suite generally leads to lower costs and higher efficiency with respect to resources used.

Over the long term, as these cost savings and efficiencies are realized, they can result in more competitive prices for the customer. This is particularly important to a company like IKEA where low cost to the customer for the value received is central to its business idea. As more IKEA suppliers take on the challenge of becoming more sustainable by moving up the environmental criteria stairs that IKEA sets, they are likely to experience cost savings associated with more efficient resource use and dematerialization. These lower costs of operations will mean IKEA can maintain the lowest possible price for the consumer and remain highly competitive in the marketplace.

The Knowledge Base and Core Competencies for the Market of the Future. In *The Living Company*, Arie de Gues contends that sometime in the 20th century, the Western world moved out of the age of capital into the age of knowledge. According to de Gues, *"Knowledge displaced capital as the scarce production factor — the key to corporate success.* Those who had knowledge and knew how to apply it would henceforth be the wealthiest members of society: the technological specialists, investment bankers, creative artists, and facilitators of new understanding. This was not merely a function of the need for people to supply technical skills under the direction of their bosses. The growing complexity of work created a need for people to be a source of inventiveness, and to become distributors and evaluators of invention and knowledge through the whole work community."[5]

Sustainable development is a knowledge-intensive endeavor. It requires new knowledge and new ways of thinking about every process, system, product, and operation of a business. It also requires that these be translated into specific competencies in design, production, distribution, and administration. De Gues points out that the successful company in this new age is one that can learn effectively — a trait of all four companies studied. To be competitive, a company's products and services need to be congruent with demands and changes in the current market, to anticipate the market of the future, and to be proactive in serving its needs. If the future market is likely to become more sensitive to environmental issues because of the economic and social trends indicated in the The Natural Step funnel, then it behooves a company to learn what that market will require and to be the first, the least expensive, or the most qualified to provide it.

As the knowledge base increases within the company regarding the designs, technologies, production processes, recyclable characteristics, and other factors that a sustainable society will require, the proactive company can play an important role in sharing that knowledge with the customer. This can serve to accelerate the pace, and often the costs, for competitors who will have to catch up as market demand for sustainability-based products and services increases.

Public Perceptions and Image. How a company is perceived in society is vital to its continued success. Ask any company that has been the focus of negative press, justified or not, about the costs. On the other hand, the benefits of a positive image are inestimable. As companies vie for the best talent, strive for employee and customer loyalty, or seek new investors or business partners, their reputation is a vital asset. As Charlie Eitel notes, "without values, you have nothing." We would add that a company also must be perceived to have those values. All the companies studied received considerable positive public recognition for their stand on sustainability. They have all received awards and positive print and television media attention for their actions.

As society moves more deeply into the funnel described by The Natural Step, the costs of not moving toward sustainability can only increase. Some companies will be put out of business by these costs. Others will spend a lot playing "catch up" — following as quickly as they can in the tracks of industry leaders or reacting to unexpected changes in public mood or legal requirements.

IKEA, Scandic Hotels, Interface, and Collins Pine demonstrate that the benefits of moving toward sustainability far outweigh the costs. Both Charlie Eitel of Interface and Roland Nilsson of Scandic say that although a company must make investments in the process, there has been no net cost associated with moving toward sustainability in their companies. In fact, the savings produced by increasing resource efficiency and reducing waste have provided the operating cash for launching other sustainable development initiatives. The result is a virtuous cycle, a positive feedback loop of benefits to the corporation.

Conclusion: A Better Way

Although the future cannot be foreseen, its principles can. The role of The Natural Step framework is to focus on understanding those principles. The role of the evolutionary corporation is to apply that understanding and to become a force that moves society in the direction of sustainability.

When explaining why Interface has made the commitment to become the prototypical company of the 21st century, Ray Anderson often includes a poem written by Glenn Thomas, an Interface associate. The poem was written after Thomas heard Anderson speak about the company's environmental mission. A few days after the speech, Anderson received an e-mail from Thomas which he describes as "one of the most encouraging moments of my life." Thomas wrote this poem:

Tomorrow's Child
Without a name; an unseen face
And knowing not the time or place
Tomorrow's Child, though yet unborn
I saw you first last Tuesday morn.
A wise friend introduced us two,
And through his shining point of view
I saw a day which you would see;
A day for you, and not for me.
Knowing you has changed my thinking,
Never having had an inkling

That perhaps the things I do
Might someday, somewhere, threaten you
Tomorrow's Child, my daughter-son
I'm afraid I've just begun
To think of you and of your good,
Though always having known I should.
Begin I will to weigh the cost
Of what I squander; what is lost
If ever I forget that you
Will someday come to live here too.

We cannot foresee the future. We don't know whether the consequences of the current unsustainable direction of society will be ours to experience directly, or whether they will be the legacy we leave to our descendants, tomorrow's children. What we can know are the first order principles — the rules of the game — of the natural/human systems we live in and that are described by The Natural Step. Guided by that knowledge, we can choose to design our future in ways that are ecologically, socially, and economically sustainable.

There is a better way. We can take responsibility, individually and collectively, for the conscious evolution of our human systems. We can hold others — individuals, corporations, and governments — accountable as well. It no longer matters "who is to blame"; what matters is that we all take responsibility for the direction and impact of our society. In this generation, in our era, humans have become integral agents of evolution. More than that, we are evolution becoming conscious of itself. Will we treat these insights as just more interesting data to be filed? Or will we, in the spirit of Archimedes, use them as a lever with which to move the world? The choice is ours.

Afterword

Paul Hawken

BRIAN NATTRASS AND MARY ALTOMARE have performed a great service in gathering and presenting the history, tenets, and early corporate results of The Natural Step. For too many years, business ecology has been a poor apprentice to the bigger ecological issues of resource conservation, habitat preservation, and species extinction. Why? Primarily because business was seen — and, in my opinion, correctly seen — as the major instigator and cause of most environmental problems.

For consumers and producers alike, such circumstances are confusing. One the one hand, we need enterprise, not necessarily as it is presently constituted or implemented, but as a provider of the essential goods and services that make us secure, civilized, and humane. But while honoring its importance in our lives, we also have seen business fail in its role as the primary negotiant between society and living systems. The planet is ebbing — all living systems are in a chaotic retreat that is accelerating.

Because human population will double in the next century and the resources available per person will drop by one-half to three-fourths, a remarkable transformation of industry and commerce must occur. If we are to develop as a civilization and to care for each other, we must create a strong economy that uses significantly less material and energy, an economy that will free up resources, increase per-capita spending on social ills (while reducing those ills), and begin to restore the Earth's damaged environment. We can endlessly debate why such damage came about, yet at the same time be relieved that there is now a growing realization in some corporations that business must become a powerful force addressing planetary degradation.

At first glance, this may seem impossible. Ask any CEO. The economic forces loose in the world make the very existence of most businesses difficult enough. Until recently, the idea that a company should take on the additional responsibility of social and environmental degradation was anathema. These new issues were not mere straws but wet haybales that would break the backs of the whole team of camels. As chronicled in these pages, the importance of The Natural Step is that it provides a framework and basis of action that can meld with extant corporate cultures, yet quickly reorient the whole enterprise system towards sustainability. For most companies encountering The Natural Step, it was the first time they could see how to make the three E's of sustainable development — economy, equity, and ecology — merge seamlessly with innovation, strategic planning, and the economic exigencies of fiscal quarters.

Writers constantly search for words or phrases that will slip past defences, cultural membranes, or the other censoring nets we use to screen out the noise of too many earnest voices. When we do read works or essays that are authentic and honest, we respond. Even in the smudged ink of a morning op-ed or letter to the editor, an alchemy of words can cut through our indifference and wake us. Similarly, Karl-Henrik's gift was to find the principles, language, and compassion that authentically convey the startling scope of global environmental and social problems, while simultaneously suggesting a means to embrace and use them for constructive change within the core business values.

Yet we can't say sustainability has happened. Far from it. But something is happening — a remarkable change in the comprehension and commitment of pioneering companies. The path from business-as-usual to sustainable development is so new that in-depth case studies are rare, and those that exist are precious even if they primarily describe the beginning of the journey. At this point, any news is valuable. For every company that has publicly committed to this path, a dozen more are watching and studying. Their success, and every move they make toward sustainability, will greatly influence and determine the future of this planet. Those lofty words are contrasted by the yeoman-like quality of the work that needs to be done. In a company, there are no charismatic species or primary forests to be saved. As shown with Scandic Hotels, the work consists of thousands of distinct tasks, daily changes in requisitions, constant alterations of specifications, the complete redesigning of products, and tens of thousands of hours of learning, questioning, and collaborating. Plenty of mistakes will be made, so we need to forgive even as we bite our lips about our impending planetary fate. As Tagore said, "If you shut your door to all errors, truth will be shut out." Companies are learning about the Earth — finally. We need to praise that.

In this process, employees are like all of us; but in the companies presented here, employees are further ahead. Their managers and associates are examining in minutiae the precise relationships of their businesses with the worlds of energy, water, wood, land, air, soil, animals, and plants. And they are changing them.

It is slow work. While breakthoughs abound, there are no miracles to be wrought. This reconstitution of the relationships between business and living systems requires a diligence and thoroughness that is the strong suit of business. Yet without an organizing framework of easily understood principles, one can get lost easily, for the natural world is so complex.

The gift of working for sustainability is its meaningfulness. By defining the boundaries that prescribe the fulfillment or demise of life, The Natural Step principles provide a critically important tool for action. Although it is important that we act against depredation, abuse, and corruption in any and all forms, we also need to act creatively to disabuse, nurture, and inspire. To paraphrase Mary Oliver, we don't want to find ourselves at the end of our lives wondering if we have made something "particular and real." The work towards a just and sustainable world is just that, particular and real. We can give thanks to those companies and institutions who apply The Natural Step for appreciating and honoring the living world, "the leaping greenly spirits of trees and a blue true dream of sky" that will ever and always be at the heart of our prosperity, happiness, and humanity.

The Natural Step is sometimes criticized for being merely words. But Buddha said: "The thought manifests as the word; The word manifests as the deed; The deed develops into character. So watch the thought and its way with care; And let it spring from love born out of concern for all beings." That is Brian and Mary's hope: that their thoughts and words develop into true character for those who understand them. And that is their gift to us.

Notes

1. The Challenge of Design: Introduction

1 Brown, L., C. Flavin, H. French, *State of the World 1998*, W.W. Norton & Company, New York, 1998, p. xix.

2 McDonough, W. and M. Braungart, "The NEXT Industrial Revolution," *The Atlantic Monthly*, October 1998, p. 82.

3 World Commission on Environment and Development (Brundtland Commission), *Our Common Future*, Oxford, Oxford Press, 1987.

4 Frankel, C., *In Earth's Company*, New Society Publishers, Gabriola Island, B.C., 1998, p. 22.

5 Elkington, J., *Cannibals with Forks*, New Society Publishers, Gabriola Island, B.C., 1998, pp. 55–56.

6 Frankel, p. 121.

7 This term was first coined by Paul Hawken.

2. A New Framework for Management

1 Morgan, G., *Images of Organization*, Sage Publications, Thousand Oaks, California, 1997, p. 28.

2 Goleman, D., *Vital Lies, Simple Truths: The Psychology of Self-Deception*, Bloomsbury Publishing, London, U.K., 1998.

3 Morgan, p. 90.

4 Ibid., p. 91. Also see publications by Senge, Senge et al., and Smith and Yanowitz in the Selected Bibliography.

5 Ibid., p. 91.

6 Hart, S.L., "A Natural-Resource Based View of the Firm," *Academy of Management Review*, 1996, Vol. 20, No. 4, p. 987.

7 Ibid., p. 98.

8 Goleman, p. 12.

9 Frankel, C., p. 37.

10 Ibid., p. 3.

11 Piasecki, B., *Corporate Environmental Strategy*, John Wiley & Sons, New York, 1995, p. 3.

12 Frankel, C., p. 39.

13 See Frankel, Chapter 6 (pp. 81 - 94), for a discussion of these four principles.

14 Holmberg, J. and Robèrt, K.H., "Back-casting from First Order Sustainability Principles — A Framework for Strategic Planning," The Natural Step, Stockholm, 1998; Dreborg, K.H., "Essence of Back-casting," *Futures*, Vol. 28, 1996, pp. 813–828.

15 Robèrt, K. H., "The Natural Step to Sustainability," *The Natural Step/U.S.*, 1997, p. 1.

16 The wording of the System Conditions has been subject to continual scientific scrutiny and consensus and has been influenced by practical application of the principles. The wording has been changed over the past decade to be more precise and to improve understanding. The wording of the System Conditions presented here was adopted by The Natural Step International (TNSI), the international co-ordinating body of national Natural Step organizations, in September, 1998. The effectiveness of this wording is being reviewed in all the countries that are part of TNSI and will be reviewed again at the meeting of TNSI in 1999. It is important to note that although the wording itself has been amended for greater clarity from time-to-time, the essential concepts remain constant.

17 The ISO standard is discussed in greater detail in Chapter 9.

18 For more on the learning organization, see Senge, P., A. Kleiner, C. Roberts, R. Ross, G. Roth, and B. Smith, *The Dance of Change - The Challenge to Sustaining Momentum in a Learning Organization*, New York, Doubleday, 1999.

19 Interface Inc., *Sustainability Report*, Atlanta: Interface, Inc., 1997.

20 Joint-declaration by scientists and engineers in attendance at the Wingspread Scientific Consensus meeting, Racine, Wisconsin, February 1997.

21 Interface, Inc., *Sustainability Report*, Part Eleven.

3. Scientific Background to The Natural Step

1 Robèrt, K. H., H. Daly, P. Hawken, and J. Holmberg, "A Compass for Sustainable Development," *The Natural Step/Sweden*, March, 1997, pp. 2–3.

2 Robèrt, K. H., "The Natural Step — A Framework for Achieving Sustainability in Our Organizations," *Innovation in Management Series*, Pegasus Communications, Inc., Cambridge, Massachusetts, 1997, p. 5.

3 Ibid.

4 Eriksson, K. E. and K. H. Robèrt, "From the Big Bang to Sustainable Societies," *Reviews in Oncology*, Vol. 4, No. 2, 1991, p. 9.

5 It is important to note that the atmosphere used to be toxic to life as we know it today.

6 Eriksson, K. E. and K. H. Robèrt, p. 9.

7 Ibid, p. 10.

8 Brower, D., *Let the Mountains Talk, Let the Rivers Run*, HarperCollins Publishers, San Francisco, pp. 18 - 19.

9 Robèrt, K. H., "The Natural Step — A Framework for Achieving Sustainability in Our Organizations," p. 6.

10 Eriksson, K. E. and K. H. Robèrt, p. 5.

11 Ibid, p. 10.

12 Robèrt, K. H., Holmberg, J., and Broman, G., "Simplicity Without Reduction — Thinking Upstream Toward The Sustainable Society," *The Natural Step*, 1997, p. 4.

13 From the perspective of the cell, concentrations of substances are very important. Cells have evolved to be healthy within a certain range of levels of concentration of substances. However, it is very difficult to predict what the exact "safe" levels are, how long it will take to cross critical thresholds, what the ultimate impact will be, whether cells can adapt quickly enough to remain healthy or whether damage done can be repaired or reversed. Depending upon the characteristics of the substance and the recipient, the critical concentrations differ. In some recipients an increasing concentration of some substances can have a positive effect before a further increase in concentration will be problematic. For this reason, simple monitoring is insufficient to guide us to sustainability. Indicators for monitoring are generally applied late in the cause-effect chain. Often damage has already occurred where concentrations linked to deleterious effects can be measured.

14 Holmberg, J., and K. H. Robèrt, "The Rationale behind the System Conditions and their Applications," *The Natural Step International Scientist's Consensus Process*, 1997, p. 5.

4. IKEA: "Nothing is Impossible"

1 It is important to note that IKEA's abbreviated adaptation of the System Conditions does not fully or accurately convey their meaning. For example, System Condition One does not suggest that society should stop using resources from the Earth's crust, but that society should use these resources in such a way that concentrations of substances from the Earth's crust do not systematically accumulate in nature. The IKEA version is included to illustrate their learning and communication process, not to suggest that this is a preferred presentation of the System Conditions.

8. Transformation by Design: Lessons, Tools, and Methodologies

1 The ecological footprint is a planning tool developed by Mathis Wackernagel and William Rees that measures the "load" imposed by a given population on nature. It represents the land area necessary to sustain current levels of resource consumption and waste discharge by that population. For more information, refer to Wackernagel, M. and W. Rees, *Our Ecological Footprint*, New Society Publishers, Gabriola Island, B.C. 1996.

9. A Compass for Environmental Management Systems

1 Susan Burns is President of Natural Strategies, a leading California-based consulting firm specializing in strategic environmental management, research, and training. This chapter was included to demonstrate the practical integration of The Natural Step with an environmental management system.

2 Kranz, D. and S. Burns, "Combining The Natural Step and ISO 14001." *Perspectives on Business and Global Change*, Vol. 11, No. 4, World Business Academy, 1997, p. 4.

3 Ibid, p. 9.

4 Ibid, p. 9.

5 An environmental aspect is defined as an element of an organization's activities, products, or services that can interact with the environment. A significant environmental aspect is an environmental aspect that has or can have a significant environmental impact.

6 Holmberg, J., *Socio-Ecological Principles and Indicators for Sustainability*, Institute of Physical Resource Theory, Chalmers University, Goteborg, Sweden, 1995. Copies available through The Natural Step/US.

7 Colborn, T., D. Dumanoski, and J. P. Meyers, *Our Stolen Future*, Penguin Books, New York, 1996.

10. The Evolutionary Corporation

1 Metzner, R., *The Unfolding Self: Varieties of Transformative Experience* Origin Press, Novato, CA, 1998.

2 Sustainable Systems Associates, *Applying Sustainable Development to Business, Realizing the Benefits*, Ministry of the Environment of Canada, Queen's Printer for Ontario, 1998.

3 Fishman, C., "The War for Talent," *Fast Company*, August, 1998.

4 Terez, T., Meaning at Work, www.meaningatwork.com/; Willard, B., *Including Sustainability in Business Agendas...Why and How*, University of Toronto, 1998.

5 de Gues, A., *The Living Company*, Harvard Business School Press, Boston, 1997, p. 18.

Resources

The Natural Step-Related Publications

Azar, C., *Long-term environmental problems: Economic measures and physical indicators*, Institute of Physical Resource Theory of Chalmers University of Technology and Göteborg University, Göteborg, Sweden, 1995.

Bradbury, H., *The Swedish Natural Step: A model for sustainable transformation*, Carroll Graduate School of Management, Boston College, Boston, Massachusetts, 1996.

Electrolux, *Electrolux and the environment 1994. Vision, policy and steps taken*, Electrolux Corporation Information and Public Affairs, Stockholm, 1994.

Eriksson, K. E. and Robèrt, K. H., "From the big bang to sustainable societies," *Reviews in Oncology*, 1991, Vol. 4, No. 2, p.5-14.

Eronn, R., "The Natural Step — A Social Invention for the Environment," *Current Sweden*, No. 401, December 1993, The Swedish Institute, Stockholm.

Fishman, C., "Sustainable growth — Interface, Inc.," *Fast Company*, April-May, 1998, Vol. 14, pp. 136–142.

Frankel, C., "The visions gap," *Tomorrow: Global Environment Business*, 1995, Vol. 5, No. 3, pp. 72–74.

Hawken, P., "Taking the natural step," *In Context*, Summer 1995, Vol. 41, pp.36-38.

Holmberg, J., *Socio-ecological principles and indicators for sustainability*, Institute of Physical Resource Theory of Chalmers University of Technology and Göteborg University, Göteborg, Sweden, 1995.

———, Robèrt, K. H., and Eriksson, K. E., "Socio-ecological principles for a sustainable society," in Costanza, R. et al (eds.) *Getting Down to Earth — Practical Applications for Ecological Economics*, Washington, Island Press, 1996, pp. 17–48.

——— and Robèrt, K. H., "The rationale behind the system conditions and their applications," *The Natural Step*, 1997.

Interface, Inc., *Sustainability Report*, Atlanta, Georgia, Interface, Inc., 1997.

Kranz, D. and Burns, S., "Combining The Natural Step and ISO 14001," *Perspectives on Business and Global Change*, 1997, Vol. 11, No. 4, pp. 7-20.

McDonald's Sweden, *McDonald's Sweden Environment Program*, Stockholm, McDonald's Sweden, 1996.

Neuwirth, R., "Eco ceo," *Metropolis*, 1998, July, pp. 68–73.

Robèrt, K. H., "Educating a nation: The natural step," *In Context*, 1991, Vol. 28., pp. 10–15.

———, "The natural step: A framework for large-scale change," *The Systems Thinker*, 1995, Vol. 6, No. 8, pp. 3-5.

————, "From framework to strategy," King Carl Gustaf's Environmental Symposium, Stockholm,, September 28, 1996, pp. 5-6.

————, "The natural step to sustainability," *Wingspread Journal*, Spring 1997, Vol. 19, No. 2, pp. 4-8.

————, Daly, H. E., Hawken, P., and Holmberg, J., "A compass for sustainable development," *International Jounral for Sustainable Development and World Ecology, 4, 1997, pp. 79-92.*

————, Daly, H. E., Hawken, P. and Holmberg, J., "A compass for sustainable development," *The Natural Step*, 1997.

————, Holmberg, J. and Broman, G., "Simplicity without reduction: Thinking upstream towards a sustainable society," *The Natural Step*, 1997.

————, *The Natural Step: A framework for achieving sustainability in our organizations.* Cambridge, Massachusetts, Innovations in Management Series, Pegasus Communications, Inc., 1997.

———— and Holmberg, J. "Back-casting from first order sustainability principles — a framework for strategic planning," *The Natural Step*, 1998.

Sånga-Säby, *Environmental Report 1996*, Stockholm, Sånga-Säby Kurs & Konferns, 1996.

Sånga-Säby Kurs, *Environmental Report 1997*, Stockholm, Sånga-Säby Kurs & Konferns, 1997.

van Gelder, S., "The Natural Step: The Science of Sustainability," *YES! A Journal of Positive Futures*, Fall 1998, Vol. 7, pp. 50-54.

The Natural Step Consensus Documents in English

The Natural Step, "An outline for municipalities working with agenda 21," Stockholm, Sweden, 1995, 25 pp.

The Natural Step, "Agriculture from a scientific perspective," Stockholm, Sweden, 1995, 20 pp.

The Natural Step, "Energy policy from an ecological perspective," (abridged version), Stockholm, Sweden, 7 pp.

The Natural Step, "Metal issues from a scientific perspective," Stockholm, Sweden, 17 pp.

The Natural Step, "Political and economic measures towards the sustainable society," Stockholm, Sweden, 41 pp.

TNS-Related Internet Articles and Sites

Altomare, Mary, Innovation Strategies, Inc., *Transformation by Design*, www.innovationstrategies.com.

Anderson, Ray, An interview with Ray Anderson by B. S. McWilliams on April 11, 1996, www.mediapool.com/offtherecord/raytran.html.

Bradbury, H., "The Swedish Natural Step: A model for sustainable transformation," Carroll Graduate School of Management, Boston College, Boston, Massachusetts, learning.mit.edu/res/wp/rtf_learning.html.

Collins Pine Company, Portland, Oregon, www.collinswood.com

Electrolux's 1997 environmental report,
www.electrolux.se/corporate/environmental/report.html.

Fishman, C., "Sustainable growth — Interface, Inc., *Fast Company*, 1998, Vol. 14, p. 136, www.fastcompany.com/online/14/sustaing.html.

Fishman, C., "Interface: their 'growth agenda,'" *Fast Company*, 1998, Vol. 14, p. 139, www.fastcompany.com/online/14/agendasg.html.

Hawken, P., "The next reformation," *In Context*, Summer, 1995, Vol. 41, p. 17, context.org/ICLIB/Icr1/hawken1.html.

Hawken, P., "Taking the natural step," *In Context*, Summer, 1995, Vol. 41, p. 36, context.org/ICLIB/IC41/hawken2.html.

IKEA, www.ikea.com.

Interface, Inc., www.interfaceinc.com.

Interface, Inc., 1997 annual report, www.ifsia.com/annual report.asp? year=1997

Kiuchi, Tachi, "What I learned from the rain forest," World Futures Society, July 19, 1997, delivered by Tachi Kiuchi, Member of the Board, Mitsubishi Electric Corporation, Chairman of the Future 500, and immediate past Chairman and CEO of Mitsubishi Electric America, www.actrix.gen.nz/users/futurestrust/rainforest.html.

Nattrass, Brian, Innovation Strategies, Inc., *Transformation by Design*, www.innovationstrategies.com.

The Natural Step/Australia, Melbourne, Victoria, www.ozemail.com.au/~natstep.

The Natural Step/US, San Francisco, California, www.naturalstep.org.

Natural Strategies, Oakland, California, www.naturalstrategies.com.

Neuwirth, R., "Eco ceo," *Metropolis,* July 1998, www.metropolismag.com.

One World Learning, www.oneworldlearning.com

Robèrt, K. H. , "Educating a nation: the natural step," *In Context*, Spring 1991, Vol. 28, p. 10, www.context.org/ICLIB/IC28/Robert.html, "Answering the king's challenge," *In Context*, Summer 1993, Vol. 35, p. 6, www.context.org/ICLIB/IC35/Robert.html.

Sånga-Säby Conference Center, "Environmental report 1997," www.sanga-saby.se.

Scandic Hotels, www.scandic-hotels.com

Scott, M., "The natural step: Sweden's commonsense green scheme comes to America," *Utne Reader*, www.utnecom/reader/magazine.html.

Selected Bibliography

Anderson, R.C., *Mid-course Correction*, Atlanta, Georgia, Peregrinzilla Press, 1998.

Argyris, C., *On Organizational Learning*, Cambridge, Massachusetts, Blackwell, 1992.

Banathy, B.B., *Designing Social Systems in a Changing World*, New York, New York, Plenum, 1996.

Beloff, Beth, *Creating Strategic Alliances from Sustainable Development Activities*, International Business Communications Conference, September 8-10, 1997.

Brower, D., *Let the Mountains Talk, Let the Rivers Run*, San Francisco, HarperCollins Publishers, 1996.

Brown, L., Flavin, C., and French, H., *State of the World 1998* and other publications in the series including *Vital Signs, World Watch Magazine, Worldwatch Papers*, and Environmental Alert book series, New York, W. W. Norton.

Colborn, T., Dumanoski, D., and Meyers, J. P., *Our Stolen Future*, New York, Penguin Books, 1996.

Daly, H. E. and Cobb, J., *For the Common Good: Redirecting the Economy toward Community, the Environment, and a Sustainable Future*. Boston, Beacon Press, 1994.

de Geus, A., *The Living Company*. Boston, Harvard Business School Press, 1997.

Dreborg, K. H., "Essence of back-casting," *Futures*, 1996, Vol. 28. pp. 813–828.

Eitel, C., *Mapping Your Legacy*, Atlanta, Peregrinzilla Press, 1998.

Elgin, D., *Awakening Earth: Exploring the Evolution of Human Culture and Consciousness*, New York, William Morrow and Company Inc., 1993.

Elkington, J., *Cannibals with Forks: The Triple Bottom Line of 21st Century Business*, Gabriola Island, B.C., New Society Publishers, 1998.

Fishman, C., "The war for talent," *Fast Company*, August.1998, Vol. 16, pp. 104-107.

Frankel, C., *In Earth's Company*, Gabriola Island, B.C., New Society Publishers, 1998.

Goleman, D., *Vital Lies, Simple Truths: The Psychology of Self Deception*, London, Bloomsbury Publishing Plc., 1998.

Hart, S. L., "A natural resource-based view of the firm," *Academy of Management Review*, 1996, Vol. 20, No. 4, pp. 986–1013.

Hawken, P. , *The Ecology of Commerce: A Declaration of Sustainability*, New York, Harper Business, 1993.

——— , "Natural capitalism: how business can restore rather than destroy our environments, natural and social," *Mother Jones*, 1997, March/April, pp. 40–61.

———, Lovins, A.B., and Lovins, H.L., *Natural Capitalism: Creating the Next Industrial Revolution*, New York, Little, Brown & Company, 1999.

Hubbard, B.M., *Conscious Evolution: Awakening the Power of Our Social Potential*, Novato, California, New World Library, 1997.

Jackson, T., *Material Concerns: Pollution, Profit and Quality of Life*, London, Routledge, 1996.

Laszlo, E., *The Choice: Evolution or Extinction? A Thinking Person's Guide to Global Issues*, New York, G. P. Putnam's Sons, 1994.

————, *Evolution: the General Theory,* Cresskill, New Jersey, Hampton Press, 1994.

McDonough, W. and Braungart, M., "The NEXT Industrial Revolution," *The Atlantic Monthly,* October 1998, pp. 82-92.

Metzner, R., *The Unfolding Self: Varieties of Transformative Experience,* Novato, California, Origin Press, 1998.

Miller, J.G., *Living Systems,* Niwot, Colorado, University Press of Colorado, 1995.

Morgan, G., *Images of Organization,* Thousand Oaks, California, Sage Publications, 1997.

Piasecki, B., *Corporate Environmental Strategy,* New York: John Wiley & Sons, 1995.

Richards, D. and Frosch, R., "Implications for Environmental Design and Management," *The Industrial Green Game,* Washington, D.C., National Academy Press, 1997.

Rogers, E.M., *Diffusion of Innovations,* 4th ed., New York, Free Press, 1995.

Salk, J., *Anatomy of Reality: Merging of Intuition and Reason,* New York, Columbia University Press, 1983.

Senge, P. M., *The Fifth Discipline: The Art and Practice of the Learning Organization,* New York, Currency/Doubleday, 1990.

————, Roberts, C., Ross, R. B., Smith, B. J. and Kleiner, A. *The Fifth Discipline Fieldbook — Strategies and Tools for Building a Learning Organization,* New York, Currency/Doubleday, 1994.

————, Kleiner, A., Roberts, C., Ross, R., Roth, G. and Smith, B., *The Dance of Change — The Challenge to Sustaining Momentum in a Learning Organization,* New York, Currency/Doubleday, 1999.

Smith, B. and Yanowitz, J., "Sustainable innovation and change: the learning path to growth," *Prism,* Fourth Quarter 1998, Arthur D. Little, pp. 35-45.

Sustainable Systems Associates, *Applying Sustainable Development to Business – Realizing the Benefits,* Ministry of the Environment of Canada, Ontario, Queen's Printer, 1998.

Terez, T., "Meaning at work," 1998, www.meaningatwork.com.

von Weizsäker, E., Lovins, A.B., and Lovins, L.H., *Factor Four — Doubling Wealth, Halving Resource Use,* London, Earthscan Publications, 1997.

Wackernagel, M. and Rees, W., *Our Ecological Footprint — Reducing Human Impact on the Earth,* Gabriola Island, B.C., New Society Publishers, 1996.

Willard, B., *Including Sustainability in Business Agendas . . . Why and How,* University of Toronto, 1998.

World Commission on Environment and Development (Brundtland Commission), *Our Common Future,* Oxford, Oxford Press, 1987.

Organizational Resources

Innovation Strategies Inc. *Transformation by Design*
Vancouver, BC and San Francisco, CA.

Innovation Strategies accelerates the movement of organizations towards sustainable development — financial, social, and ecological. ISI employs the disciplines of organizational design, organizational learning, natural systems thinking, scenario building, conflict resolution, and financial modelling. The principals of ISI are among the world's leading authorities on the organizational training and implementation of The Natural Step framework for sustainability. They bring a powerful combination of disciplines and experience to the analysis and solution of organizational challenges on the path to sustainability.

Contact: Brian Nattrass, President
Mary Altomare, Vice-President
Tel: 604.886.0957 Fax: 604.886.0967
email: innostrat@aol.com   www.innovationstrategies.com

Natural Strategies
Oakland, CA
Natural Strategies helps organizations achieve long-term, "bottom-line" results through the application of sustainability principles in strategic and tactical decision-making and action. Natural Strategies helps organizations improve efficiency and quality at all levels. Expertise includes environmental performance measurement and reporting, environmental management systems, benchmarking and product design, analysis and support.

Contact: Susan Burns, President
Tel: 510.839.8879 Fax: 510.834.9202
email: innostrat@aol.com   www.innovationstrategies.com

The Natural Step National Organizations

The Natural Step/Australia
Tel: 61356.642.359 Fax: 61356.642.369
4 Koala Drive Koonwarra, Victoria, Australia 3954
email: natstep@ozemail.com.au
Contact: Leigh Crocker
www.ozemail.com.au/~natstep

The Natural Step/Canada
Tel: 604.886-0937 Fax: 604.886.0967
R.R. #6, S-1, C-48, Gibsons, B.C. V0N 1V0 Canada
email: tnscanada@aol.com
Contact: Brian Nattrass and Mary Altomare
www.naturalstep.org

The Natural Step/Netherlands
Tel: 31.70.365.32.83 Fax: 31.70.364.4934
Zeestrat 71, 2518 AA Den Haag
The Netherlands
email: tnsnl@hvanh.nl
Contact: Ernst van Hezik

The Natural Step/New Zealand
Tel: 64.4.380.0432 Fax: 64.4.380.0926
C/-8 Coolidge Street, Brooklyn, Wellington, NZ
Contact: Ms. Pam Williams
email: natstep@extra.co.nz

The Natural Step/Sweden
Tel: 46.8.789.2900 Fax: 46.8.789.2939
Wallingatan 22 111 24, Stockholm, Sweden
email:magnus.huss@detnaturligasteget.se
Contact: Magnus Huss
www.detnaturligasteget.se

The Natural Step/UK
Tel: 44.1242.262.744 Fax: 44.1242.524.445
9 Imperial Square, Cheltenham, Gloschester GL50 1QB
email: davidcook@tnsuk.demon.co.uk
Contact: David Cook

The Natural Step/US
Tel: 415.561.3344 Fax: 415.561.3345
P.O. Box 29372, San Francisco, CA 94129-0372
email: tns@naturalstep.org
Contact: Catherine Gray
www.naturalstep.org

The Organizing Committee for The Natural Step in Japan
Tel: 03.5643.6221 Fax: 03.5643.6220
c/o Nippon Environment Research Co., Ltd.
Naitoh Building, 2-25-1 Nihonbashi-Hamacho
Chuo-ku, Tokyo 103, Japan
email: stakami@ner.co.jp
ekumano@sumieto.co.jp
Contact: Eisuke Kumano and Sachiko Takami

The Organizing Committee for The Natural Step in South Africa
Tel: 27.21.686.2845 Fax: 27.21.686.2845
Suite 250, Private Bag x 18, Rondebosch 7701,
Cape Town, South Africa
Contact: Kerry Sandison
email: Kerryson@iafrica.com

Index

Numbers following the letter "n" refer to endnotes with chapter numbers in superscript where needed.

ABOUT THE AUTHORS

Brian Nattrass combines the qualities of senior executive, corporate lawyer, scholar, and environmental educator. Having served as both CEO of a public company and chairman of an international environmental organization, he brings a balanced understanding and expertise to the business/environment relationship. He has extensive experience in conflict resolution and complex, multi-party consensus processes. His doctoral studies investigated organizational learning and change with a focus on the dynamics of sustainable development. As President of Innovation Strategies Inc., he consults to corporations across North America on creating long-term wealth and shareholder value through the implementation of effective organizational change initiatives utilizing natural systems thinking, including The Natural Step. His previous book, *Raising Money* (with Douglas Gray), 1993, concerned business finance for entrepreneurs.

Mary Altomare is the Vice-President of Innovation Strategies Inc., advising corporate and non-profit clients on organizational development, project planning, and the design of innovative training programs. She has conducted extensive research on socio-economic development and contributed to training programs for the US Agency for International Development. At both Yale and Duke Universities she was instrumental in the creation of international educational and policy research programs. She has contributed to a number of policy, research, and training publications including *Tools for Effective Policy Dialogue*, 1990, prepared for the Research Triangle Institute, Research Triangle Park, N.C., and US AID, Washington, D.C.

Both live on the Sunshine Coast near Vancouver, British Columbia, where they enjoy an active outdoor life of ocean and mountain sports.

CONSCIENTIOUS COMMERCE

The Natural Step for Business:
Wealth, Ecology and the Evolutionary Corporation
is one of New Society Publisher's
CONSCIENTIOUS COMMERCE
series of books.

This series aims to appeal equally to both
corporate executives seeking to bring their
companies into the 21st century, and to
activists, officials, and citizens wanting to know
more about the ways in which business is
responding to the challenges of sustainability.

Other volumes in the series include:
In Earth's Company:
Business, Environment and the Challenge of Sustainability,
by Carl Frankel
and
Cannibals with Forks:
The Triple Bottom Line of 21st Century Business,
by John Elkington.

To order, or for a full list of NSP titles,
call 1-800-567-6772,
or check out our web site at:
www.newsociety.com

NEW SOCIETY PUBLISHERS